LIVERPOOL'S
LAST OCEAN LINERS

LIVERPOOL'S LAST OCEAN LINERS

THE GOLDEN AGE

JOHN SHEPHERD

The History Press

'Now, Voyager, sail thou forth,
to seek and find'

Walt Whitman
1819–1892

First published 2009

The History Press
The Mill, Brimscombe Port
Stroud, Gloucestershire, GL5 2QG
www.thehistorypress.co.uk

Reprinted 2011, 2012

British Library Cataloguing in Publication Data.
A catalogue record for this book is available from the British Library.

ISBN 978 0 7524 4915 9

Typesetting and origination by The History Press
Printed in Great Britain

CONTENTS

ACKNOWLEDGEMENTS 7

AUTHOR'S NOTES 8

FOREWORD 10

CHAPTER 1

ANCHOR LINE 11

Circassia 13

Cilicia 14

Caledonia 16

CHAPTER 2

BOOTH LINE 17

Hilary 18

Hildebrand 22

Hubert 23

Anselm (ex-Baudouinville, ex-Thysville) 24

CHAPTER 3

CANADIAN PACIFIC 25

Empress of France (ex-Duchess of Bedford) 27

Empress of Canada (ex-Duchess of Richmond) 37

Empress of Scotland (ex-Empress of Japan) 42

Empress of Australia (ex-De Grasse) 52

Empress of Britain   54

Empress of England   65

Empress of Canada   70

CHAPTER 4

CUNARD LINE   76

Scythia   77

Franconia   79

Ascania   81

Samaria   86

Britannic   89

Georgic   91

Media   94

Parthia   96

Saxonia   99

Ivernia   99

Carinthia   102

Sylvania   121

CHAPTER 5

ELDER DEMPSTER   130

Accra   131

Apapa   135

Aureol   136

CHAPTER 6

PACIFIC STEAM NAVIGATION COMPANY   140

Reina Del Pacifico   141

Reina Del Mar   147

CHAPTER 7

UNION CASTLE   153

Windsor Castle   152

ACKNOWLEDGEMENTS

I should like to thank the following for all the assistance they have given me in the preparation of this book:

Alan Woodhouse for meticulously proof-reading the early drafts of my text, and correcting my clumsy spelling, grammar, punctuation and syntax.

Malcolm McRonald for allowing me access to his comprehensive archive of press cuttings covering the 1950s and '60s which was a valuable source of information covering many long-forgotten incidents.

Peter Elson, Senior Features Writer at the *Liverpool Daily Post*, for writing the chapter dealing with the Birkenhead-built *Windsor Castle*.

Peter Clowes, Ted Morris, J.C. Moffatt, Brian Scott and Guy Stafford for sharing their memories of life aboard some of Liverpool's last passenger liners.

And finally to the officers and crew of the Cunard Liners *Carinthia* and *Sylvania* in the 1960s, with whom I spent the most enjoyable time of my life.

Front cover image: The *Duchess of Bedford* (from 1948 the *Empress of France*) alongside Princes Landing Stage on the occasion of her maiden voyage, 1 June 1928. (Photo: Canadian Pacific)

Back cover image: The Cunard liner *Carinthia* at anchor off the Pier Head, Liverpool, August 1959.

AUTHOR'S NOTE

L iverpool's Last Ocean Liners started out as a talk I gave to the Liverpool Nautical Research Society in March 2005. It was suggested to me that there was enough content for a book on the subject, and so, four years on, this is the result.

I was brought up in Merseyside in the 1940s and '50s. Some of my earliest memories are of being taken by my father for trips on the Overhead Railway to the Pier Head on a Sunday morning. The grandstand view of the docks, packed with ships, fascinated me and when we walked down to the Princes Landing Stage there was invariably a passenger liner alongside. After the Overhead Railway closed down in December 1956, access to Liverpool docks was easiest on a Sunday morning, and my father's car would invariably be waved through the dock gates at Gladstone by a friendly policeman and we would make for the river entrance lock where, if we were very lucky, the *Empress of Scotland* would be arriving, or maybe the *Britannic* might be sailing.

I resolved that I would go to sea, and although I stayed on at school to gain three very mediocre 'A' Levels, I became word-perfect in the *Regulations for the Prevention of Collisions at Sea*, which was not of much use in a French literature exam! My eyesight was not good enough to become a deck cadet, so in March 1962 I joined Cunard's *Queen Elizabeth* as a purser's clerk and remained there for nine months, after which I joined the Liverpool-based *Carinthia* as an assistant purser. I remained with the ship for four years, followed by two years on the *Sylvania*. Looking back, they were the best years of my life. In the early 1960s it was a way of life which seemingly had no end, but towards the end of the decade it disappeared, almost overnight. Six almost new Liverpool-based passenger liners became redundant due to competition from the airlines; appalling industrial relations both amongst ships' crews and shore labour, and, further exacerbating the situation, the ever-escalating cost of fuel oil.

The passenger liners described in this book are those which used Liverpool as their homeport, and any one of which, on an average day, might have been seen alongside the Princes Landing Stage landing or embarking passengers. Liners such as the *Caronia* and the *Mauretania* are not included as their visits to Liverpool were very few and far between, usually for winter overhaul. Companies such as Blue Funnel and Bibby carried relatively small numbers of passengers in some of their larger ships, but these were basically cargo/passenger liners and did not sail from the landing stage.

Eleven of the ships described in this book were built before the outbreak of the Second World War in September 1939. Without exception they all saw distinguished war service and this is here described in full. After the cessation of hostilities in May 1945 (the date I have used as the starting point for this book), the liners began to be released from their repatriation and troop-carrying duties, and after extensive refits following six years of intensive wartime operation, they slowly returned to their designed routes in the North Atlantic passenger trade.

The author at Cape
Town in 1969.

A massive rebuilding programme began in the late 1940s and continued throughout the 1950s, commencing with Elder Dempster's *Accra* and *Apapa*, and Cunard's *Media* and *Parthia* in 1947/48. A total of fourteen new passenger liners were built for Liverpool-based passenger services, culminating in the *Empress of Canada* in 1961. It was a bold move, given that competition from the airlines was making its presence felt from the mid-1950s.

The 1950s and 1960s were decades of appalling industrial relations in the shipping industry, both ashore and at sea. The sixteen-week strike of boilermakers at Liverpool in 1961 was the reason cited by Cunard for the early withdrawal of the *Media* and the *Parthia*. Passengers simply did not know if their ship would sail on time or, indeed, at all. Crossing the North Atlantic by sea became nothing short of a lottery. The whole sorry mess culminated in the forty-two-day seamen's strike of May and June 1966 when the entire British Merchant Navy was strikebound. This was the catalyst, but by no means the only reason for the total disappearance of Liverpool's passenger liners by early 1972.

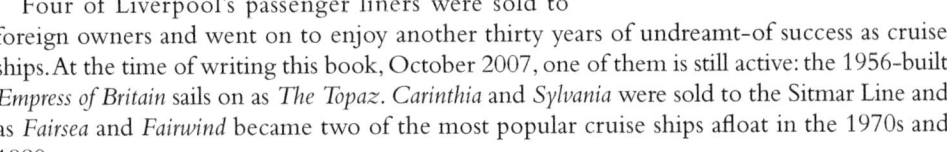

Four of Liverpool's passenger liners were sold to foreign owners and went on to enjoy another thirty years of undreamt-of success as cruise ships. At the time of writing this book, October 2007, one of them is still active: the 1956-built *Empress of Britain* sails on as *The Topaz*. *Carinthia* and *Sylvania* were sold to the Sitmar Line and as *Fairsea* and *Fairwind* became two of the most popular cruise ships afloat in the 1970s and 1980s.

Sadly, the two Liverpool liners sold to British interests – the *Reina del Mar* and the *Empress of England* – enjoyed only a further five years of active service after they left Liverpool due to on-going crew problems and ever soaring fuel oil prices.

It was never the intention of this book to provide a photograph album of the Liverpool liners. That has been attempted several times before with photographs (often repetitions of previous publications) and a few statistics culled from *Lloyd's Register*.

The purpose of this book is to tell the story of Liverpool's last passenger liners, incorporating as much material as possible from people who actually sailed on them as crew members or passengers. There were numerous great characters who crewed the Liverpool liners and I have mentioned as many of them as possible, especially in my autobiographical chapter, *A Year with the Carinthia*.

Liverpool now has a new landing stage to accommodate visiting cruise ships, and this was inaugurated by the *Queen Elizabeth 2* on 21 September 2007. Whilst the era of the passenger liner (i.e. a ship sailing from Liverpool to New York or Montreal for the specific purpose of getting passengers to their destinations) has gone for ever, it is pleasant to see today's cruise ships back in the Mersey.

If this book can recall the halcyon days of the passenger liners which sailed from the Mersey, a way of life that has disappeared for ever, then it will have achieved its aim.

John Shepherd

FOREWORD

I t is with great pleasure that I offer this foreword to John Shepherd's fine, wide-ranging account of the last Passenger Liners of Liverpool. Over more than thirty years of the closest friendship with John, I have learned all that I know of the sea and the ships of the Mersey. My younger years were spent landlocked in the Yorkshire Pennines; the Mersey and the last of its grand succession of liners came as a wonderful surprise and new treasure when I settled in Wallasey in 1955. A more dramatic first encounter is hard to imagine. I remember vividly, on drawing the curtains one morning, the shock and delight, almost surreal to me, of seeing for the first time, riding at anchor waiting to proceed to the Pier Head, a Cunarder not one hundred yards from my window. For many months this remained a keenly anticipated event. I find the magic of these sights vividly elaborated in John Shepherd's splendid tributes.

This volume is a precious mine of information, entertainment, humour and experience. All John's enthusiasm, personal service, technical understanding, and sheer admiration for these vessels and those who sailed in them, combine to make this account so rich. I find the book admirable in its compass; because the writer has not simply focussed upon the two great transatlantic rivals, but he gives due attention and appreciation to the smaller brethren and the more exotic as well. My own favourite vessel became the beautiful *Aureol*, the Elder Dempster ship, lovely in name and form, which always recalled to me Conrad's note of the landlubbers' appreciation of the *Narcissus* as 'that pretty grey ship'.

Prosaically, I close this tribute to John's workmanship with an acknowledgement of responsibility. If any errors of language or syntax remain, the seaman/author must not be blamed. My own inadequacy as corrector and proof reader will be the cause! I commend John's work. His volume will bring not only increased knowledge and understanding but, more importantly, great pleasure to all his readers.

Alan Woodhouse

1

ANCHOR LINE

The Anchor Line was founded by Nicol and Robert Handyside, who in 1838 set up as shipbrokers and merchants in Glasgow and established a thriving business with Russia and other Baltic ports. Thomas Henderson joined the company about 1855 and the company's *Tempest* sailed from Glasgow for New York in October 1856 with Thomas's brother, John, in command. This Atlantic service was known as the Anchor Line of Steam Packets – the first time the title Anchor Line was used.

John Henderson was made a partner in 1859 and his other two brothers, David and William, founded the Finnieston Steamship Works Co., later to become known as D. & W. Henderson Ltd. Among the early steamers of the Anchor Line were several built by Tod & McGregor, but their engines, wherever possible, were bought from the Finnieston Works.

Anchor Line publicity brochure from the 1950s.

The imposing main lounge on the *Caledonia*.

A service between Glasgow and Liverpool to Bombay was commenced in 1875, and services to Calcutta were commenced in 1882 and proved to be very profitable. The Cunard Company purchased the ordinary capital of the Anchor Line in 1911 and not long afterwards the Anchor Line acquired a controlling interest in Thos. & Jno. Brocklebank to operate the Anchor–Brocklebank service to Calcutta. In 1916 the Anchor Line acquired the Donaldson Line passenger steamers and Anchor–Donaldson was formed to operate them.

As a result of the worldwide depression, in April 1935 the Anchor Line went into liquidation and the assets were transferred to a new company to be known as Anchor Line Ltd (1935), in which Cunard had no interest. Runciman (London) Ltd were appointed managers and the new company had Lord Runciman as chairman. The Anchor Line was completely rejuvenated and the *Circassia*, the first of three passenger motorships for the Indian services, was commissioned.

In December 1949 the United Molasses Co., already substantial shareholders, made an offer for the balance of the ordinary capital and the preference capital was purchased in 1953 when the company became a wholly owned subsidiary of United Molasses.

In July 1965 the Anchor Line was sold to the Moor Line of Newcastle. The time had come when a firm decision had to be made on the replacement of the passenger ships employed in the UK–India trade. Considerable market research was undertaken and it became apparent that the inroads made into the passenger business by air travel made it unrealistic to justify the high capital cost of building new vessels and it was announced that the service would cease at the end of 1965, thereby breaking a passenger link between Great Britain and India which had extended over ninety years.

CIRCASSIA

Built by the Fairfield Shipbuilding & Engineering Co. of Govan in 1937.   **Yard No:** 661
Official Number: 165916   **Signal Letters:** G Z M D
Gross Tonnage: 11,170   **Nett:** 6,534   **Length:** 483.5ft   **Breadth:** 66.4ft
Owned by the Anchor Line Limited, registered at Glasgow.
Twin screws, Doxford diesels, service speed 16½-knots, maximum 18-knots.

The *Circassia* was launched on 8 June 1937 and sailed on her maiden voyage from Glasgow and Liverpool to Bombay on 14 October of that year. She could carry 300 passengers in first class and eighty in steerage. The Anchor Line chairman, Philip Runciman, was on board for the Glasgow to Liverpool leg of the voyage and told the *Liverpool Daily Post*, 'This ship is our message to Liverpool. What finer message could we send to any port?'

Spectators who had assembled at the Princes Landing Stage to watch the new *Circassia* depart on her maiden voyage were disappointed. She was late in completing her loading and embarked her passengers in the Alexandra Dock, from where she sailed direct to sea, under the command of Captain William Gemmell.

Following the outbreak of war *Circassia* was converted into an armed merchant cruiser, but was transferred to trooping duties in 1942. The following year she was rebuilt as a Landing Ship Infantry. *Circassia* was engaged in the Sicilian landings and was commanded by Captain (later Sir) David Bone at the Salerno invasion. She also took part in the south of France landings of 1944.

A three-berth 'A' deck cabin.

On the completion of her war duties, the *Circassia* was returned to the Anchor Line in May 1947 and resumed service on the Liverpool to Bombay route on 21 August of that year. Among the *Circassia*'s 298 first-class passengers who sailed from Liverpool for Bombay in September 1948 were the sixty members of the British Olympic team, and Sir Ness Wadia, a wealthy seventy-seven-year-old Bombay businessman, who was on his 99th voyage between India and Britain.

In March 1958 the *Circassia* arrived at Liverpool flying the yellow quarantine flag. Professor Andrew Semple, Liverpool's Medical Officer of Health at that time, went on board and confirmed a case of smallpox in a lascar seaman. A team of doctors vaccinated the liner's 300 passengers and crew of 145.

On 13 January 1966 the *Circassia* left Glasgow and Liverpool for Bombay on the Anchor Line's final passenger sailing, under the command of Captain Angus Colquhoun. She received an emotional 'goodbye' from hundreds of dockers, seamen and other spectators as she left the Ballard Pier, Bombay, for the last time, flying a long, white paying-off pennant.

On her arrival back at Liverpool on 15 March 1966 the *Circassia*'s 300 passengers and 187 crew members were met on the landing stage by sixty-year-old Wallasey piper David Renton, of the Liverpool Clan Macleod Pipe Band, who played *Will Ye No Come Back Again?* But the *Circassia* was not to return to the Mersey again.

After completing the discharge of her cargo at Birkenhead on 25 March, the *Circassia* sailed for Glasgow. She made a short cruise in Scottish waters carrying present and past directors of the Anchor Line, and then sailed for Alicante where she arrived on 25 April 1966 to be broken up. The Anchor Line had sold its last passenger liner for scrapping for just £140,000.

CILICIA

Built by the Fairfield Shipbuilding & Engineering Co. of Govan in 1938.   **Yard No:** 664
Official Number: 165934   **Signal Letters:** G D G L
Gross Tonnage: 11,157   **Nett:** 6,538   **Length:** 483.6ft   **Breadth:** 66.4ft
Owned by the Anchor Line, Limited, registered at Glasgow.
Twin Screws, Doxford diesels, service speed 16½ knots, maximum 18 knots.

The *Cilicia* was launched on 21 October 1937 and left Liverpool on her maiden voyage to Bombay on 14 May 1938. Like her sister, the *Circassia*, she could carry 300 passengers in first class, and eighty in steerage. She had hardly settled into a routine when the Second World War broke out and the *Cilicia* was requisitioned as an armed merchant cruiser on 31 August 1939.

She served in this capacity for the next four and a half years. In 1940 the *Cilicia* was in collision with the Cunard liner *Carinthia*, also serving as an armed merchant cruiser. Both vessels were travelling at speed and were blacked out. There was no radar fitted at the time. The *Carinthia* cut into the *Cilicia* almost to her centreline in way of No.2 hold, and left her jackstaff on board. But for the fact that the *Cilicia*, like all armed merchant cruisers, carried a large number of empty drums in her hold for buoyancy purposes, she would probably not have been able to make her way back to Belfast. From the position of the collision, she left behind a continuous trail of empty drums! The *Carinthia*'s jackstaff was retained on board the *Cilicia* and in fact 'decorated' the anteroom of the wardroom throughout her service as an AMC.

On 25 March 1941, whilst on patrol in the Atlantic, the *Cilicia* received a radio message from another Anchor Line ship, the *Britannia* (b.1926, 8,799 tons), reporting that she was being attacked by a surface raider some 750 miles west of Freetown. The surgeon of the *Cilicia* was Dr Thomas Miller, whose daughter Nancy was surgeon of the *Britannia*. As no further signal was received, it was clear that the raider's attack had been successful.

The dining saloon on the *Cilicia*.

Three days later the *Cilicia* sighted a small steamer at 6.25 a.m., and at 7.15 a.m. she sent away a boarding party to investigate. She proved to be the Spanish steamer *Bachi*, and a signal came from the boarding party that she had picked up sixty-three of the *Britannia*'s survivors. By 9.30 a.m. they were alongside the *Cilicia*, and the first to reach the deck was Dr Nancy Miller, to be greeted by an overjoyed father. The *Cilicia* landed the survivors at Freetown and in 1942 Dr Nancy Miller was awarded the MBE, and in 1943 Lloyd's Medal for her services in attending the passengers and crew of the *Britannia* during the shelling and sinking of the vessel by the German raider *Thor*. In the encounter 127 passengers and 122 crew from the *Britannia* lost their lives.

In 1942 HMS *Cilicia* was instrumental in establishing a meteorological station on the island of Tristan da Cunha, which became known as HMS *Atlantic Isle*. Tristan da Cunha [37°10′S, 12°20′W] is in fact the top of a symmetrical volcanic cone rising to 6,760ft above sea level. The meteorological station was established at Edinburgh Settlement on a small ledge four and a half miles long and half a mile wide.

After the plans for the station, known as 'Job 9', had been formulated, matters were complicated by the Admiralty's instruction that wives and families of naval personnel should accompany their husbands, and that all members of the party should be most carefully selected. 'Job 9' involved the transportation and erection of a township, the weather station itself being only part of the huge task. In all over 2,000 tons of cargo was transported from Cape Town to Tristan. As ships could not approach the shore closer than half a mile, everything had to be landed in ships' boats on an open beach and in heavy surf. With the possibility of enemy interference an ever present threat, the work of discharging cargo was a long and hazardous undertaking for the AMCs allocated to the task. An idea of the weather conditions prevailing can be gleaned from the fact that when HMS *Cilicia* arrived off Tristan on 9 May 1942 to land 1,426 tons of cargo using her own boats, she remained there until 9 June, as only seven and a half days produced favourable conditions for working cargo. The meteorological station HMS *Atlantic Isle* was eventually commissioned in 1943.

In 1969, the *Cilicia* was depicted on a *6d* stamp issued by Tristan da Cunha. The stamp was significant in that it was the only occasion on which a British merchant ship was featured on a stamp in wartime guise – in the *Cilicia*'s case as an armed merchant cruiser. The stamp serves as a tribute to all armed merchant cruisers and the men who served in them.

In March 1944 the *Cilicia* was sent to Mobile, USA, for overhaul and conversion into a troopship. She left Liverpool for Port Said on 16 December 1944 with 2,400 troops. By the end of hostilities she had made four trooping voyages, carrying a total of 16,035 troops and prisoners-of-war.

The *Cilicia* was returned to the Anchor Line in 1946 and was given a complete refit by her builders. She reopened the Indian passenger service from Liverpool on 31 May 1947.

In November 1965 the *Cilicia* was sold for £170,000 for use as a floating hostel for training stevedores at Parkhaven, Holland. She was renamed *Jan Backx* in this capacity. She remained in use until August 1980 when she was towed by the tug *Zwarte Zee* to Bilbao for breaking up. For this final voyage she reverted to her original name of *Cilicia*, and except for a broad orange band round her hull, she was still in Anchor Line colours.

CALEDONIA

Built by the Fairfield Shipbuilding & Engineering Co. of Govan in 1948.   **Yard No:** 732
Official Number: 182083   **Signal Letters:** G C K R
Gross Tonnage: 11,252   **Nett:** 6,547   **Length:** 483.6ft   **Breadth:** 66.4ft
Owned by the Anchor Line, Limited, registered at Glasgow
Twin screws, Doxford diesels, service speed 16½ knots, maximum 18 knots.

The loss of the Britannia in 1941 and the extreme age of the *Castalia* necessitated the Anchor Line building a third passenger vessel of the *Circassia*'s class. It was originally intended that the third ship (to be named *Caledonia*) should be a much larger vessel, but because of India's impending independence, it was felt that there would be a downturn in passenger traffic, and in the event an almost identical ship to the two earlier sisters was built.

The *Caledonia* was launched by the Marchioness of Linlithgow on 12 March 1947 and left Liverpool on her maiden voyage to Bombay on 23 March 1948, replacing the ageing *Castalia* of 1906.

She would appear to have led a charmed existence and remained on her designed route until withdrawn at the end of 1965. On 29 December 1965 the *Caledonia* arrived at Amsterdam for use as a floating hostel by students of Amsterdam University. She remained in this capacity until March 1970 when she was towed to Hamburg for demolition by the Ritscher Co. of Hamburg.

The *Caledonia* entering the Alfred Lock at Birkenhead. (Photo: Anchor Line)

2

BOOTH LINE

The brothers Alfred and Charles Booth started steamship services from Liverpool to North Brazil and the mouth of the River Amazon in 1866. Their ships sailed to Para (later Belem) where passengers and cargo were transferred to smaller vessels for transportation to upriver destinations.

The company was known to seafarers as 'Maggie Booths', after a lady of the family who took a kind and motherly interest in the crews of the Booth Line ships. She would visit their wives when their husbands were away at sea, ensuring that allotments were being sent home. She became a much-loved figure in Birkenhead and Bootle.

The business thrived sufficiently for the Booths to commence a service from New York to Para via West Indian ports. By 1890, a direct service was up and running from Liverpool to Manaus, 1,000 miles up the Amazon.

In 1901 the Booth Line became a limited company (Booth Steamship Co. (1901) Ltd) and amalgamated with the Red Cross Line, enabling an extensive passenger and cargo business with Spain and Portugal to be built up. At this time there was a boom in Amazon rubber which boosted cargo carryings.

In 1903 the Booth Steamship Co. acquired the Maranham Steamship Co., strengthening its North Brazilian connection, and finally in 1913 it took over the Iquitos Steamship Co., enabling it to extend its own services to Iquitos in Peru, some 2,300 miles upriver. Transhipment into smaller vessels for onward passage to Iquitos took place at Manaus.

There was considerable demand for passenger accommodation and the 4,600-ton *Ambrose* was built in 1903. Two years later she was followed by the 5,400-ton *Anselm* and in 1907/08 the trio of 6,300-ton liners *Antony*, *Lanfranc* and *Hilary* appeared on the Liverpool – Amazon route. In 1911 the 6,995-ton *Hildebrand* was built. This was indeed the heyday of the Booth Line as after the First World War, only the *Hildebrand* was to return to the Amazon.

In 1931 the new *Hilary* joined the Booth fleet, slightly larger than the *Hildebrand*. The two ships sailed together for just one year, but the depression of the early 1930s took its toll and the *Hildebrand* was sold in 1932, leaving the *Hilary* to carry on the service alone.

Family ownership of the Booth Line continued until 1946 when, dismayed at the task of rebuilding a fleet that had been reduced to just four ships by war losses, the Booth Line was sold to the Vestey Group, which already included the Blue Star Line and Lamport and Holt, both operating to South America. The Booth Line's Brazilian services tied in neatly with the rest of the group.

The Booth Line continued to operate passenger services under the slogan '1,000 Miles up the Amazon' until 1964, by which time competition from the airlines had made the services uneconomic. The last Booth Line-owned cargo vessels were withdrawn in 1986, and chartered ships operated on Booth Line routes until 1992 when the company ceased trading. The Booth Line, which had done so much to open up vast areas of Brazil to trade, was but a memory.

HILARY

Built by Cammell Laird & Co. Ltd at Birkenhead in 1931
Official Number: 162350   **Signal Letters:** G Q V M
Gross Tonnage: 7,420   **Nett:** 4,286   **Length:** 424·2ft   **Breadth:** 56·2ft
Owned by the Booth Steamship Company Limited, registered at Liverpool
Single screw steamer, triple-expansion engine, speed 14 knots.

Ordering the passenger-cargo liner the *Hilary* at the height of the depression was a mark of considerable faith by the Booth Line, and the placing of the order locally in Merseyside was much appreciated.

The *Hilary* was launched on 17 April 1931 and was completed by August. She sailed on her maiden voyage from Liverpool to Para and Manaus on 14 August. The new *Hilary* could be easily recognised by her distinctive three-note triple-chime steam whistle.

First-class single-berth rooms were on the promenade deck, double and three-berth on the upper deck, and there were four deluxe rooms with private bath and toilet. The third-class passengers were accommodated in two and four-berth cabins on the main deck, in compliance with Portuguese emigrant ship requirements.

The crew and stewards were quartered forward on the main and upper decks, while the captain and officers were in a house at the fore end of the boat deck.

A sister ship to the *Hilary* was built in 1935 – the *Anselm* – slightly smaller and with a cruiser stern. However, she was lost on 5 July 1941 when she was torpedoed by *U-96*, some 300 miles off the Azores.

The *Hilary* was aground twice in the Amazon during her early years. The first occasion was in November 1935, some 170 miles below Manaus, and in April 1936 she grounded two miles east of Goiabel on the notorious Mandahy Bank. One is reminded of the story attributed to Mark Twain, who, when asked by a passenger if he was the man who knew where the sandbanks were, replied, 'No, I'm the man who knows where the sandbanks ain't!'

Far more serious was the occasion when the *Hilary* ran aground on rocks near Holyhead , Anglesey, in dense fog at 12.45 a.m. on Easter Sunday, 9 April 1939. Because of the fog it was several hours before assistance arrived, but her 100 passengers were eventually taken off safely. The *Hilary* had sprung a leak forward, but was refloated and towed to Liverpool. It was an unfortunate experience for her master, Captain Lewis Evans of Pwllheli, who was due to retire at the end of the voyage.

On the outbreak of the Second World War, the *Hilary* was initially left to her owners' commercial service, but in January 1941 she was sent to South Shields and there converted for use as an armed boarding steamer. In May 1941 she sighted two Italian oil tankers off the Azores. One of these was scuttled before the *Hilary* had a chance to put a boarding party on board, but the other, the *Gianna M* was taken safely to Belfast by a prize crew from the *Hilary*.

In April 1942 the *Hilary* ceased to operate as an armed boarding steamer and was returned to Booth Line management, but under Ministry of War Transport orders. On 16 October 1942 she was acting as commodore ship of a convoy bound for New York when her engine room was struck by a torpedo. Luckily for the *Hilary*, the torpedo failed to explode. The story is best told in the words of her then master, Captain A. Elliott:

> We had been followed by enemy submarines for about twenty-four hours, but had not been attacked. However, on the morning of 16 October, at about 10.30am, we heard an explosion and felt a rather heavy tremor in the ship, just as if some other ship in the vicinity had been torpedoed.
>
> The commodore gave an anxious look round his convoy but everything seemed very quiet and peaceful, with the ships all plodding along in their rightful stations. It suddenly struck

me that we ourselves might have been hit, although our engines were still turning to the revolutions required. I thought I should send officers to check, and I myself went down to the after-end of the ship, but no damage could be seen.

As I came forward again the chief engineer met me and took me down to the dynamo platform where he showed me a large dent in the ship's plates. Some rivets had been sheared off, but there was no leak.

We had been hit by a torpedo in a very vulnerable part of the ship, but although the pistol had gone off, the main charge of the torpedo had failed to explode. If the mechanism had functioned there would have been very little chance of the ship surviving.

In March 1943 the *Hilary* was again requisitioned, this time as an infantry landing ship. The conversion was carried out by Cammell Laird at Birkenhead. Her passenger accommodation became mess decks, her public rooms communication and control centres, and six landing craft replaced her lifeboats. Armament included a 6-inch gun on her forecastle and a number of Oerlikons; a radar tower was built on the bridge and a searchlight platform constructed between the bridge and the funnel. The *Hilary*'s funnel, masts and superstructure were all left intact and not cut down or removed as with so many converted merchant ships.

With her hull and superstructure painted grey, the *Hilary* sailed for the Mediterranean where she was based on Algiers, and on 10 July 1943 took part in Operation Husky, the invasion of Sicily, acting as headquarters for Rear Admiral Sir Philip Vian. Two months later the *Hilary* was present at the Salerno landing, and in December 1943 she returned to Portsmouth, ready for the invasion of Europe.

In June 1944 the *Hilary* took part in the Normandy landings as flagship of Force 'J' under Commodore G.N. Oliver. On 23 June, Admiral Vian transferred his flag to the *Hilary* after his cruiser HMS *Scylla* had been damaged by a mine.

The *Hilary* returned to the Mersey in January 1945 and was handed back to her owners. Cammell Laird refitted her for her old commercial trade and provided accommodation for ninety-three first-class and 138 tourist-class passengers. By the end of 1945 *Hilary* was once again sailing 1,000 miles up the Amazon for the Booth Line. She retained her pre-war appearance, but in 1947 the Booth Line houseflag was painted on each side of her funnel. In 1949 *Hilary* was converted from a coal burner to an oil burner, and in 1951 she was joined on the Amazon by a new running-mate, the *Hildebrand*.

When she was twenty-five years old, the *Hilary* was sent to Antwerp for a four-month major refit, and reappeared with an all-white hull, the only Booth liner ever to be so treated. She resumed service in April 1956 with her regular route now including calls at Barbados and Trinidad. Later in 1956 the *Hilary* was chartered to Elder Dempster for three round voyages to West Africa.

On the *Hilary*'s arrival back at Toxteth Dock, Liverpool, on 14 December 1956, Special Branch detectives boarded the ship to investigate the jamming of her steering gear in the Atlantic a week previously. The *Hilary* had been on her way home from West Africa via Las Palmas with 170 passengers. Third Officer James Turley was on the bridge and had given orders to turn to port when he saw another vessel approaching, but the *Hilary* would not answer her helm.

The master, Captain T.E. Williams, was summoned, and 'not under command' lights hoisted. An investigation revealed that an eighteen-inch wheel key, used to control heat in the galley, was missing from its usual place, and it was later found jammed in the steering mechanism. It was quickly removed. The wheel key, a heavy instrument three quarters of an inch in diameter, with two lugs at one end for fitting in the locks of steam pressure doors, had been taken from the galley.

For twenty minutes the *Hilary* was drifting in a busy sea lane. Captain Williams reported that other incidents had taken place during the voyage. Some electrical cables had been found cut or disconnected. The loudspeaker system had failed and the spare parts could not be found and an alarm instrument on the turbine gear was found smashed.

Hilary, with Elder Dempster funnel colour. (Photo: K.P. Lewis)

After two hours of investigation, Inspector Albert Allen of the Home Office Forensic Science Department ruled out the sabotage theory and said that no further police action was necessary. Captain Williams commented: 'There must have been a lunatic on board'.

The loss of the *Hildebrand* in 1957 gave the *Hilary* a reprieve from the breakers' yard until 1959, when she was sold for scrap. On 12 September of that year she left the Mersey for the last time, under her own steam, bound for the Firth of Forth where she was broken up by Thos. W. Ward at Inverkeithing.

1,000 MILES UP THE AMAZON ON THE *HILARY*

Extracts from the Booth Line brochure for 1932

If a tramcar started from London or Liverpool and made a circle of 11,800 miles at a charge of two pence a mile, the travelling public would be amazed at both the achievement and the price. Yet this is exactly what has been accomplished; only a magnificent liner takes the place of the tramcar, and the charge of two pence a mile includes not only transport but the services and cuisine of a first-class hotel.

A cruise on an ocean liner is not only a new innovation, but when 2,000 of these miles are accomplished in a luxuriously fitted 7,000-ton vessel on the great Amazon – the river of mystery – and the heart of the South American continent is penetrated through the equatorial forests of Brazil without a change of cabin from the time of leaving Liverpool to the day of the return to the Mersey, then it becomes not only unique as a cruise, but also a historic achievement in maritime transport and luxurious travel.

Days are spent in quaint cities. Curious natives in the palm thatch dwellings of their jungle homes are passed at many points. Hours speed by swiftly in gliding on tropical rivers through forests of vivid colours alive with bright plumed birds and gorgeous butterflies.

However, before this wonderland of Amazonia is entered there are scenes of beauty and enjoyment under the blue skies of Portugal, amid the romantic mountains of Madeira and on tropical seas where gales are almost unknown and the broad sunlit ocean is ruffled only by the fresh trade wind and the shoals of flying fish.

These distant lands, seas and rivers of beauty, warmth and mystery can be reached and enjoyed on the comfortably seated, broad decks, or in the palatial staterooms of a 7,000-ton liner, the specially equipped Royal Mail Steamer *Hilary*.

When the island of Madeira disappears in the deep blue of the sea and sky, muslin dresses and white drill suits make their first appearance on the decks. Delightful days of rest and pleasure, deck sports and reading, are spent; interspersed with moonlight nights of concerts, dances and lectures. New friendships, new scenes, new thoughts – away from the bustle, hum and smoke of great cities.

From out of the tropical haze has appeared a low shore. It is the first glimpse of the mysterious Amazon which has already changed, with its outflow, the colour of the sea around from deep blue to pale yellow-green.

Soon we are in the Para River, one of the mouths of the mighty Amazon, here nearly 200-miles broad but filled with forest-clad islands. Then the great ship, which has brought us across the Equator into the Southern Hemisphere, comes to a momentary rest for official visits from the authorities of the Port of Para – the gateway to the Amazon.

The *Hilary* penetrates further into the heartland of Brazil. The immense tropical forest is all around and natives in their dugout canoes cease paddling to gaze in awe at the huge vessel towering above their frail craft.

There is a great mystery in the Amazonian night. Scarcely has the sun disappeared in golden glory behind the interminable walls of the forest, before all around is plunged into darkness. Troops of howling monkeys hold a conversation before retiring. Sometimes the indigo vault is ablaze with the lightning from soundless electric storms.

The town of Obidos is passed during the night. Somewhere in this comparatively narrow section of the river the *Hilary* often passes a sister ship coming downstream. The occasion is one for saluting the house flag.

Some nine miles from Manaus the *Hilary* leaves the main stream of the Amazon and enters the Rio Negro. The meeting of the waters of these two giants provides a scene of extraordinary interest. As its name implies, the Negro is comprised of blue-black water, and this forms huge dark patches and miniature whirlpools in the middle of the Amazonian flood. So distinct is the cleavage that the bows of the ship are floating in the dark water whilst the stern is still supported by the yellow of the Amazon proper.

There appears to be a certain rivalry between Para and Manaus as to which town shall give the more hearty welcome to those who cruise on the *Hilary*. For whereas Para welcomes the ship with rockets and shots fired in the air, Manaus sends a band onto the quay and residents appear *en masse* with cheers, spotlessly clean white suits, straw hats and immense bouquets of flowers.

It is easy to write lightly of this hearty welcome, but when one grips the hands of Englishmen in this isolated town, a thousand miles from civilisation – and yet, like an oasis in the desert, possessed of all modern conveniences such as electric light, trams, theatres, cafes and daily newspapers – there is a feeling of pride because English, Scots and Irishmen have had no small share in the achievement.

Manaus is a clean town and one is not afraid to eat its food or drink its water. No one could remain long on the ship, or be lonely in hospitable Manaus.

The leave takings from this remote town are mingled with regret. There is a feeling of sadness as the end of the outward cruise is reached, at a distance of over 5,000 miles from Liverpool, and the *Hilary* turns her bows downstream.

The same course is followed on the homeward journey and time ashore is usually available at Para, Madeira, Lisbon and Oporto for completing the work of sightseeing. Fancy dress balls on the decorated decks, concerts in the music room and open-air dances lend enchantment to tropical nights.

When the *Hilary* returns to the broad and busy River Mersey, and this unique cruise is drawing to a close, the traveller will feel that he has been away in fairyland, so many and so unusual have been the sights, sounds and sensations. The Amazon is a river of mystery and provides food for thought and romance long after trips to other lands have faded from memory.

HILDEBRAND

Built by Cammell, Laird & Co. Ltd at Birkenhead in 1951
Official Number: 185422   **Signal Letters:** G K T K
Gross Tonnage: 7,735   **Nett:** 4,368   **Length:** 420·5ft   **Breadth:** 60·3ft
Owned by the Booth Steamship Co. Ltd, registered at Liverpool
2 steam turbines, double-reduction geared to single screw shaft.   **Speed:** 14 knots.

The *Hildebrand* was launched at Birkenhead on 20 July 1951, and sailed on her maiden voyage from Liverpool to Lisbon, Para and Manaus on 28 December of that year. On 15 June 1953 the *Hildebrand* represented the Booth Line at the Coronation Review of ships at Spithead.

The *Hildebrand* had a very short career with the Booth Line. On 25 September 1957 she was attempting to approach Lisbon in thick fog and ran aground on Cascais Point at the mouth of the River Tagus. Despite every effort by the tugs *Herakles* and *Em. Z. Svitzer*, the *Hildebrand* could not be refloated and she was declared a total loss on 28 October. All her 164 passengers and her crew were saved and her cargo was removed.

As a result of the subsequent inquiry, the captain of the *Hildebrand* had his master's certificate suspended for twelve months. In presenting the findings of the court of inquiry, the Wreck Commissioner said that much of what was passing through the mind of the master during the last half-hour before the stranding must remain obscure, but there was strong evidence that he was a tired man.

The Booth Line steamer *Hildebrand*, 1951. (Photo: *Shipbuilding and Shipping Record*)

This unfortunate incident raised the whole question of the shipmaster's responsibilities in bad weather at sea, particularly in fog. No one questions that the ultimate responsibility must rest with the master, but it may pertinently be asked how far the bearing of this ultimate responsibility must take the traditional form, which involves the presence of the master on the bridge throughout, without respite of any kind.

The loss of the *Hildebrand* provided the ageing *Hilary* with a two-year reprieve from the breaker's yard.

HUBERT

Built by Cammell Laird & Co. Ltd at Birkenhead in 1955
Official Number: 185510   **Signal Letters:** G S B F
Gross Tonnage: 7,905   **Nett:** 4,452   **Length:** 439ft   **Breadth:** 60·4ft
Owned by the Booth Steamship Co. Ltd, registered at Liverpool
2 steam turbines, double-reduction geared to single screw.   **Speed:** 14 knots.

The *Hubert* was designed as a consort for the *Hildebrand*, but had slight modifications made in the light of experience. She was launched on 31 August 1954 and had the distinction of being the largest ship ever built for the Booth Line, but she was not the largest ever owned by the company. This honour goes to the *Anselm* of 1961.

The *Hubert* sailed on her maiden voyage from Liverpool on 11 February 1955, calling at Leixoes, Lisbon, Madeira, Barbados, Para and Manaus. She had accommodation for seventy-four first-class passengers and ninety-six in tourist class.

The Booth Line ceased carrying passengers in 1964 and the *Hubert* was transferred to the Blue Star Line who placed her on charter to the Austasia Line and renamed her *Malaysia*. In 1976 she was sold to the Atlas Shipping Agency of Singapore and renamed *Khalij Express*. Eight years later the old *Hubert* was broken up at Alang.

The last of the Booth passenger liners: the *Hubert*, 1955. (Photo: *Shipbuilding and Shipping Record*)

ANSELM (EX-BAUDOUINVILLE, EX-THYSVILLE)

Built by Soc. Anon. Jhn. Cockerill at Hoboken in 1950 for Cie. Maritime Belge.
Gross Tonnage: 10,990   **Nett:** 5,910   **Length:** 479ft   **Breadth:** 64·8ft

The *Baudouinville* was launched on 4 March 1950 and sailed on her maiden voyage from Antwerp to Matadi on 19 September. On 1 June 1957 her name was changed to *Thysville* and she continued in service with Cie. Maritime Belge until in 1960 she became redundant following the independence of the Belgian Congo.

The vessel was acquired by the Booth Line in 1961 and renamed *Anselm*, and on 16 June sailed on her maiden voyage from Liverpool. She was the largest merchant ship ever to sail 1,000 miles up the Amazon and had accommodation for 135 first-class passengers and 101 in tourist class. Considerations which affect the size of ships trading to Manaus are relative to length rather than to tonnage or draft, since there are many sharp bends to be negotiated on the river passage. The *Anselm* had an overall length of 505ft and she was the longest vessel ever to proceed to Manaus, with the exception of the British light cruiser *Apollo*, which navigated the Amazon in 1938.

The *Anselm*'s service with the Booth Line lasted for only two years and in 1963 she was transferred to the Blue Star Line and became the *Iberia Star*. Two years later she was transferred to the Austasia Line and, in 1965, renamed *Australasia* and put on the Singapore to Melbourne service. She remained in this capacity for seven years before being sold for demolition in December 1972.

3

CANADIAN PACIFIC

The Canadian Pacific Railway Co. was incorporated on 16 February 1881, and the 2,900 miles of track from Montreal to the Pacific coast were opened in 1886.

Canadian Pacific commenced its passenger liner operations in 1889 when the company was awarded a mail contract worth £60,000 a year for a monthly service across the Pacific. Initially chartered tonnage was used on the route, but in 1891 the first three Empress liners entered service.

The trans-Pacific route was only part of a wider scheme to provide a through link from England by steamers capable of crossing from Plymouth to St John, New Brunswick or Halifax, Nova Scotia, in not more than five days. It was not until 1902 that any progress was made when it was announced: 'At the request of the Canadian Ministers now in London, the Canadian Pacific Railway Co. today telegraphed an offer to establish and work a weekly fast passenger service composed of four steamers of modern equipment, with a speed of 20 knots, from Liverpool to Quebec and Montreal in the summer, and to Halifax in the winter'.

In March 1903 Canadian Pacific bought the Canadian interests of Elder Dempster, who had been involved in the Canadian trade since the early 1890s, and who had acquired the Beaver Line in 1899. Canadian Pacific's red and white chequered house flag was raised on the *Lake Champlain* on 6 April 1903, and this vessel took the first Canadian Pacific Liverpool to Montreal passenger service a week later on 14 April. With its entry into North Atlantic passenger operations, Canadian Pacific was now in control of the westbound route from Europe to Japan and China.

In December 1904 Canadian Pacific placed orders for two large express steamers which were launched as the *Empress of Britain* and the *Empress of Ireland*. They were by far the largest and fastest vessels in the Canadian trade. Canadian Pacific obtained control of its archrival on the transatlantic route, the Allan Line, in 1909.

Perhaps the blackest day in Canadian Pacific history was 24 May 1914 when the *Empress of Ireland* collided with the Norwegian steamer *Storstad* in dense fog in the Gulf of St Lawrence and sank with the appalling loss of 1,014 lives. A court of inquiry found the *Storstad* entirely to blame.

In April 1922 Canadian Pacific transferred its principal express passenger service from Liverpool to Southampton. For several years Canadian Pacific's European terminal was Hamburg, and its *Empress* liners operated to Quebec, calling at Southampton and Cherbourg. On 11 June 1930 the Prince of Wales launched the *Empress of Britain*. With a gross tonnage of 42,348 and a service speed of 24 knots, the new *Empress* was the largest ship ever built for the Canadian trade. Sadly Canadian Pacific's magnificent flagship was bombed on 26 October 1940 whilst in the Western Approaches after a voyage from Egypt via the Cape. Although taken in tow, the *Empress of Britain* was torpedoed and sunk by *U-32* on 28 October. She had the dubious distinction of being the largest merchant ship lost in the war.

Towards the end of the 1920s, Canadian Pacific launched four Duchess cabin-class liners, specifically for the Liverpool service. These were the *Duchess of Bedford*, *Duchess of Atholl*, *Duchess of Richmond* and *Duchess of York*. Each of the new ships had a tonnage of just over 20,000, a service speed of 18 knots and accommodation for 580 cabin, 480 tourist and 510 third-class passengers.

Two of the Duchess liners were lost during the Second World War. The *Duchess of Atholl* was torpedoed and sunk by *U-178* on 10 October 1942, some 200 miles east of Ascension Island. On 11 July 1943 the *Duchess of York* was bombed and sunk by enemy aircraft off the Spanish coast.

Canadian Pacific never resumed its transpacific services after the Second World War, and the surviving pre-war Empress, the *Empress of Scotland*, and the two surviving Duchesses returned to the Liverpool–Montreal service on the completion of their war duties.

EMPRESS OF FRANCE (EX-DUCHESS OF BEDFORD)

Built by John Brown & Co. Ltd at Clydebank in 1928. **Yard No:** 518.
Official Number: 160482   **Signal Letters:** G N T V
Gross Tonnage: 20,448   **Nett:** 11,335   **Length:** 581·9ft   **Breadth:** 75·2ft
Owned by the Canadian Pacific Railway Co. (Canadian Pacific Steamships – Managers)
6 steam turbines, single reduction geared to twin-screws.   **Speed:** 17½ knots.

The *Duchess of Bedford* took the concept of the 'cabin-class' ship to its highest point. She was one of four sisters, the others being the *Duchesses of Atholl, Richmond* and *York*. The *Duchess of Atholl* was intended to be the first in service, but an accident involving one of her turbines when she was fitting out meant that this honour fell to the *Duchess of Bedford*, whose completion was speeded up so that she could take the first sailing on the advertised date of 1 June 1928.

The *Duchess of Bedford* was launched on 24 January 1928 by Mrs Stanley Baldwin, wife of the then prime minister. The new liner had a deadweight capacity of 8,750 tons, which included 2,725 tons of fuel oil, and she could very easily exceed her designed service speed of 17½ knots. Her original passenger accommodation was for 580 in cabin class, 480 in tourist class and 510 in third class. A crew of 510 was carried.

On her second westbound voyage the *Duchess* established a new record for the passage between Liverpool and Montreal of six days, nine and a half hours, saving nearly a full day on the previous best. Although she was only intended to make 17½ knots, she could average 18-knots without the least difficulty, and could steam at almost 20 knots for considerable periods.

At the beginning of 1933 the *Duchess of Bedford* was on charter to Furness, Withy & Co. and sailed on the New York–Bermuda service whilst the *Queen of Bermuda* was being completed. On 8 May 1933 the *Duchess* was the subject of an absolutely unfounded rumour that she had foundered after striking an iceberg off the Newfoundland coast with passengers and about £500,000 of gold bullion on board. The distress that this must have caused to the relatives of those on board was not alleviated until 2 a.m. the following day when the liner radioed from mid-ocean that all was well with her.

The Empress of France as she appeared after her 1948 refit. (Photo: *Shipbuilding and Shipping Record*)

Two months later, on 13 July 1933, the *Duchess of Bedford* actually did strike an iceberg in the Belle Isle Strait between Newfoundland and Labrador, but fortunately was undamaged and six years later, in June 1939, she brought thirty-two French seamen whose barquentine had sunk after striking a berg off Newfoundland safely to Liverpool.

On the outbreak of the Second World War the *Duchess of Bedford* was requisitioned for service as a troopship for which she was admirably suited by her original design. Just before the fall of Singapore in January 1942 she arrived with 4,000 Indian troops and forty Indian nurses. Packed with refugees, including 875 women and children, she got away five days before the surrender. Later in 1942 the *Duchess of Bedford* arrived at Liverpool with the first US troops: 673 officers and 6,507 men. She was given the credit for sinking a submarine by gunfire about this time, and the *Duchess* finished a very eventful year stranded during the French North African operations. The Irish Sea packets *Ulster Monarch* and *Royal Ulsterman* had to tow her free.

The first-class cocktail bar on the *Empress of France*. (Photo: Canadian Pacific)

The first-class lounge on the *Empress of France*. (Photo: Canadian Pacific)

After North Africa came the Sicilian and Italian operations. In 1943 the *Duchess of Bedford* was the first transport in at the Salerno landings. In the spring of 1945 she carried to Odessa a large number of Russian prisoners who had been liberated by the Allied advance in Europe, and returned with Allied prisoners whom the Russians had rescued. Considering the extent and variety of her war work, covering some 350,000 miles and carrying 231,000 troops, it was remarkable that the *Duchess of Bedford* escaped any damage, although she had very many narrow escapes.

After the war the *Duchess of Bedford* was employed in repatriating troops, service wives and children to Canada, and arrived at the Fairfield yard at Govan to be reconditioned in 1947. She was renamed *Empress of France* (although the original intention had been to change her name to *Empress of India*), and her accommodation was rebuilt to carry a total of 400 passengers in first class and 300 in tourist class.

The machinery was thoroughly overhauled, new propellers were fitted, and she was painted in Canadian Pacific's new Atlantic colours of white hull with green riband and boot-topping, with buff funnels having the company's houseflag painted on either side. She returned to the Liverpool to Montreal service on 1 September 1948.

It was intended that Princess Elizabeth and the Duke of Edinburgh would sail to Canada at the start of their 1952 tour on board the *Empress of France*, but the King's illness forced these arrangements to be cancelled, and the royal couple went by air. However, Captain Ben Grant, master of the *Empress of France*, was not forgotten and he was invited to a reception at London's Guildhall where he met the royal couple on their return from Canada on board the *Empress of Scotland*.

During one of her refits in the late 1950s, the *Empress of France* was given what was claimed to be a more modern appearance; her two funnels were tapered and raked tops were added. This did not particularly suit her and many of her admirers felt that her profile had been ruined.

The *Empress of France* with her new modern funnels after her 1958 refit. (Photo: *Shipbuilding and Shipping Record*)

The long gallery connecting the public rooms on the *Empress of France*.

The library and writing room on the *Empress of France*.

The *Empress of France* lasted until 1960, making her last voyage in October of that year. On Monday 19 December 1960 she left Liverpool under her own steam for Newport, where she was broken up by John Cashmore & Sons. It was a time of sad farewells on the Mersey, for just three days previously the *Britannic* had left Liverpool, also for the breakers' yard.

LATE FOR HIS OWN FUNERAL – LITERALLY!

by Ted Morris

In the run up to Christmas 1948 I was serving as Fourth Officer in RMS *Empress of France*. Shipment of mail that year was particularly heavy and stowage in the secure lockers became problematical as the time for sailing from Liverpool approached. The safe carriage of the mail and any 'special' parcels and items was my responsibility, and I had already accepted a crated coffin, containing the remains of a gentleman and destined for discharge at Quebec, and which was now resting in the specials locker.

Within the limits of practicability we always afforded such situations the utmost reverence but on this particular occasion a late arrival of mail for Montreal left me no choice of stowage space other than the said locker. The mail was duly loaded but because of the excessive number of bags, the crate in question was very unfortunately overstowed.

A first-class start to the day: breakfast on the *Empress of France*, Monday 1 August 1960.

I was sometimes fascinated by various remarks made and questions asked by relatives of deceased persons whose remains were travelling with us. They seemed to have the impression that the casket would be serenely mounted on a catafalque with the traditional candles at head and foot or, perhaps, armed guards at the four corners, resting on their reversed arms! Not so, I fear, but I had to be happy with the existing situation and console myself that there was no real breach of ethics.

A turbulent westbound passage caused a late arrival at Wolfe's Cove, Quebec and an ultra-fast disembarkation of passengers and discharge of ancillaries. Air temperatures were falling and this was definitely the last voyage of the season and everything was hurry, hurry, hurry.

In quick time we were off the berth and heading upriver at best speed on our way to Montreal, more than satisfied with our endeavours, but imagine the scene as my particular complacency was shattered when the Staff Captain informed me (in dulcet tones, of course) that a message had been received from Quebec that a BODY had gone missing and that funeral directors had called for collection – in vain!

The situation was awesome, and now ethics were fighting economics in my mind! All sorts of reasons and excuses relative to our quick stay at Quebec could be given, but the facts could neither be denied nor forgiven. The remains of the deceased must now stay with us to Montreal, and then be transported back to Quebec by some means or other.

Distress to relatives would be inevitable, not to mention the obvious enormous expense involved and the awful fact that, as mentioned in the title of this anecdote, the gentleman in question really had missed his own funeral!

This must be the nearest I ever came to a 'Decline to Report' – I think!

LIFE ON THE *EMPRESS OF FRANCE* IN 1949

by Captain J.C. Moffatt

I joined the *Empress of France* as fifth officer in Gladstone Dry Dock, Liverpool in November 1949. The ship was undergoing refit, having completed her first post-war year on North Atlantic service.

The taxi driver helped me to carry my luggage on board and I reported to the chief officer. He welcomed me on board and showed me to my cabin which was small but well-appointed: a bunk, settee, desk, wardrobe and a washbasin with hot and cold running water. A far cry from the old compactum-type washbasin in my last ship, the *Clan Macneil*.

I was introduced to the first and third officers who were standing-by the ship. Although we were sleeping on board there was no victualling and we were paid seven shillings a day to feed ourselves. The chief officer then told me he was about to cook a light meal for the stand-by officers, probably beans on toast. At the time I thought this was a bit strange as I had never known a chief officer do the cooking before!

After unpacking I went on ship rounds with the third officer. Being new to passenger liners I soon realised I was fortunate to join the ship in refit as I quickly got to know my way about. On my first morning aboard I joined the others in the wardroom where the chief officer (who held an Extra Master's Certificate) dished up a superb breakfast of porridge, boiled eggs, toast and marmalade. 'I don't suppose you have experienced this arrangement before, have you?' he asked me. He then went on to explain we had a steward in the daytime to make our bunks, clean our rooms, the wardroom and wash up the dishes. The rest of the time we looked after ourselves. I was also informed that it was my job as the most junior officer to go to the local grocery store in Seaforth every Friday armed with cash, grip-bag, ration cards and a list of groceries to be purchased for the wardroom.

The *Empress of France* left the dry dock on 29 December 1949. The chief officer took me to meet the captain. I was shaking in my shoes. On being introduced I was immediately made to feel at ease and was welcomed to the ship.

The atmosphere on board was friendly and after six weeks I had settled into harbour routine. After leaving the dry dock we secured in No.2 branch Gladstone Dock to commence loading. Ship's Articles were opened on 2 January 1950 and the next day we commenced to feed on board. The food was very good and there was plenty of it.

The ship now had a full complement of officers: Master, six deck, four radio, four pursers, twenty plus engineers (including electrical and sanitary engineers), chief and second stewards, a Canadian rail traffic officer and a nursing officer.

Fire and lifeboat drills including an abandon ship exercise were carried out under the eagle eye of the BOT Surveyor and the ship was granted her Safety Certificate. Over the next ten days the Empress was stored and general cargo loaded. Twenty-four hours before departure hundreds of bags of mail arrived.

A leisurely luncheon in the first-class restaurant on the *Empress of France*, Friday 28 August 1959.

Luncheon

Chilled Juices :   Clam   Tomato   Apple   Grapefruit

Sardines in Oil   Herrings in Cream   Salade Americaine   Eggs Tartare
Artichoke Fonds Vinaigrette   Heart of Palm Ravigote
Cornichons   Aubergines Italienne   Antipasto
Assorted Continental Sausages

Consommes : Nature, Vermicelli   Pea Soup Habitant
Clam Chowder Manhattan

Broiled Fillet of Haddock   Butter Sauce
Cold : Gaspe Salmon Mayonnaise, Sliced Cucumber

Omelettes :   Mushroom   Savoury   Espagnole

Raviolis au Parmesan
Fresh Vegetable Plate
Irish Stew with Dumplings
Curried Fruits Bangalore

Boiled Wiltshire Gammon, Julienne of Parsnips

FROM THE GRILL AND TO ORDER (10 to 15 minutes)
Lamb Loin Chop Vert Pre   Slip Sole Saute Meuniere

VEGETABLES
Boston Succotash   Creamed Spinach
Potatoes :   Mashed   Baked   Jacket   Pont Neuf

COLD BUFFET
Prime Roast Ribs of Beef   Canadian Ham   Terrine of Duckling
Spiced Beef   Raised Pie   Pressed Corned Pork   Galantine of Veal
Home Made Brawn   Roast Turkey   Jellied Ox Tongue

SALADS
Tossed Romaine Lettuce with Chives & Celery
Lettuce   Tomato   Potato   Beetroot   Cole Slaw   Grated Carrot   Combination
Dressings : French   Roquefort   Thousand Island   Sweet

DESSERTS
Rusk Custard Pudding   Compote of Pineapple Whipped Cream
Apricot Pie
Ice Cream :   Vanilla,   Orange
Raspberry Puffs

CHEESE
Canadian Red   Kraft   Danish Blue   Cherry Hill Wine
Gorgonzola   Black Diamond   Oka   Philladelphia Cream
Gruyere   Edam   Cheddar   Imperial

CRACKERS VARIOUS
Tea   Iced Tea & Coffee   Coffee

Coffee is also served in the Public Rooms
Special and Dietetic Dishes may be ordered as desired
EMPRESS OF FRANCE   Friday, 28th, August 1959
IC

On Tuesday 10 January 1950 we left Gladstone Dock at 10 a.m. and were secured alongside Princes Landing Stage by 11.30. The ship was gleaming and stewards were buzzing about in preparation for the embarkation of 600 passengers. The junior officers were on gangway duty throughout the period of embarkation. At 1 p.m. I went down to the first-class dining saloon for lunch and experienced my first meal dining from the first-class menu. I thought to myself, 'I am going to enjoy life in this ship!'

Embarkation was completed by 4 p.m. and half an hour later we sailed for Halifax, Nova Scotia, and St John, New Brunswick.

I was to keep watch with the second officer on the 12 to 4. After dinner I turned in at 8.30 p.m. to get some sleep before I was called at quarter to midnight. I spent most of my first watch on the bridge wing as the *Empress of France* proceeded down the St George's Channel. It was a bitterly cold night. Visibility was excellent and there were a large number of ships

Menu

Chilled Honeydew Melon Frappe

Canape Suedoise

Smoked Salmon   Salted Cashews   Eggs Farci Monaco
Ripe Olives   Table Celery   Queen Olives

Consomme Trois Filets   Creme Marie Louise

Supreme of Turbot Sauce Mousseline
Fried Silver Smelts Tartare

Glazed Apple Fritters Melba
Emince of Beef Tenderloin Palace
Heart of Palm Mornay

SPECIAL TO ORDER
Wiener Schnitzel

Quarter of Lamb Roasted, Mint Sauce or Jelly
Roast Young Turkey Chestnut Dressing Cranberry Jelly

VEGETABLES
Brussels Sprouts au Beurre   Fried Egg Plant
Potatoes: Boiled New   Rissolees   Marquise

COLD SELECTION
Raised Pie   Jellied Ox Tongue
Galantine of Capon

SALADS
Heart of Lettuce   Tomato   Waldorf
Dressing :   French   Mayonnaise   Thousand Islands

DESSERTS
Bachelor Pudding

Fruit in Jelly   Coupe Africaine
Vanilla Ice Cream au Menthe
Chocolate Gateaux   Petit Fours

SAVOURY
Croute Dianne

Fresh Fruits   Coffee

Coffee is also served in the Public Rooms

EMPRESS OF FRANCE   Tuesday, 25th August, 1959

The tourist-class dinner menu on the *Empress of France*, Tuesday 25 August 1959.

proceeding towards Liverpool and Glasgow. My senior on the watch was very good, giving me much valuable advice both on the working side and what was expected of one socially on an Empress at sea.

The watch passed quickly and at 4 a.m. we handed over to the first and fourth officers. The second officer had informed me earlier that the 12 to 4 watch was not required to do a breakfast relief and that I could stay in my bunk until 10 a.m. I thought he was joking and just smiled. I turned in at 4.20 a.m. and was somewhat surprised when the steward called me at 10 a.m. with a breakfast tray. He said: 'You hadn't left any instructions, sir. Therefore I thought it would be a good idea to call you at the same time as the second.' This was definitely a different type of life from cargo ships!

As we steamed west the weather started to deteriorate and forty-eight hours after leaving Liverpool we were pitching heavily into a head sea. Twenty-four hours later the temperature started to drop and it continued to do so as we approached the Grand Banks. Apart from watchkeeping duties at sea, I did not have much extra work. I was responsible to the chief officer for the upkeep of stationery and all signalling equipment.

Social life at sea was good. Junior officers were not allowed in the public rooms, except on cinema night, but were expected to entertain passengers during morning coffee and afternoon tea.

Two nights before arrival at Halifax was 'Gala Night'. This was *the night* of the voyage, with extra special dressing up. The orchestra played in the dining room and the menu was out of this world!

On Monday 18 January we entered Halifax harbour. It was bitterly cold; in fact I have never felt so cold in all my life. I realised that I would have to get some extra gear as soon as we arrived at St John. We were alongside at Halifax for five hours and a number of passengers disembarked and transferred to the Canadian Pacific Railway for the final part of their journeys to the Canadian interior.

With mail and baggage discharged and water tanks topped up, we sailed at 1 p.m. When we secured alongside our berth at St John the next day the snow was at least a foot deep. During passenger disembarkation the fourth officer and myself did gangway duty. By noon the passengers had all gone and we commenced harbour routine. Along with the third and fourth officers I was required to do twelve hours on and twenty-four hours off.

Throughout our stay at St John we worked cargo and tended moorings (the tidal range was over 20ft). Over the weekend large numbers of local people came down to the docks to see the 'White Empress' – it was always a great occasion when we docked at St John.

On 24 January 1950 we embarked our eastbound passengers, completed loading cargo, baggage and mail, bunkering and topping up of water tanks, and at noon we sailed for Halifax and Liverpool. The weather was foul on the passage home and we were six hours late arriving at Liverpool. I enjoyed my time on the *Empress of France* and I was very sorry some months later when I was transferred to another ship of the line.

PROUD SHIP ON THE MERSEY – CANADA RUN

by a *Liverpool Echo* reporter, April 1958

Walk on board the Canadian Pacific liner *Empress of France* in Gladstone Dock and it will seem strangely quiet. It is the day before sailing and the lounges and cocktail bars are deserted in marked contrast to the gay scenes there when the ship is at sea.

But do not be misled by the quietness. Without any fuss the staff onboard are diligently attending to their duties. Two orderly queues are formed up on one of the decks. This is signing-on day and the crew are presenting their discharge books to the shipping master and company officials before signing the ship's Articles of Agreement.

As dockside cranes lower cargo into the holds, sixty-two-year-old Patrick McAleavey, first-class cocktail bar steward from Blundellsands, puts a few finishing touches to the already mirror-clean fittings and furniture. He's been with Canadian Pacific for forty years and has probably served enough cocktails to float the Empress.

First Officer John Walker of Great Crosby checks over documents in his cabin. They show that the *Empress of France* brought in 2,100 tons of cargo, 70 first-class passengers and 370 tourist-class passengers on her last eastbound voyage. And now for the forthcoming voyage the ship is loading 1,000 tons of exports. The last of the consignment of 'Hot Rod' racing cars for the Canadian market is lifted from the quay and gently lowered into the forward hold. Inside the dock shed lorries are still being loaded with the inward cargo from Montreal.

In the first-class dining saloon Arthur Wilson of Wallasey notes that there will be 601 passengers on the outward trip and that 127 are travelling first class. He'll spare a moment to tell you that he first joined the *Empress of France* in 1936 and has sailed with her on every voyage except one. Arthur will tell you that when the ship (then the *Duchess of Bedford*), made her first voyage of the war to Bombay, she had a skirmish with submarines. On another voyage, from Liverpool to Boston, the ship was credited with sinking one U-boat and badly damaging another. The damage to the enemy was done using a First World War vintage gun mounted on the stern.

The *Empress of France* is indeed a proud ship with a proud record. If time permits, Arthur Wilson will describe the time the Empress was the last ship to leave Singapore after the capitulation. But she did not escape without damage from Japanese shrapnel bombs. Arthur was there when the *Empress of France* took part in three invasions – North Africa, Salerno and Anzio. She was carrying American commandos to Salerno and was HQ ship under the command of Captain 'Pony' Moore. The American commander of the invading force was so pleased that he ordered 'splice the mainbrace'.

Not one man was lost during the ship's wartime trooping career. She steamed 322,543 miles and carried 149,166 people. She was lucky the night she dropped anchor in the Mersey during the ten day Blitz on Liverpool in May 1941. Bombs rained down and the ship was one of the special targets. As the Empress was swinging with the tide a stick of bombs fell near the starboard side, but she escaped damage. The next morning the ship was ordered to the Clyde.

Chief pastrycook is Thomas Patten of Plymouth, aged fifty-four, who first went to sea in 1924 after learning his trade ashore. He recalls one occasion when he made a cake 4ft x 2½ft x 1ft high. It was in the form of a football pitch complete with players. This was in 1937 when the famous amateur champions, Islington Corinthians, travelled in the ship. Everyone on board received a piece of the cake as a memento.

A man with a lot of responsibility on board the *Empress of France* is Thomas Mercer who lives near Chester. He's the chief steward and has been with the company for twenty-seven years.

The *Empress of France* has a happy crew, many of whom have had the opportunity of moving on to other ships, but preferred to remain with 'the last of the four sisters'. Her master is Captain John Soame who says, 'I am very proud to sail in the *Empress of France*. She is a fine old ship with plenty of life left in her, and she is very popular with passengers and crew.'

EMPRESS OF CANADA (EX-DUCHESS OF RICHMOND)

Built by John Brown & Co. Ltd, at Clydebank in 1929. **Yard No:** 523.
Official Number: 160631   **Signal Letters:** G S V R
Gross Tonnage: 20,022   **Nett:** 11,238   **Length:** 600ft   **Breadth:** 75·1ft
Owned by the Canadian Pacific Railway Co. (Canadian Pacific Steamships – Managers)
6 steam turbines, single-reduction geared to twin screws.   **Speed:** 18 knots, maximum 19.

The *Duchess of Richmond* was launched on 18 June 1928 and sailed on her maiden voyage from Liverpool on 26 January 1929, this taking the form of a six-week cruise to the Atlantic Islands and the west coast of Africa. Among her passengers were the Chief Scout, Lt. General Sir Robert Baden-Powell, and Lady Baden-Powell. The new Duchess could carry 580 passengers in cabin class, 480 in tourist class and 510 in third class with a crew of 510.

The *Duchess of Richmond* settled into her regular service runs on the Canadian route when she left Liverpool on 15 March 1929 for St John, New Brunswick. A month later she grounded in fog at St John on 28 April, and her passengers were transferred to the *Montcalm*.

In November 1932 the *Duchess of Richmond* was in collision in fog with the Cunard liner *Alaunia* off Sorel, Quebec, and three years later carried the Duke and Duchess of Kent on their honeymoon cruise.

The *Duchess of Richmond* had more than her fair share of relatively minor incidents. On 18 December 1935 she was at Gibraltar and involved in a collision which necessitated temporary repairs being carried out and her 748 passengers missed their Christmas at home in the UK due to the delays. Some eighteen months later, in April 1937, the Duchess broke away from her moorings in Haifa harbour during a full gale, and her 1,000 passengers, pilgrims to the Holy Land, were stranded on shore until the gale abated.

On 14 February 1940 the *Duchess of Richmond* was requisitioned as a troopship and left Liverpool for Suez. During the invasion of North Africa, the Duchess was close to the P&O liner *Strathallan* when that ship was sunk by two torpedoes on 21 December 1942. In March 1945 she sailed to Odessa carrying 3,700 Russians who had been held prisoner in France.

The *Empress of Canada* following her post-war refit in 1947. (Photo: Canadian Pacific)

Eight months later the *Duchess of Richmond* arrived at Liverpool from Rangoon with the last of the prisoners-of-war from Sumatra and Singapore. On her return from Bombay in March 1946, the *Duchess* was held in quarantine until four smallpox cases among the service personnel on board were removed into isolation. Coincidentally, the *Georgic* also arrived at Liverpool with a smallpox case at this time, and these incidents resulted in nearly 10,000 people taking part in the largest mass vaccination of passengers and crew ever undertaken at Liverpool.

In May 1946 the *Duchess of Richmond* was sent to the Fairfield Yard at Govan for complete refurbishing. She reappeared as the *Empress of Canada*, and her passenger complement was reduced to 397 in first class, and 303 in tourist class. On 16 July 1947 the *Empress of Canada* sailed on her first post-war commercial voyage from Liverpool to Quebec and Montreal under the command of Captain E.A. Shergold. On her return passage one of the *Empress*'s passengers was Tommy Handley of I.T.M.A. *(It's That Man Again)* fame.

On 10 January 1953 the *Empress of Canada* entered Gladstone Dock for her routine winter overhaul. She was due to return to service on 11 February. But this was a date that she was unable to keep. On Sunday 25 January, whilst lying in Gladstone No.1 Branch Dock, the *Empress* caught fire and, in spite of tremendous efforts of firemen from all over the north-west of England, she eventually slid on to her side and became a burnt out hulk.

Work to right the liner commenced immediately as she was completely blocking a much needed deep-water berth at Liverpool. Her masts, funnels and much of the superstructure had to be cut away and it was not until over a year later, on Saturday 6 March 1954 that the salvage operation was successfully completed. It was the greatest operation of its kind ever tackled in Europe and was a feat of skill rivalled only by the salvage of the *Normandie* at New York and the battleship *Oklahoma* at Pearl Harbour.

The height of the blaze on the *Empress of Canada*, 25 January 1953. (Photo: Captain H.J. Chubb)

The salvage operation to right the ship, 6 March 1954. (Photo: Captain H.J. Chubb)

The hulk of the *Empress of Canada* was uprighted by a combined system of parbuckling and buoyancy. The Mersey Docks & Harbour Board, responsible for the cost of the salvage, pledged an expenditure of £380,000 to tackle the problem. When the sixteen hawsers took the pull, the *Empress* began moving without the slightest protest. Six pontoons, each filled with 104-tons of water, pulled down on the exposed starboard side. Eleven other pontoons, filled during the previous night with compressed air, pushed upwards on the submerged port side. The wreck moved silently and quickly towards her point of balance. It took only thirteen minutes to come from 88 degrees to 44½.

Then, however, a snag was encountered which the experts had allowed for in their plans. The liner had slid twenty feet along the mud of the dock bottom, rather more than they had anticipated, and the blocks on the winch purchases had come together. Adjustments took twenty minutes and with a final pull of only 70 tons, the *Empress of Canada* righted herself. When the operation ended, just fifty-five minutes after it had begun, the liner was sitting on the mud of the dock bottom at an angle of only nine degrees.

The deadweight pull which had been needed to right the *Empress* was 15,000 tons. There now remained the patching of her port side and the actual refloating; an operation which would take about ten weeks. The *Empress of Canada* was taken into Gladstone Graving Dock on 30 June 1954 to be made seaworthy for her last voyage to the breakers' yard. Four Alexandra Towing Co. tugs carried out the delicate manoeuvre. The *Empress* had a displacement of 45,000 tons and was drawing 40ft 9in, giving her a clearance of only 2ft over the entrance sill to the dry dock.

The hulk of the *Empress of Canada*, a mass of blackened and rusty steel, left Liverpool on 1 September 1954 under the tow of the 836-ton ocean-going Dutch tug *Zwarte Zee*, commanded by sixty-one-year-old Captain Thomas Vet. Watching her leave the Mersey was Commandante Enrico Accame, who had paid £130,000 for the hulk and was said to have paid another £12,000 for the 2,200 mile tow to La Spezia.

The salvage operation had cost the Mersey Docks & Harbour Board £466,000, plus the loss of a deep-sea berth for eighteen months. The Board sold the propellers separately for about £8,000.

Commandante Accame stated that he was happy with his purchase. The hulk of the *Empress of Canada* would be completely broken up in between nine and ten months and would be 'fed' to the large Italian steel plants.

Twelve Dutch seamen, supplied by the towing company, sailed on board the *Empress*. Accommodation had been built into the wreck, close to where the old luxurious Empress Room had been situated. A coal galley stove, toilet facilities and a motor-driven dynamo for lighting had also been installed.

Captain Vet of the *Zwarte Zee* estimated that the tow would take between twenty-one and forty days, dependent on the state of the weather. He said that he would be happy to maintain an average speed of 5 knots. The towing gear comprised 6-inch wire cables, 600 yards long, and 22-inch manilla ropes, 160 yards in length.

The tow to La Spezia presented some serious difficulties. After rounding the Skerries the *Zwarte Zee* encountered a full gale and off Tuskar Rock the tow rope parted, leaving the *Empress* adrift. After reconnecting the tow the hulk was taken to Dublin Bay, and it was intended that she would then go to Belfast for repairs to the pumps and the makeshift crew quarters. This proved to be too difficult and so the wreck was diverted to the Clyde for necessary repairs. After these had been completed the *Zwarte Zee* once again headed south and more gales were encountered. The hulk of the *Empress of Canada* eventually arrived at La Spezia for demolition on 10 October 1954, forty days after leaving the Mersey.

The hulk of the *Empress of Canada* enters Gladstone Gravin Dock, 30 June 1954. (Photo: Captain H.J. Chubb)

The hulk leaves Liverpool for tow to Genoa, 1 September 1954. (Photo: Captain H.J. Chubb)

THE FINDINGS OF THE COURT OF INQUIRY INTO THE LOSS OF THE *EMPRESS OF CANADA*

The Court of Inquiry into the loss by fire of the *Empress of Canada* at Liverpool on 25 January 1953 concluded on 8 January 1954. The findings of the Court were issued in mid-March 1954 in the course of which it was stated that the probable cause of the fire was a cigarette discarded in a cabin.

The Court stated that the Working Party on *Fire Prevention and Firefighting in Ships in Port Report*, 1950, was a comprehensive study of the problem of fire risks aboard ships in port. It contained a number of valuable recommendations which, although there was no statutory sanction behind them, deserved the closest study by all parties concerned. It was therefore regrettable to have to record that no attempt was made to consider the recommendations in detail or to carry any of them into effect with regard to the Canadian Pacific Railway Co.'s ships sailing into Liverpool.

Had the *Empress of Canada* been in commission, there is no reason to doubt that the fire precautions would have been effective.

It was clear that no liaison had been established between the ship owners and the fire brigade in relation to the ship, and there was no direct telephone between the ship and the fire brigade. Fire patrols were below the recommended standard and no personal alarms for each patrol man were supplied. The ship's fire main had not been maintained under pressure and no adequate alternative had been arranged.

This last omission was due to the action of the assistant chief engineer who stated that the pump had not been restarted since the vessel came out of dry dock. No attempt had been made to connect up to the shore main. The treatment of this important matter by the chief officer and the assistant chief engineer appeared to have been casual in the extreme. The chief officer appeared to have accepted the fact that there was no water instantly available, while the assistant chief engineer did not make sure that all his juniors were informed of what was to be done in an emergency.

The Court was satisfied with the evidence of a witness, a worker on a grain elevator berthed across the dock from the *Empress of Canada*, in which he said he saw smoke issuing from the starboard shell door between 3.25 p.m. and 3.30 p.m. on 25 January 1953. This man hailed the Empress but no notice was taken. Such inaction was tragic in the extreme. The first discovery of the fire was not made inside the ship until 4.10 p.m..

The Court was satisfied that at the time of the first arrival of the fire brigade the fire had already obtained such a firm hold and was spreading aft and upwards with such rapidity, that all that could be done was to attempt to box it in. This was done with some measure of success, but by 8.35 p.m. it became necessary to stop pumping any more water for stability reasons.

The Court of Inquiry considered that clandestine smoking was the most likely cause of the fire. The most probable explanation was that a cigarette end had been discarded in a cabin within the range B39 to B53. It was difficult to explain non-detection over a period of time which resulted in a build-up of heat and gases sufficient to create this debacle. The Court felt that the patrolling system, particularly on a Sunday afternoon, was less than effective. It was clear from the evidence that smoking was carried on to a considerable extent on board the *Empress of Canada*, and the Court appreciated just how difficult a problem this was, especially when driving the practice underground might in itself have increased the fire risk.

THE NIGHT OF THE FIRE

by Ted Morris

I sailed in the *Empress of Canada* as 3rd Officer on her last fateful voyage, leaving Princes Landing Stage at 4.00 p.m. on Christmas Eve, 1952. The weather from the start and during the entire westbound crossing was abominable, and very few passengers enjoyed the festive celebrations.

We spent New Year's Eve at St John, NB, sailing for home on New Year's Day, and upon our return to Liverpool I was standing-by during the refit before being relieved at noon on Saturday, 24 January 1953 – the day prior to the tragedy.

At the time I was living in Wallasey in one of the roads which run down to the Mersey. When my father telephoned me following the BBC Home Service *Ten O'clock News* on the Sunday evening, I could easily see the loom of the fire from my bedroom window. I did not have (neither could I afford it!) a car in those very different days, and I gladly accepted his offer to take me over to Gladstone Dock where I remained all night on the quayside with all those concerned. A sad and awesome experience to watch helplessly as the Empress was devoured by the flames of her demise (and most of my gear with her!)

EMPRESS OF SCOTLAND (EX-EMPRESS OF JAPAN)

Built by the Fairfield Shipbuilding & Engineering Co., Govan in 1930. **Yard No:** 634.
Official Number: 161430   **Signal Letters:** G M L V
Gross Tonnage: 26,313   **Nett:** 14,486   **Length:** 644ft   **Breadth:** 83·8ft.
Owned by the Canadian Pacific Railway Co. (Canadian Pacific Steamships – Managers)
6 steam turbines, single-reduction gearing to twin screws.   **Speed:** 21 knots, maximum 23.

Of all the passenger liners that have ever operated across the North Pacific, the *Empress of Japan* of 1930, the second vessel to carry this name in the Canadian Pacific fleet, was undoubtedly the finest, largest and fastest.

She was built at the Fairfield yard at Govan at a cost of about £1·5 million. The ship's twin screws were driven by Parsons' single-reduction geared turbines. Six Yarrow oil-fired water tube boilers supplied steam at 425lb psi and 725° superheat. The main engines developed 30,000shp on five boilers (leaving one in reserve) for a normal 21 knots; 33,000shp was maximum for 23 knots. The third funnel was a dummy but served as a ventilator for the engine room and the first and second-class galleys.

When the *Empress of Japan* entered service she could carry 268 first-class passengers; 131 interchangeable; 164 second-class; 100 third-class and 510 steerage. For cargo she had space for 212,000 cubic feet of general; 33,000 cubic feet for insulated, and 59,000 cubic feet. in her silk rooms.

The *Empress of Japan* was launched on 17 December 1929 and was completed in June 1930. She ran her trials in the Firth of Clyde and achieved a maximum speed of 23 knots on the Skelmorlie Mile. On 8 June she was delivered to Canadian Pacific, a truly magnificent ship, beautifully proportioned, graceful, and yet with a look of tremendous power.

On 14 June 1930 the *Empress of Japan* left Liverpool on her maiden voyage to Quebec, returning to Southampton. On her return passage she averaged 21 knots on 26,100shp. Her fuel consumption was 168 tons per day. On 12 July she left Southampton for Hong Kong via Suez, and from Hong Kong she commenced her transpacific service to Vancouver via Shanghai,

The *Empress of Japan* as she appeared on the Pacific services in the 1930s. (Photo: *Shipbuilding and Shipping Record*)

Kobe and Yokohama, joining her running mates the *Empress of Canada*, *Empress of Asia* and *Empress of Russia*.

Normally there would have been a balancing pair of sister ships, but the world depression was affecting policy, and with the advent of its new transatlantic flagship, the *Empress of Britain* of 1931, Canadian Pacific Steamships had enough on its plate.

The *Empress of Australia* had left the Pacific route in August 1927, returning to the Fairfield yard to be re-engined. She had not been a success on the Pacific due to her slow speed of about 17 knots maximum, but she had made a great name for herself by her rescue work following the Yokohama earthquake. Following re-engining she was transferred to the Atlantic.

Along with the *Empress of Canada* of 1922, the *Empress of Japan* had sufficient speed to include a call en route at Honolulu, lengthening the passage by a considerable amount and bringing the new ship into direct competition with the American and Japanese liners on the Pacific.

The *Empress of Japan* lost little time in capturing the speed record for the transpacific passage in both directions. In October 1930 she averaged 21.02 knots from Yokohama to Race Rocks, Vancouver, completing the passage in eight days, six hours and twenty-seven minutes, beating the *Empress of Canada*'s previous record by four and a half hours. In 1931 she reduced this time to seven days, eight hours and twenty-seven minutes. The largest and fastest ship on the Pacific, the *Empress of Japan* was for eight years extremely popular and before the end of 1939 she had completed fifty-eight round voyages.

On 26 November 1939 the *Empress of Japan* was requisitioned for service as a troopship. She had been in Shanghai when was war declared, and after a crossing to Honolulu and Vancouver she sailed to Esquimalt where a certain amount of work was carried out to fit her for trooping. Her hull and superstructure were painted grey and she then left for Sydney, arriving on 22 December.

Shortly afterwards she sailed for Suez with a contingent of Australian troops. Returning to Melbourne, she sailed again with troops to Suez in the company of the *Queen Mary*, *Aquitania*, *Mauretania*, *Empress of Britain* and *Empress of Canada*. In 1941 the *Empress of Japan* completed

Cocktail bar in the *Empress of Scotland*, showing the extensive window space. (Photo: *Shipbuilding and Shipping Record*)

The tourist-class smokeroom on the *Empress of Scotland*. (Photo: *Shipbuilding and Shipping Record*)

trooping voyages from Glasgow to the Cape and Singapore, returning to the UK via Panama; 35,000 miles in 141 days.

Following the entry of Japan into the Second World War, the *Empress of Japan* was renamed *Empress of Scotland*, ten months after the attack on Pearl Harbour. At this time, changes of ships' names were prohibited, but Winston Churchill said that in the case of the *Empress of Japan* 'it is a nonsense', and so on 16 October 1942 she became the *Empress of Scotland*, second of that name in the Canadian Pacific fleet, the first having been the ex-*Kaiserin Auguste Victoria* in 1921.

In 1942, under heavy air attack, the *Empress of Scotland* took 1,700 women and children away from Singapore to Colombo. During 1943/44 she was on a trooping service from Halifax, NS, New York and Newport News to Liverpool and to Casablanca, carrying a total of 30,000 American troops.

On 9 November 1944 the *Empress of Scotland* was subject to an air attack off Northern Ireland, three bombs being such near misses that they actually glanced off the ship's rail and a lifeboat, exploding in the sea. Captain J.W. Thomas had given evasive-action orders to the quartermaster who swung the wheel whilst lying on his stomach to avoid machine gun bullets which were raking the bridge! Both men were later decorated for their bravery.

Following the cessation of hostilities the *Empress of Scotland* continued trooping, repatriating troops and their families until she was released on 3 May 1948 at Liverpool. During the years 1939/48, the *Empress of Scotland* had steamed three times round the world, twice westbound and once eastbound, had sailed five times to South Africa and Singapore, and visited Australia and New Zealand five times. She had called at Canadian and US ports on twelve occasions, eight times to India and post-war twice to Japan. In all the *Empress of Scotland* had steamed 713,000 miles on war service and had carried 292,000 troops as well as other passengers.

When released, the *Empress of Scotland* was the only Empress left in the Canadian Pacific fleet. The *Empress of Russia* had been burnt out at Barrow-in-Furness in 1945 whilst refitting. The *Empress of Asia* was sunk in 1942 off Singapore by Japanese aircraft. The *Empress of Canada* had been torpedoed and sunk in the South Atlantic when homeward bound from Durban, and the *Empress of Britain*, completed in 1931, was set on fire by air attack in October 1940, and subsequently torpedoed whilst under tow. The *Empress of Australia* remained a troopship until sold to breakers in 1952 and was never returned to Canadian Pacific.

Of the four Duchesses completed in 1928/29, only two remained after the war, the *Duchess of Bedford* and the *Duchess of Richmond*. In 1947 these two ships were elevated to Empresses with white hulls and green ribands and renamed respectively *Empress of France* and *Empress of Canada*. Given this state of affairs, Canadian Pacific abandoned its Far East Vancouver service and accordingly the *Empress of Scotland* was refitted for the North Atlantic.

The *Empress of Scotland* was sent back to her builders, the Fairfield Yard at Govan, for a full refit for the Liverpool–Quebec mail service, and also for winter cruising. After eight years as a troopship, this was a job which took from June 1948 until May 1950.

The passenger accommodation was completely transformed. No space was now needed for Asiatic steerage passengers and this enabled very great improvements to be made to the crew accommodation. The ship was refitted for 458 first-class passengers and 205 tourist-class. All deck coverings had to be renewed and the promenade deck was glassed-in for its whole length, this being more appropriate for typical North Atlantic conditions.

Externally the *Empress of Scotland* was repainted with a white hull and yellow funnels, but the previous blue riband of the 1930s was changed to green, and the company's red and white chequered houseflag was painted on all three funnels. The propelling machinery remained the same but was given a complete overhaul and new propellers were fitted. On trials on the Arran Mile, after the completion of the refitting process, she reached a very creditable 22½ knots.

The *Empress of Scotland* left Liverpool on 9 May 1950 on her first post-war commercial voyage to Quebec, with a call at Greenock. She was the only Empress to make the Scottish

The *Empress of Scotland* after her return to service in May 1950. (Photo: *Shipbuilding & Shipping Record*)

call until the advent of the newer ships in the mid-1950s. On her second eastbound crossing she broke the record for the St Lawrence–Clyde passage by seven hours, with a time from the pilot station at Father Point in the Gulf of St Lawrence to the Clyde pilot station off Little Cumbrae of five days and forty-two minutes at an average speed of 21.3 knots.

Later in the summer of 1950 the *Empress of Scotland* bettered these passage times by using the Belle Isle Strait (between the northern tip of Newfoundland and the south of Labrador), rather than sailing south-about Newfoundland via Cape Race. This route cut the distance from 2,728 miles to 2,558 miles, and she sailed from the Clyde Pilot to Father Point in four days, fourteen hours and forty-three minutes, at an average speed of 21 knots.

In November 1951, Princess Elizabeth and the Duke of Edinburgh returned from their Canadian tour on the *Empress of Scotland*. The *Empress* had left Quebec at 4.13 p.m. on 9 November and arrived off Portugal Cove in Conception Bay, Newfoundland, at 7.30 a.m. on 12 November.

There was a north-easterly gale blowing, as a result of which the *Empress of Scotland* was unable to anchor and was skilfully manoeuvred by Captain C.E. Duggan whilst constantly being driven towards the shore.

The Royal couple had a rough one and a half mile passage out to the *Empress* on board the 140-ton ferry *Maneco* which took forty-five minutes. Photographers and officials on two fishing trawlers which accompanied the *Maneco* were soaked to the skin! The *Maneco* was alongside the *Empress of Scotland* at 1.10 p.m., and after the royal couple had boarded and their entire luggage had been transferred, the *Empress* sailed at 1.46 p.m.

Princess Elizabeth and the Duke of Edinburgh occupied the main suite on 'A' deck which had been partitioned off under constant guard by selected stewards to ensure privacy. It was hardly necessary, however, for word had been passed round tactfully amongst the other passengers during the two-day passage from Quebec and round to Conception Bay that the Princess and the Duke would like to relax and enjoy themselves as ordinary passengers. And so it was.

For about forty miles out from Conception Bay the *Empress of Scotland* was escorted by HMCS *Ontario* and the destroyer *Micmac* and it had been planned that they would man ship to give the traditional naval farewell, but in the prevailing heavy seas this was abandoned as being too dangerous. The destroyers *Zambesi* and *Creole* met the Empress off the Ulster coast to escort her into the Mersey, but they too were forced to break station because of bad weather in the confined shipping lanes of the Irish Sea.

The *Empress of Scotland* arrived alongside Princes Landing Stage at 6 a.m. on 17 November 1951 where the Royal couple disembarked.

In April 1952 the *Empress*'s masts were shortened by 44ft to allow her to proceed up the St Lawrence to Montreal, necessitating passing under both the Quebec Bridge (about five miles upstream from Quebec City), and the Jacques Cartier Bridge at Montreal. The channel to Montreal had by this time been deepened and the *Empress of Scotland* became the largest vessel ever to dock in Montreal.

Cruising in the winter months became a regular part of the schedule and in December 1950 the *Empress of Scotland* made her first cruise from New York to the West Indies, resuming Canadian Pacific's pre-war cruising programme. A 17-ton swimming pool was hoisted on board for the benefit of cruise passengers.

CANADIAN PACIFIC STEAMSHIPS LIMITED

"EMPRESS OF SCOTLAND"
Captain C. E. DUGGAN, R.D., R.N.R.
Staff Commander N. W. DUCK, D.S.C., R.D., R.N.R.

- ABSTRACT OF LOG -

QUEBEC TO LIVERPOOL, VIA CONCEPTION BAY — SAILED NOVEMBER 9, 1951.
Distance—Quebec to Liverpool—2,922 miles.

Date	Latitude NORTH	Longitude WEST	Dist.	Wind	Force	Weather Remarks, Etc.
Nov. 9						4.13 p.m. left Berth, Wolfe Cove.
„ 10	49.05	64.13	345	SW	4	0.36 a.m. Departure Father Point. Moderate sea, overcast and clear.
„ 11	46.47	56.49	328	SW	3	Slight sea, fine and clear. 11.13 p.m. Passed C. Race.
„ 12	Arr. Portugal Cove		265	S	3	7.30 a.m. Arrived at Conception Bay. Slight sea. misty patches.
„ 12	At Portugal Cove		27	N x W	7	7.30 a.m. - 1.46 p.m, Manoeuvring off Portugal Cove. 1.10 p.m. T.R.H. Princess Elizabeth and Duke of Edinburgh boarded. 1.46 p.m. proceeded. 2.12 p.m. Departure Portugal Cove.
„ 13	50.54	44.21	390	NNW	7	Very rough sea, heavy NNW swell. cloudy and clear, fierce squalls.
„ 14	53.33	33.27	430	WNW	9-4	High to moderate sea and swell, cloudy and clear, squalls.
„ 15	55.02	21.33	425	ENE	8-3	High to moderate sea, heavy swell, overcast, clear.
„ 16	55.28	7.47	471	S	4	Slight to rough sea, heavy swell, cloudy and clear. 1.00 p.m. passed Inishtrahull.
„ 16	Arrival Pt. Lynas		190	S	5	Due Lynas Point 10.00 p.m.
„ 17	To Liverpool		51			Prince's Landing Stage, Liverpool.

BEAUFORT WIND SCALE.—0 Calm. 1 Light Air. 2 Light Breeze. 3 Gentle Breeze. 4 Moderate Breeze. 5 Fresh Breeze 6 Strong Breeze. 7 Moderate Gale. 8 Fresh Gale. 9 Strong Gale. 10 Whole Gale. 11 Storm. 12 Hurricane.

W. S. W. Main, R.D., R.N.R., Chief Officer   J. N. Thomson, O.B.E., Chief Engineer   A. W. M. Stark, Purser
J. Prendergast, M.B., Ch.B., B.A.O., B.Sc., B.A., B. Litt., Surgeon   W. Parr, Chief Steward

Abstract of log for the Royal voyage from Conception Bay to Liverpool, November 1951.

Left to right: Mr Biggart, first officer; Staff Commander Duck; Captain Duggen; and Mr W.S. Main, cheif officer. Senior officers on the *Empress of Scotland* for the Royal voyage. (Photo: *Shipbuilding and Shipping Record*)

In April 1956 the new *Empress of Britain* entered service, followed a year later by the *Empress of England*. With the *Empress of Scotland* and the *Empress of France*, there were again four Empresses on North Atlantic service. With a new *Empress of Canada* due to join the fleet, these newcomers spelt the end for the older two ships. The *Empress of Scotland* was sold first and the *Empress of France* went to the breakers in 1960. On 8 November 1957 the *Empress of Scotland* left Liverpool on her final voyage for Canadian Pacific. She arrived back in Liverpool for the last time in a chill wintry mist on 26 November 1957 under the command of Captain S.W. Keay, and after disembarking her 213 passengers at Princes Landing Stage, she was laid up in the Gladstone Dock.

Captain Keay was interviewed by a reporter from the *Liverpool Echo* and commented that, 'Occasions such as these are always sad. Members of the crew have been sailing on this route for many years, and everyone is feeling the parting very much today.' There was a farewell party on board on the last night of the voyage and a member of the crew said, 'It was the quietest party I have ever seen on a ship. Everyone seemed to be too sad to make merry'.

For three members of the crew, the occasion was a doubly poignant one. As well as parting with the *Empress*, they were also finishing their seafaring life. The three men were William Campbell, first radio officer, John Butterworth, second radio officer, and William Lombard, the ship's dispenser. Mr Campbell had been at sea with Canadian Pacific since 1922, and Mr Butterworth was retiring after forty-five years at sea. Mr Lombard was the first dispenser ever to be appointed by Canadian Pacific and after completing thirty-seven years he said:

> There is no life like one at sea. It has gone like a flash and I can hardly realise that it is time for me to retire. I am glad that I am going at the same time as the *Empress of Scotland*. She has been a grand ship to sail in.

Just before the New Year she was sold to the Hamburg Atlantic Line and left Liverpool on 31 December 1957 for Belfast where she arrived on New Year's Day, 1958. Following a dry docking and survey, she was accepted by her new owners and was handed over to them at Belfast on 17 January 1958.

The *Empress of Scotland* having her masts shortened in April 1952. (Photo: *Shipbuilding and Shipping Record*)

On 19 January the old ship left Belfast under the German flag and with the temporary name of *Scotland*. Two days later she arrived at the Howaldtswerke Co.'s yard at Hamburg. Here she was renamed *Hanseatic* and reconstructed and 'modernised' during a six-month overhaul which cost 43 million Deutschmarks.

The Hamburg Atlantic Line was a final attempt to run a transatlantic passenger service from Hamburg after HAPAG had given up passenger carrying. With the growth of the post-war German merchant fleet it was strongly felt during the mid-1950s that the time was ripe for Germany to re-enter the traditional transatlantic passenger service with a Hamburg-owned liner. In 1957 the Hamburg–Atlantic Linie G.m.b.H. was formed. A decision was made to start with a second-hand vessel and shortly afterwards the *Empress of Scotland* appeared on the market for sale.

The funnel colours of the *Hanseatic* were red with a black top and a white logo in the red sector. The hull was painted black. The passenger accommodation was rebuilt to carry 85 first-class and 1,165 tourist-class passengers. The third funnel was removed and replaced by two shorter and more modern ones. For some reason it was thought worthwhile to alter her bow, giving it a slightly raked curve at the top, which increased the overall length by about six feet.

The rebuilding took about six months and on 21 July 1958 the *Hanseatic* left Cuxhaven for New York via Le Havre, Southampton and Cobh. In 1959 the ship made twelve round transatlantic voyages and went cruising in the winter months. By 1965 competition from the airlines meant that the New York voyages were reduced to eight and the *Hanseatic* spent most of her time cruising.

On 7 September 1966, whilst lying at New York, fire broke out in the *Hanseatic*'s generator room, caused by oil leaking from a fractured pipe line. It took 200 firemen to bring the blaze under control, by which time great damage had been done. Not only had the generators been ruined, but the engine room had suffered considerably from the intense heat and the water, while smoke and water had caused great damage to much of the accommodation. The *Hanseatic*'s passengers were transferred to the *Queen Mary*, whose sailing time was delayed by some four hours whilst they were embarked.

The *Hanseatic* was towed to the Todd shipyard at Brooklyn for survey, and as a result Hamburg Atlantic decided to have her towed back to the Howaldtswerke yard at Hamburg for possible repair. On 3 October 1966 she left New York under tow by two of Bugsier's latest tugs, the *Atlantic* and the *Pacific*, for the seventeen-day tow. In Hamburg the damage was found to be too severe to be worth repairing and she was sold for scrap to Elkhart & Company on 2 December for 15 million Deutschmarks.

Such then, was the sad end of the last Pacific Empress, thirty-six years old. She had served her country and her company supremely well. The *Empress of Scotland* was an utterly magnificent ship, perhaps the finest ever to grace the Mersey.

The *Hanseatic*, ex-*Empress of Scotland*. (Photo: *Shipbuilding and Shipping Record*)

WESTERN OCEAN INTERLUDE

by Captain Brian Scott

At the end of my four-year cadetship with the Clan Line in 1956, I wanted to attend Liverpool Technical College to obtain my first certificate. However, my timing was wrong – the College was due to close for the summer holidays. Remembering what a third mate had told me about his experience of being seconded to Canadian Pacific Steamships as an uncertificated fifth officer, I decided to follow suit.

I joined the *Empress of Scotland* at Liverpool in June 1956, put on my boiler suit, and as junior cargo officer on six-hour port watches did exactly the same as when I was a cadet. Cargo work was hectic on the *Empress of Scotland* due to the quick turnaround. There was tank cleaning after discharging tallow, hold cleaning after grain, plus the requirement to work out the vessel's stability morning and evening due to ballasting/deballasting, refuelling and taking on fresh water. Outward cargo consisted of high value goods such as mails, crockery, textiles, woollen goods, motor cars and machinery.

When sailing day arrived it was no watch below and no rest as the second mate and myself had amended the crew boat and fire station lists during the previous night, and then the M.O.T. surveyor was present for the crew boat drill. We next moved from Gladstone Dock to Liverpool Landing Stage with the company pilot and five tugs. Gangway duty was tourist class for the fifth officer and first class for the fourth officer. Then we were on our way, calling at Greenock where we disembarked the Liverpool pilot, embarked more passengers, lowered all lifeboats into the water and took some of them for a run around the anchored ship.

On arriving and sailing, my station was on the bridge with the Captain, Staff Captain and Second Officer, who was my senior on the 12 to 4 watch at sea. This was not a problem for me as for part of my cadetship I had been bridge cadet for arrivals and departures. When no fourth officer had been carried on my Clan Line voyages, I was frequently on watch with the chief officer on his 4 to 8 watch.

After leaving Greenock we settled into our watchkeeping routine. The first (navigator) and fourth officers on the 4 to 8, the second and fifth on the 12 to 4, and the third officer (who held a master's certificate) on the 8 to 12, with the day worker chief officer on stand-by to go on the bridge if the weather or visibility became poor. The captain and staff captain always appeared to be busy with heads of other departments, and the four radio officers laboured away with high speed Morse messages for the ship's daily newspaper, ice reports and six-hourly weather reports to shore stations.

My days and nights were busy. Before each bridge watch I mustered my deck watch at the emergency boat (No.1 or No.2). After each watch we held fire drill and each day I went along a different deck with my plug-in telephone testing the fire alarms. This ensured that junior officers knew every nook and cranny on board. The fourth officer was the met. officer and had plenty to keep him busy as well as the boat drills. Life was well ordered.

The watchkeeping officers dined in an alcove in the first-class dining saloon. However, being on the 12 to 4, I had brunch brought to my cabin at 10a.m., skipped lunch and had dinner at 6.30 p.m. In between times there was always plenty of tea, coffee and sandwiches available on the bridge. Sometimes the quartermasters got the lion's share of the sandwiches!

On my two voyages the weather was fine, a little ice but quite a lot of cargo ship traffic. Passenger ships stuck to the Atlantic routing/separation lanes of longstanding to avoid head-on situations with each other, as at 22 knots the closing speed was quite intimidating. As a safety measure, at the start of each watch, a note book with the vessels dead-reckoning positions for the next four hours, complete with local and GMT was handed to the duty radio officer.

The *Hanseatic* at Malta whilst on a Mediterranean cruise in September 1963. (Photo: *Shipbuilding and Shipping Record*)

We stopped at Quebec to disembark some passengers and then proceeded to Montreal where the remainder left. We discharged cargo, had more boat drills, and then loaded grain, sawn timber, apples, bulk tallow, mail and gold and silver bullion for Liverpool. The passengers boarded and we sailed for Quebec and Liverpool.

On completion of my two relief voyages, the regular fifth officer returned from leave. For my part, I had learned a lot with regard to shipboard organisation, the routine of ocean navigation on fast ships, the use of Loran, ice and weather reports, plotting of such information on special charts, and practical ship's stability. The experience paid dividends, for some years later I wanted a summer fill-in job prior to attending nautical school, and was fortunate enough to be appointed as relief fourth officer on both of the new sister ships *Empress of Britain* and *Empress of England*.

EMPRESS OF AUSTRALIA (EX-DE GRASSE)

Built by Cammell Laird (Shipbuilders & Engineers) at Birkenhead in 1924.   **Yard No: 886**
Official Number: 185887   **Signal Letters:** G Q M Q
Gross Tonnage: 19,379   **Nett:** 10,296   **Length:** 552·0ft   **Breadth:** 71·1ft
Owned by the Canadian Pacific Railway Co. (Canadian Pacific Steamships – Managers)
4 steam turbines, single-reduction gearing to twin screws.

Canadian Pacific purchased the *De Grasse* from the French Line in 1952 and renamed her *Empress of Australia*. She was intended as a stop-gap replacement for the burnt-out *Empress of Canada*. The *Canada* had been fully booked for the forthcoming coronation of Queen Elizabeth II, and the purchase of the *De Grasse* (renamed *Empress of Australia* on 24 April 1953) enabled these bookings to be honoured, although the cost was high.

The *De Grasse* was completed by Cammell Laird at Birkenhead in 1924. She had been laid down as the *Suffren* for the French Line on 23 March 1920, but was launched as the *De Grasse* on 23 February 1924. Due to long interruptions to the building work, cancellation of the

The *Empress of Australia*, ex-*De Grasse*. (Photo: *Shipbuilding and Shipping Record*)

contract was considered at one stage. Because of ongoing industrial unrest at Cammell Laird, the new ship was towed to St Nazaire to be completed. Her first transatlantic service was between Le Havre and New York, commencing on 21 August 1924. Between November 1924 and January 1925 she was taken in hand by Penhöet and was given a complete overhaul of her engines and boilers, and later the *De Grasse* proved to be one of the most reliable cabin liners on the North Atlantic, and was used extensively for cruising.

Between September and October 1934, and again from June to September 1935, the *De Grasse* made a number of voyages between Marseille and New York. On 29 May 1937 she opened a new service from Le Havre to New York and Boston, via Southampton and Cobh.

During the invasion and occupation of France in the early days of the Second World War, the *De Grasse* was taken over by the Germans and was used as an accommodation ship in the Gironde, near Bordeaux. She remained under German requisition until 4 June 1942 when she was returned to the French to become a training ship for merchant service apprentices. The *De Grasse* was not to escape the ravages of war, however, for during the German withdrawal on 30 August 1944 she was sunk by depth charges exploded by a passing 'E'-boat in shallow water. A year later the *De Grasse* was salved and put in the hands of the Chantiers et Ateliers Saint-Nazaire-Penhöet for complete reconditioning. In the course of this refit her interior was entirely rebuilt and her two original funnels were replaced by one of generous proportions in an effort to modernise her appearance.

On 12 July 1947 the *De Grasse* returned in her new guise to the Le Havre–New York service and had the distinction of reopening the transatlantic service of the Cie Générale Transatlantique. In 1951 she was transferred to the Le Havre–Southampton–West Indies service, being retained on that route until being handed over to Canadian Pacific at Le Havre on 28 March 1953. She sailed for Liverpool on the same day.

The *De Grasse* arrived at Liverpool on 30 March and she sailed from the Mersey on her first voyage as the *Empress of Australia* on 28 April 1953, bound for Quebec and Montreal. One feature of her refit was the shortening of her masts by 25ft to permit her to pass under the Quebec Bridge and the Jacques Cartier Bridge.

The ship's career for Canadian Pacific was largely uneventful although she did experience one or two passages involving heavy weather damage. One such occasion brought about a bad leak in the stern gland, and a diver had to assist in its repacking whilst the vessel lay afloat at Montreal.

Towards the end of 1955 the *Empress of Australia* was chartered for troop movements between Canada and Europe and it became clear that she would not be returning to Canadian Pacific's trans-Atlantic services on completion of the charter. On 12 December 1955 she arrived at Liverpool and shortly afterwards sailed to the Gareloch to be laid up pending disposal.

When the *Empress of Australia* was advertised for sale it was stated that she had accommodation for 220 first-class passengers and 444 tourist-class passengers, as well as having a deadweight capacity of 6,566 tons. She was purchased on 16 February 1956 by Sicula Oceanica S.p.A. of Palermo, a subsidiary of Fratelli Grimaldi of Naples. Taking delivery of the ship on the Clyde, her new owners renamed her *Venezuela* and placed her on the Naples–La Guaira, Venezuela service. On 17 March 1962 she ran aground off Cannes and a month later was refloated but was assessed as being beyond economic repair. On 16 August 1962 the *Venezuela* was sold for demolition at La Spezia.

EMPRESS OF BRITAIN

Built by the Fairfield Shipbuilding & Engineering Co. Ltd, Govan.   **Yard No:** 731
Official Number: 187376   **Signal Letters:** G V C N
Gross Tonnage: 25,516   **Nett:** 13,681   **Length:** 640ft   **Breadth:** 85·2ft
Owned by the Canadian Pacific Railway Co. (Canadian Pacific Steamships – Managers)
6 steam turbines, double reduction gearing to twin screws

After the Second World War, replacements were urgently needed for Canadian Pacific's ageing passenger fleet, and the situation became more serious in 1953 following the loss by fire of the *Empress of Canada*. In 1951 the Cunard Line, Canadian Pacific's great rival on the Liverpool to Montreal service, had announced its intention to build a class of passenger liner for the Canadian service. Canadian Pacific was faced with the very real need to meet the Cunard challenge in order to maintain a viable presence on the route.

Canadian Pacific waited until the first of the new Cunarders, the *Saxonia*, had entered service before placing an order for a new ship which would become the *Empress of Britain*. There is no doubt that Canadian Pacific paid very close attention to the new Cunard liner before placing

Queen Elizabeth II launching the *Empress of Britain* on 22 June 1955. (Photo: *Shipbuilding and Shipping Record*)

an order with the Fairfield Shipbuilding & Engineering Co. at Govan for the new *Empress* which was launched by the Queen on 22 June 1955. The *Empress of Britain* had the distinction of being the first Canadian Pacific liner, and the first Fairfield-built vessel, to be named by a reigning monarch.

The Queen and the Duke Edinburgh were entertained to lunch in the shipyard boardroom, and following the loyal toast, Vice-Admiral E. W. Longley-Cook, the managing director of the Fairfield Co. pointed out that the new *Empress of Britain* would be the twenty-first ship built by his company for Canadian Pacific, a total which included six Empresses and eight Princesses. The association between the two companies went back fifty years to when the first *Empress of Britain* was built at the Govan yard.

On 28 October 1955, just four months after the launching of the *Empress of Britain*, Canadian Pacific Airlines ordered three Bristol Britannia 300LR airscrew-turbine air liners, with an option for a further five. The age of the trans-ocean airliner was dawning!

The new *Empress* left the Clyde on 1 March 1956 and entered the Gladstone Graving Dock at Liverpool the following day, before returning to the Clyde on 8 March to carry out her speed trials. These were run over the Arran Mile on the next two days, following which the *Empress of Britain* was berthed in Glasgow's King George V Dock for almost three weeks. At noon on 29 March 1956 the new ship underwent further trials on the Firth of Clyde before being handed over to Canadian Pacific Steamships at a ceremony held that evening whilst the vessel was at anchor at the Tail of the Bank.

The *Empress of Britain* sailed to Southampton on a 'shake-down' cruise, leaving Liverpool on 9 April with 400 guests of the company on board. On her way down the Mersey she passed the new *Reina del Mar*, arriving from her sea trials. After arriving at the southern port on 10 April, the *Empress* disembarked her passengers and took on another 400 guests for the return passage to Liverpool, arriving back in the Mersey on 12 April to prepare for her maiden voyage which left Liverpool on 20 April.

One shipping journalist who had been on board for the cruise described the *Empress of Britain* as 'Britain's most interesting ship of the decade'. She was in fact the first completely air-conditioned passenger liner to have been built in Britain. *Lloyd's List* enthused:

> For comfort and real quality in ship decoration and furnishing – indeed, luxury in many respects – Canadian Pacific's new flagship sets the highest possible standard in North Atlantic

The *Empress of Britain* on trials on the Arran Mile in March 1956. (Photo: *Shipbuilding and Shipping Record*)

travel. This applies particularly to tourist class and the *Empress of Britain* is primarily a tourist class ship. The distinction between the two classes is virtually negligible, and the generous tourist class public rooms, to say nothing of most of the cabins, are in literal truth of first-class standard.

Although essentially a passenger liner, the new *Empress* could also carry 3,000 tons of cargo with a large provision of refrigerated space for fruit and other Canadian produce. Bearing in mind that, for at least part of the year, the ship would encounter ice conditions in the St Lawrence, the hull was suitably strengthened.

The *Empress of Britain* embarked a full complement of 150 first-class passengers and 900 tourist-class passengers and left Liverpool on her maiden voyage on 20 April 1956, arriving at Quebec on 25 April and at Montreal on 26 April. The call at Greenock, traditionally part of the Canadian schedule, was omitted.

There were some minor machinery problems in June and July, but generally all went well, and the new liner settled down into her transatlantic schedule. On 11 September 1956, Canadian Pacific announced that the *Empress of Britain* had broken both the eastbound and westbound records between Liverpool Bar and the St Lawrence pilot station at Father Point with an average speed of 21.43 knots.

St John, New Brunswick, was the winter terminal port between November and March when the St Lawrence was impassable due to ice.

The *Empress of Britain* docked at Liverpool on 18 January 1957 after experiencing some trouble with her port engine off the Mersey Bar. She was due at Princes Stage at 6.30 a.m., but sailed directly to her berth in Gladstone Dock where she arrived shortly before 3 p.m. The *Empress* had arrived off the Bar at 2.35 a.m. and was met by the Alexandra Towing Co.'s

The Sun Lounge on the *Empress of Britain*. (Photo: Canadian Pacific)

The drawing room on the *Empress of Britain*. (Photo: Canadian Pacific)

North Light. A Canadian Pacific official said that he understood that the port engine had not failed, but was 'unreliable'. The *Empress of Britain* had left St John, N.B. six days earlier with 270 passengers.

The new *Empress of England*, the slightly younger sister of the *Empress of Britain*, entered service in April 1957. The new ship was to become Canadian Pacific's cruise liner during the winter months, leaving the *Empress of Britain* to maintain the winter transatlantic schedule. In 1958 the call at the Tail of the Bank, off Greenock, was introduced into the *Empress of Britain's* schedule.

An ice jam in the St Lawrence in mid-April 1959 caused problems. The *Empress of Britain* was damaged trying to force her way though ice at Sorel, some thirty miles from Montreal. The *Empress*, along with Cunard's *Carinthia*, was trapped at Montreal for some days until the jam broke up.

The *Empress of England's* winter cruising programme had been such a success that Canadian Pacific decided it would be far more profitable to send the *Empress of Britain* cruising as well, rather than to retain one of them for a winter transatlantic service. Cunard was having similar difficulties in profitably employing its four Canadian ships in the winter months, and the Canadian Pacific ships lent themselves far more readily to cruising than the Cunarders which were primarily emigrant carriers with only very partial air-conditioning.

Both the new Empresses were overhauled at Liverpool in December 1959 and sailed for New York, where they arrived in mid-January 1960 for three months of cruising to the Caribbean.

The year 1960 was severely disrupted by industrial action at the height of the passenger season. When the *Empress of Britain* arrived at Liverpool on 19 July, most of her crew joined the unofficial strike over pay and hours. However, efforts to recruit a full crew for her departure scheduled for 22 July succeeded and she left Princes Landing Stage at noon and anchored

Above: The tourist-class dining saloon on the *Empress of Britain*. (Photo: Canadian Pacific)

Below: The tourist-class library on the *Empress of Britain*. (Photo: Canadian Pacific)

The *Empress of Britain* in the Mersey. (Photo: *Shipbuilding and Shipping Record*)

in mid-Mersey to await the Greenock passengers who were on a special train to Riverside Station, and who were taken out to join the liner by tender. The crew situation could not be resolved for the 12 August departure from Liverpool, and the *Empress of Britain*'s sailing was cancelled and her 600 passengers travelled with Canadian Pacific Airlines. The unofficial strike action dragged on into September, and over 1,000 passengers booked to sail on the *Empress of Britain*'s 2 September voyage had to accept alternative ways of reaching Canada. It was not until 10 September that the *Empress of England* was able to resume the sailing schedule, and it was 24 September before the *Empress of Britain* sailed, having lost two round voyages at the peak of the season.

The *Empress of Britain* docked at Quebec on 5 April 1961 with 525 passengers after being delayed for a day by thick pack ice in the Gulf of St Lawrence. The voyage did not proceed to Montreal, and the *Empress* left Quebec with 800 passengers on schedule.

More unofficial industrial action dogged the *Empress of Britain* in 1961. Her 18 April departure was delayed for twenty-four hours by members of the National Seamen's Reform Movement. Engine trouble delayed her sailing from Montreal on 19 May, and her 14 November departure from Liverpool was set back for thirty-six hours by renewed unofficial strike action.

Some 200 crew members were demanding the dismissal of the boatswain and walked off the ship at the landing stage. The 350 passengers on board were looked after by the remainder of the crew. In a statement Canadian Pacific said, 'It is clear that the whole affair has been engineered by the same subversive elements who have taken similar action in the past and whose avowed intention is to disrupt British shipping'.

The *Empress of Britain* sailed in the early morning of 16 November with a full crew who had been signed-on during the night. The 200 crew members who had walked off, and who had been told by strike leaders that 'she can't sail without us' arrived for a meeting on the landing stage to find that she had sailed without them! Jim Scott, the general secretary of the National Union of Seamen, said, 'These men had fair warning. They were told to return to the ship on an assurance of an investigation of their complaints. Their discharge books have been stamped

"Voyage Not Completed" and now they will have to go into the pool to take their turn for jobs'. The *Empress of Britain* cut out her Greenock call to make up time, and her Scottish passengers were switched to the *Carinthia*. Mr Norris R. Crump, chairman and president of the Canadian Pacific Railway Co., said that his company must reserve the right to leave the port of Liverpool for some other port where continuity of operation could be obtained.

The *Empress of Britain* continued to operate a winter trans-Atlantic schedule until 13 January 1962, after which time Canadian Pacific abandoned all attempts at operating such sailings which had become unprofitable due to low passenger numbers. After completing her annual overhaul the Empress went cruising from the UK until returning to her designed route from Liverpool to Montreal for the 1962 summer.

The three Canadian Pacific Empresses made thirty-three round voyages between Liverpool and Canada in 1962 – never again would such an extensive schedule be operated. From January to April 1963 the *Empress of Britain* was employed on a cruising programme from the UK and it was not until 30 April that she returned to her Liverpool to Montreal route. Passenger numbers on the North Atlantic began an accelerated terminal decline in 1963, and the *Empress of Britain* made her 108th and final round voyage to Canada, leaving Liverpool on 24 September.

South African entrepreneur Max Wilson had set up the Travel Savings Association (TSA) in 1963, promoting cheap 'no frills' cruises. Potential passengers paid instalments into TSA's savings scheme, eventually using the money to buy inexpensive cruises. Initially the scheme seemed to meet with great success. Canadian Pacific acquired a fifty-one per cent controlling interest in the new company and both the *Empress of Britain* and the *Empress of England* went on charter to TSA.

The Empress Room on the *Empress of Britain*. (Photo: Canadian Pacific)

The tourist-class smoking room on the *Empress of Britain*. (Photo: Canadian Pacific)

On 25 October 1963 the *Empress of Britain* sailed from Liverpool on her first TSA cruise. On 4 December she left for South Africa, carrying 570 emigrants travelling under the South African government's assisted passage scheme. The *Empress* arrived at Cape Town on 19 December and two days later sailed on her first cruise across the South Atlantic to South American ports.

TSA's original charter of the *Empress of Britain* had been for five years, but early in 1964 it exercised its option to terminate the charter as from 5 January 1965. Shortly afterwards it was announced that the TSA would cease trading at the end of 1964 as it had not developed into the success that had been envisaged. On 13 February 1964 the *Empress of Britain* left Cape Town for Liverpool, where she arrived on 28 February.

Canadian Pacific stated that 'the economics of passenger operations are not what they should be', and by the time that the *Empress of Britain* had arrived back in the Mersey she had been sold to the Goulandris-owned Greek Line for $8 million. The *Empress* spent the next six months undertaking cruises under her TSA charter, and arrived back at Liverpool on 22 August 1964. She was temporarily laid up, awaiting her delivery to the Greek Line. For the ship herself, this was a new beginning. She had more than proved her versatility both as an Atlantic liner and as a cruise ship.

The *Empress of Britain* was renamed *Queen Anna Maria* and left Liverpool under this name on 18 November 1964, bound for Genoa where she arrived on 22 November. The ship was flying the Greek flag and three painters had been employed to paint the new name in Greek characters on the stern and bows. Just before sailing time the painters were back, reinstating the English lettering, because the new owners felt that this was in accordance with accepted practice. An official of the marine surveyor's office at the Ministry of Transport commented, 'As far as we know, there is no compulsion for a Greek ship to have her name in English lettering.'

The former *Empress of Britain* spent the next three months at the Mariotti shipyard where the cabin accommodation was increased and the ship was made more suitable for a Mediterranean Atlantic service, rather than the North Atlantic. The total passenger complement increased to 1,313 on the Atlantic run, and 742 whilst cruising. The original steam turbines were retained. The outward appearance was little changed, except at the stern, where a large night club and lido deck were constructed. The overall character remained and the essentially British-styled North Atlantic liner décor was retained intact.

The *Queen Anna Maria's* refit was completed on 6 March 1965 and she arrived at Piraeus three days later. Her first Atlantic crossing for the Greek Line left Piraeus on 23 March and she called at Naples, Palermo and Lisbon. A call was made at Halifax, NS, and the *Queen Anna Maria* arrived at New York on 5 April. She settled into a routine of spending the summer on the Atlantic and cruising in the winter. On 19 February 1967, whilst arriving at Kingston, Jamaica, the *Queen Anna Maria* ran aground and was not refloated until a week later. Towards the end of 1967 three-night 'cruises to nowhere' from New York were slotted in between Atlantic crossings.

The Greek Line worked the *Queen Anna Maria* hard. Her summer seasons on the Atlantic run became increasingly short and cruising became her principal occupation. In the early 1970s the Greek Line was struggling to remain viable in the face of ever escalating costs, but following the death of its owner and chairman, Basil Goulandris, the company seemed to lose its vigour and momentum. The four-fold increase in the price of fuel oil over the winter of 1973/74 was the final blow. The *Queen Anna Maria* sailed on in 1974 amidst mounting debts, and in January 1975 the Greek Line issued a statement to the effect that financial difficulties have made it impossible to continue with the cruise program.

As one of the Greek Line's only two assets (the other was the *Olympia*), the *Queen Anna Maria* was tied up at New York and the creditors made arrangements to seize her. However, forewarned that this was about to happen, her crew prepared for a quick and unannounced departure on 11 January 1975. It was a particularly ignominious farewell. On 22 January the *Queen Anna Maria* arrived at Piraeus and was laid up, along with many other redundant passenger liners, at Perama.

With the Greek Line in receivership, the Chase Manhattan Bank, which held the mortgage on the *Queen Anna Maria*, was anxious to dispose of her and made her available for sale at a very low price.

In January 1972 Ted Arison had completed arrangements for purchasing the *Empress of Britain's* younger sister, the *Empress of Canada*, and then laid up at Tilbury. On 21 February the *Empress of Canada* was renamed *Mardi Gras* and five days later she sailed for Miami to be operated by the newly formed Carnival Cruise Lines. Three years later Ted Arison was looking for a running-mate for the *Mardi Gras* and inspected the *Queen Anna Maria*. The Sitmar Line (purchaser of Cunard's *Carinthia* and *Sylvania*) was also interested and Arison had to move fast. He bought the *Queen Anna Maria* (ex-*Empress of Britain*) for $3 million. The ship was immediately prepared for sea and arrived at Miami on New Year's Day, 1976, and was renamed *Carnivale*. In mid-February 1976 the *Carnivale* entered service for Carnival Cruise Lines, sailing in company with her younger sister, the *Mardi Gras*, ex-*Empress of Canada*. Of the two ships the *Carnivale* was better suited to cruising, given the extensive rebuilding carried out by the Greek Line.

The *Carnivale* was still an Atlantic liner at heart and during her first months with Carnival she underwent upgrading and refitting. Both the *Carnivale* and the *Mardi Gras* were marketed as 'fun ships' and became phenomenally successful on the seven-day circuit from Miami, calling at San Juan, St Maarten and St Thomas. The two ships had enjoyed some measure of success with Canadian Pacific, but this had been rather short-lived due to the changing patterns of transatlantic travel. Under the guiding hand of Ted Arison the two former Empresses achieved undreamed-of success.

The Carnivale (ex-*Empress of Britain*) sailing for Carnival Cruise Lines. (Photo: Carnival Cruise Lines)

The *Carnivale* sailed on as part of the Carnival Cruise Lines' ever expanding fleet until October 1993 when she was renamed *FiestaMarina* and transferred to a Carnival subsidiary, FiestaMarina Cruises. The former *Empress of Britain* was now thirty-eight years old, and after eighteen years of popularity and success with Carnival, she could not compete with the newer and much larger purpose-built cruise ships. The *FiestaMarina* was based at San Juan for three months but this proved to be a costly failure, after which she returned to her more familiar Miami base. In September 1994 the old ship sailed on her final cruise after which FiestaMarina Cruises was wound up and the ship laid up.

The former *Empress* was quickly purchased by the Greek Epirotiki Lines and left Miami for the Mediterranean on 14 September 1994 where she was renamed *Olympic*. She was in impeccable condition, having been flawlessly maintained by Carnival over the years. A correspondent sailed on her in August 1997 and reported that, 'the *Olympic*'s public rooms are a mix of vintage Canadian Pacific and 1990 Carnival glitz. The cinema remains untouched from the ship's Canadian Pacific days, with its polished wood and leather-trimmed bulkheads, plastic acoustic ceiling and vivid red seating'.

The *Olympic* was based at Piraeus and operated three and four-day cruises in the Aegean. Such was her success that there was speculation that her younger sister, the former *Empress of Canada*, which was at this time languishing in lay up at Perama Bay, near Piraeus, might join her. However, at the end of the 1997 cruising season, Epirotiki Lines announced the disposal of the *Olympic* and she was sold to a Panamanian-registered company, Topaz International.

On 19 January 1998 the forty-three-year-old ship was taken to the Skaramanga shipyard for a refit. She was renamed *The Topaz* and was chartered to Thomson Holidays. *The Topaz*'s first cruise was a transatlantic crossing to Port Everglades, but unfortunately her entry into service was marred by bad publicity generated by passenger complaints. It would appear that the final stages of the refit had been hurried, and that the crew had not sufficient time to familiarise themselves with the ship. As a result, by the time that *The Topaz* arrived at Malta, Thomson had received many complaints about problems with meals, poor service and run-down facilities, and the 756 passengers were taken off the ship.

Fortunately this proved to be a temporary blip and *The Topaz* quickly became one of the most popular cruise ships. During the summer of 1999 Thomsons based *The Topaz* at Palma, but on 28 October she sailed for the Caribbean for a six-month cruising season. She returned to Palma in April 2000 for a further programme of Mediterranean cruising for Thomsons.

In May 2002 it was announced that Thomsons' five-year charter of *The Topaz* would come to an end in May 2003 and would not be renewed. With the best will in the world, *The Topaz*, one of the oldest operational cruise ships, could just no longer compete and Thomsons had negotiated a charter of the former Holland–America cruise ship *Nieuw Amsterdam* to replace her. It seemed that the writing was on the wall for the former *Empress of Britain*.

In early November 2002 came the news that *The Topaz* was to be chartered by the Japanese educational organisation Peace Boat. She was scheduled to make four round-the-world cruises for them, the first to commence on 14 June 2003, and the Peace Boat charter would extend until 2006.

The Topaz arrived in Tokyo on 10 June 2003 and shortly afterwards sailed on her first cruise for Peace Boat. This involved revisiting some of her old haunts: for instance she sailed into New York on 8 August for a three-day stay, after an absence of twenty-eight years. On 31 August 2003 *The Topaz* entered the harbour at Vancouver, the first time that an *Empress* liner had been in the port for over sixty years. In 2004 *The Topaz* called at Piraeus on 13 August, the first day of the Athens Olympic Games, and a couple of weeks later she made a call at Tilbury. *The Topaz* was back in the Irish Sea on 31 July 2007 when she called at Dublin on a voyage from Bergen to New York.

In the spring of 2008 news came that the Peace Boat Organisation would not be renewing the charter, spelling the end for Liverpool's longest-serving ocean liner. The reason cited was high fuel costs. After the termination of the charter, *The Topaz*'s owners, Kyma Shipping, immediately sold the old *Empress* as scrap metal prices were at an all-time high. The former *Empress of Britain* was beached at Alang, India, on 4 July 2008 for demolition, almost fifty-two years to the day after her maiden voyage from Liverpool.

When the Queen launched the *Empress of Britain* back in 1955, nobody could possibly have envisaged the way things would turn out. The transatlantic market entered rapid and terminal decline within five years of her maiden voyage, but the *Empress of Britain* has sailed on, and apart from eleven months of inactivity following the collapse of the Greek Line, the ship has been was in almost continuous operation from the day of her maiden voyage in April 1956 – an incredible fifty-two years.

The Topaz, on charter to the Peace Boat Organization, is still easily recognisable as the former *Empress of Britain*.

EMPRESS OF ENGLAND

Built by Vickers-Armstrongs (Shipbuilders), Walker-on-Tyne.   **Yard No:** 155
Official Number: 187544   **Signal Letters:** G V S U
Gross Tonnage: 25,585   **Nett:** 13,725   **Length:** 640ft   **Breadth:** 85·4ft
Owned by the Canadian Pacific Railway Co. (Canadian Pacific Steamships – Managers)
6 steam turbines, double-reduction gearing to twin screws.   **Speed:** 20 knots.

Lady Eden, the wife of the Prime Minister, launched the *Empress of England* on 9 May 1956. Speaking after the launch, Lady Eden said:

> This must be a day of satisfaction and pride for Canadian Pacific. War brought the almost complete annihilation of the Empress' class of ships and I believe it is true that no other line suffered as heavily as yours. We in Britain will never forget the brave part your ships played in the dark years. They brought your soldiers to these shores and they helped to keep this island supplied. They made resistance possible.

Mr A.C. MacDonald, the managing director of Canadian Pacific Steamships, said that tenders for a third new Empress would be sought later in the year.

A strike that would shut down all British shipyards was due to start at noon on 16 March 1957, the day the new ship was due to sail for her sea trials. In the event the *Empress of England* left the Tyne with just half an hour to spare before becoming caught up in the unrest. She sailed to the Firth of Clyde for speed trials on the Arran Mile and then spent some time at Glasgow before arriving at Liverpool on 26 March.

The new *Empress* was to all intents and purposes an exact sister to the slightly older *Empress of Britain*. She sailed on her maiden voyage from Liverpool to Quebec and Montreal on 18 April 1957 with a full complement of 158 first-class and 900 tourist-class passengers.

Both the new Canadian Pacific liners carried a full crew of 464. They both had 380,650 cubic feet of cargo space, of which 80,000 cubic feet were refrigerated. As with Cunard's *Saxonia*-class, this massive capacity was never full utilised, given the strict timetable of the passenger schedule.

As was the case with the *Empress of Britain*, both first and tourist-class passengers shared the ship's principal public room, the Empress Room. The ship was fully air-conditioned and all the tourist class cabins on 'A' Deck were equipped with private showers and toilets – two decided advantages over the Cunard sisters. Denny–Brown stabilisers were fitted, which, it was claimed, could reduce an eighteen degree roll to one of less than six degrees.

The *Empress of England* on trials off the Isle of Arran on 19 March 1957. (Photo: *Shipbuilding and Shipping Record*)

With the entry into service of the *Empress of England*, Canadian Pacific operated four passenger liners on the North Atlantic in 1957. The new ship had some engine problems on her second voyage, resulting in her being two days late arriving back to Liverpool. On 29 August 1957 she was in collision with the ore carrier *Sept Îles* at Quebec.

The new *Empress of England* was sent cruising to the Caribbean from New York between 15 January and 28 March 1958, but she was back on the Canadian service on 18 April. The *Empress of Britain* had been left to maintain a winter service from Liverpool to St John, New Brunswick.

From 1958, a call at Greenock was reintroduced into Canadian Pacific's sailing schedules. This had been dropped in post-war years in an attempt to speed up passage times.

The *Empress of England*'s winter cruising programme from New York was highly successful and she was joined by the *Empress of Britain* in January 1960.

In the summer of 1960, strike action severely disrupted Canadian Pacific sailings from Liverpool. The *Empress of England* had two voyages cancelled at the height of the season – in July and August – as a result of members of the National Union of Seamen refusing to sail unless their demands for higher basic pay and a shorter working week were met. Many intending passengers were forced to fly the Atlantic, and it was not until 10 September 1960 that the *Empress of England* resumed service. With a full complement of passengers, the Empress was short of crew and, although she was delayed for twelve hours at Greenock whilst additional stewards were signed-on, it was still not enough to provide the traditional Canadian Pacific service. Each passenger was given a letter from the company pointing out the difficulties. The letter stated: 'The entire ship's company will do all they can to give you service and assistance during the voyage, but because of the shortage of staff, meals may have to be curtailed and personal service may not always be as readily available as on a normal voyage.'

Whilst the *Empress of England* was in Montreal a series of fires broke out in five passenger cabins and arson was suspected.

In January 1962 the *Empress of England* operated Canadian Pacific's first cruises out of Liverpool since before the war.

The *Empress of England* was overhauled as usual at Liverpool at the end of 1962 and in severe gales on 17 December the liner broke adrift after ripping a mooring bollard out of the quay. Members of the skeleton crew on board fought to save her from extensive damage as she swung round on her bow moorings. As the *Empress* swung across the dock basin her sirens sounded a warning and the tugs *Aysgarth* and *Hazelgarth* went to her assistance. The chief officer, Mr Wylie, ordered the stern anchor to be dropped.

The liner struck the knuckle between the entrance to Hornby lock and the Gladstone river entrance, causing a 20ft gash in her side, just forward of the bridge. The *Empress of England* was made fast in the position in which she had come to rest, blocking both the Hornby lock and the river entrance, and trapping the tug *Aysgarth* in the lock chamber. After jamming the Gladstone dock system for twelve hours, the *Empress* was pulled off the knuckle and edged into No.1 branch dock.

The year 1963 marked acceleration in the rapid and terminal decline of the number of passengers crossing the North Atlantic by sea. Canadian Pacific reached the inevitable conclusion that it could no longer justify employing three liners on its Liverpool–Montreal service. It has to be said that Canadian Pacific had been involved in airline operations for many years, as part of its claim to be 'the world's most complete transportation system'. Other shipowners purchased interests in airlines, notably the Cunard/BOAC association.

When Max Wilson and his Travel Savings Association (TSA) arrived on the scene in 1963, Canadian Pacific was only too happy to charter both the *Empress of England* and the *Empress of Britain* to operate TSA cruises, and to acquire a 51 per cent interest in the business. On 28 November 1963 the *Empress of England* sailed for Cape Town on TSA charter and operated cruises across the South Atlantic to Brazil and Argentina, and also along the east coast of Africa.

The *Empress of England* in her traditional Canadian Pacific colours. (Photo: *Shipbuilding and Shipping Record*)

The TSA bubble quickly burst and by April 1964 the *Empress of England* and the *Empress of Canada* were back in St Lawrence. The *Empress of Britain* was sold to the Greek Line at the end of her TSA charter. With a two-ship service on the North Atlantic, passenger occupancy improved with an average of 930 passengers on westbound sailings and 735 on eastbound crossings being achieved. Many business travellers flew to Canada and then returned to the UK by ship. Canadian Pacific's European passenger manager was in 'gung-ho' mood when he said in September 1964, 'As far as Canadian Pacific is concerned, we are prepared to stay on the North Atlantic as long as business is profitable. Demand may well outstrip supply. Canadian Pacific is staying in the passenger business!'

Following another winter of cruising, the *Empress of England* resumed service between Liverpool and Montreal in April 1965. There were still crew problems and in an effort to minimise these, the *Empress of England* became the first British liner to carry National Union of Seamen shop stewards and a union convenor in July 1965. 'This is a new page in maritime history,' enthused one union official. The year's statistics for 1965 showed that 26,000 passengers had crossed the Atlantic by sea to Canada, whilst 350,000 had travelled by air.

On 8 November 1965 the *Empress of England* collided with the 12,000-ton Norwegian tanker *Lifjord* in St Lawrence at the height of a fierce blizzard. The *Empress*'s bows were holed and her stern damaged, resulting in five days of temporary repairs which were carried out at Quebec. The liner returned to Liverpool on 4 December for her annual overhaul before starting another winter cruising program.

In 1966 the *Empress of England* sailed for Canada on 26 April and returned to Liverpool on 12 May, just in time to coincide with the start of the six-week seamen's strike on 15 May. With the Atlantic passenger trade in terminal decline this strike, at the height of the season, was nothing less than a death blow. It was not until 14 July that the *Empress of England* resumed her sailings.

In 1967 the Cunard Line announced its withdrawal from operating passenger services to Canada. Its liners on the route, the *Carinthia* and the *Sylvania*, were not up to Canadian Pacific standards and were not suitable for winter cruising.

The *Empress of England* operated her by now usual pattern of winter cruises. Christmas and New Year cruises sailed from Liverpool to the Atlantic Isles and on 8 January 1968 she sailed on her annual long winter cruise to the Caribbean. On 2 April the *Empress* returned to her Liverpool–Montreal service and completed thirteen round voyages during the year.

Canadian Pacific's final call at the Tail of the Bank, off Greenock in the Firth of Clyde, was made on 13 November 1968 by the *Empress of England*, so breaking a forty-year link between Scotland and Canada. It was a sad occasion with a pipe band playing *Will Ye No Come Back Again?*

At the end of 1968 the Candian Pacific fleet was treated to a new corporate image. The famous buff funnel with the red and white chequered houseflag disappeared to make way for a new funnel design made up of two shades of green depicted in curious shapes on a white background. Canadian Pacific described the new corporate painting (graffiti?!) as 'a triangle to represent motion, a circle for global operations, and a square for stability'! The narrow green sheer line on the hull was repainted in a much broader form, with the legend 'C P Ships' painted in large green letters amidships. Maybe the Canadian Pacific directors had been a little high on Lily the Pink's medicinal compound when they authorised this atrocity which met with universal disapproval.

Canadian Pacific's public relations representative, John D. MacGregor, commented:

It would be a pity if we have given the impression that we have just slapped a new coat of paint in strange colours over our two ocean liners and left it at that. This has not been just an isolated 'paint job'. The entire Canadian Pacific transportation complex is undergoing a profound change to draw together under a unique symbol all the diverse entities that make up the whole. These major changes affect not only our liners but the cargo fleet, international airline, railway system, hotels, trucking and express operations. The purpose of this mammoth task which will take up to five years to complete is to bring a clear and identifiable picture for all to see of this company's worldwide activities.

Fancy!

The *Empress of England* in Canadian Pacific's new 'corporate image', applied in 1969. (Photo: *Shipbuilding and Shipping Record*)

In 1969 the *Empress of England* was the mainstay of the St Lawrence service and she completed fourteen round voyages. She left Liverpool on what was to prove her final crossing to Canada on 14 November. On 20 January 1970 Canadian Pacific announced its decision to dispose of the liner on 1 April, following the completion of her winter cruise programme.

The ship was immediately sold to Shaw Savill for £5 million. Chairman Robert Russell said, 'When the *Empress of England* became available we decided immediately that she would be a most satisfactory partner to join the *Northern Star* and the *Southern Cross* in our extremely popular round-the-world service'.

On 4 April 1970 the *Empress of England* was renamed *Ocean Monarch* and a week later left Liverpool on her first voyage for Shaw Savill. She was bound for Australia via South Africa and arrived at Sydney on 15 May. This was immediately followed by a thirty-nine-day cruise to Yokohama to allow her passengers to visit the World Exposition. Following more cruising from Sydney, the *Ocean Monarch* sailed back to the UK on a liner voyage, arriving at Southampton on 11 August.

It was planned to give the *Ocean Monarch* a £2 million refit at Cammell Laird's Birkenhead yard. The project manager, Mr William Cooke, said, 'The conversion is an extremely big job and has to be carried out in a comparatively short time. I would say that our chances of improving on the time schedule are slim, compared with our chances of over-running it!' The *Ocean Monarch* arrived at Birkenhead on 17 September 1970. The refit was beset with problems, labour unrest and strikes. The liner was scheduled to be back in service on 23 April 1971, but it was 17 September 1971 before the refit was complete. As a result Shaw Savill had to cancel seven out of the eight planned summer cruises of the *Ocean Monarch* and lost an estimated £12 million in passenger revenue. The final cost of the refit doubled to £4 million, and Cammell Laird lost an estimated £1¼ million, due to its underestimation of the refit costs.

The *Ocean Monarch* sailed from Southampton on 16 October 1971, fully booked on the first and last cruise of her original summer schedule. On 5 November she sailed from Southampton 'westabout' to Sydney, from where she cruised to New Zealand and the South Pacific islands. A liner voyage back to the UK followed where she arrived on 4 April 1972, and eight days later the *Ocean Monarch* left on a seventy-four-day, round-the-world voyage.

Crew unrest continually dogged the *Ocean Monarch*. On 22 January 1973 half her crew staged a walk-off at Sydney. Replacements were flown out from the UK. In 1974 persistent

The *Ocean Monarch*, ex-*Empress of England*, during her brief spell with Shaw Savill. (Photo: Shaw Savill)

boiler problems occurred requiring a large amount of costly and time-consuming work to rectify.

On 1 April 1975 Shaw Savill announced that it would be withdrawing the *Ocean Monarch* from service. The company said that passenger shipping was no longer a viable option as a result of inflated manning and bunkering costs. It had been necessary to raise cruise fares by thirty per cent and further increases were inevitable. Following the *Ocean Monarch's* arrival at Southampton on 5 June 1975, the ship was sold to Taiwanese shipbreakers. She left Southampton on 13 June and reached Kaohsiung on 17 July 1975 for demolition.

Speaking at Shaw Savill's Annual General Meeting in June 1975, Chairman Lord Beeching said:

> Ships such as the *Ocean Monarch* inspire a strong sentimental attachment, and I am sure that many of our shareholders will regret her passing, just as we do. Nevertheless, it must be said that from a financial point of view the *Ocean Monarch's* disposal gives rise to nothing but a sigh of relief. She has become a loss-making worry and there can be no surer way of improving profitability than by withdrawing her from service.

EMPRESS OF CANADA

Built by Vickers–Armstrongs (Shipbuilding) Ltd, Walker-on-Tyne.   **Yard No:** 171
Official Number: 302597   **Signal Letters:** G H L A
Gross Tonnage: 27,284   **Nett:** 14,240   **Length:** 650ft   **Breadth:** 86·9ft.
Owned by the Canadian Pacific Railway Co. (Canadian Pacific Steamships – Managers)
6 steam turbines, double-reduction gearing to twin screws.   **Speed:** 20 knots

The keel of the third new post-war Canadian Pacific Empress was laid in January 1959 at Vickers–Armstrongs' yard at Newcastle upon Tyne. Seventeen months later the new ship was launched by Mrs Diefenbaker, the wife of the Canadian Prime Minister, on 10 May 1960, and named *Empress of Canada*. In February 1961 the vessel was moved into the dry dock at Swan Hunter & Wigham Richardson's yard at Wallsend, and a month later, on 7 March 1961, she left for trials in the Firth of Clyde.

The *Empress of Canada* carried out her speed trials over the Arran Mile on Saturday 10 March and achieved 23 knots, which was two knots above her designed service speed. After her trials were successfully completed, the new *Empress* returned to the Tyne for final adjustments by her builders, and arrived at Liverpool for the first time on 27 March, 1961. She remained there for a month and was open for inspection by the shipping press and the travel trade. The new *Empress of Canada* was enthusiastically received with one correspondent writing: 'The new vessel matches in speed, grace and luxurious passenger accommodation everything that is best in British shipbuilding'.

The ship was the first Canadian Pacific liner to be equipped with a bulbous bow, which, it was said, would aid in reducing pitching. She had Denny–Brown stabilisers and full air-conditioning. In first class there was accommodation for 192 passengers, and 856 could be carried in tourist class. Another correspondent wrote, 'The *Empress of Canada* is undoubtedly the ship whose general décor, furnishings and accommodation are something which we have been waiting for in a big liner for some time'. Over 70 per cent of the tourist-class cabins had private toilets, a vast improvement over other ships on the Canadian service. There were 262,000 cubic feet of cargo space and a crew of 510 was required to man the ship when she was fully booked.

The *Empress of Canada* left Liverpool on her maiden voyage on 24 April 1961.

The *Empress of Canada* on her trials on the Arran Mile, 10 March 1961. (Photo: Canadian Pacific)

The London train, pulled appropriately by the engine *Empress of Canada*, arrived at Riverside Station with over 400 passengers including the author Nicholas Monsarrat. Promptly at 6.47 p.m. the moment for which the thousands of spectators on the landing stage and the waterfront, the millions watching on television, and the 800 passengers on board, had been waiting for finally came. Slowly at first, as though shy to leave, but growing bolder with a churn of white water at her stern, the new *Empress* moved gracefully down the Mersey as the tugs drew back. She was saluted by an armada of tugs, dredgers, liners, freighters and ferry boats as she slid down the river into the mist after the most impressive send-off Liverpool had seen for many years. The new ship immediately ran into severe gales. She proved herself to be a fine seaboat and arrived at Quebec on 1 May.

With a fleet of three modern passenger liners, Canadian Pacific was in an ideal position to offer extensive winter cruises. As flagship, the *Empress of Canada* operated the prestige cruises out of New York. She left Liverpool on 12 December 1961 and made her maiden arrival at New York a week later on 19 December. There was no elaborate welcome for her as the city was shrouded in dense freezing fog.

In 1962 the three Canadian Pacific Empresses made a total of thirty-three round voyages between Liverpool and Montreal. The *Empress of Canada* was more extensively employed in cruising in the winter and spring of 1963 and in addition to her Caribbean cruises from New York she sailed on a sixty-day, twenty-four port Mediterranean cruise on 20 February.

After performing flawlessly for over two years, the *Empress of Canada* suffered some engine trouble in September 1963 and was thirty hours late in arriving at Liverpool. Her next voyage was hit by a strike of longshoremen in Canada and after arriving off Quebec on 8 October she was not permitted to berth. After two days at anchor she sailed for Halifax, NS, to discharge her passengers and cargo.

The 1966 strike of the National Union of Seamen affected the *Empress of Canada* when she arrived back at Liverpool on 20 May, and she was strikebound until the end of the dispute on 1 July, sailing again for Montreal on 4 July.

The *Empress of Canada* was involved in a couple of mishaps in 1967. On the 8 February she ran aground at San Juan, Puerto Rico, but fortunately suffered no damage and on 4 May she struck a whale which became impaled on her bow. Her captain ordered 'full astern' on the engines and the whale was dislodged.

At the end of 1968 the *Empress of Canada* suffered the indignity of being painted in Canadian Pacific's new corporate logo (described in the chapter dealing with the *Empress of England*).

Faced with dwindling passenger numbers on the North Atlantic, Canadian Pacific extended the *Empress of Canada*'s New York-based Caribbean cruising programme into the summer of 1969, when she operated a total of thirteen cruises. The Empress was back in Liverpool on 10 June and sailed on one round voyage to Montreal. Following that she undertook a cruise to Norway and the North Cape, and this was followed by four more transatlantic round voyages on the Canadian route.

Following the announcement of the disposal of the *Empress of England* in early 1970, the chairman of Canadian Pacific Steamships, Mr W.J. Stenason, said that his company would continue to operate the *Empress of Canada* on Caribbean cruises and on the North Atlantic, and was confident that there was a viable economic future for the liner.

The *Empress of Canada* had a shorter than usual New York cruising season in 1970 and on 6 April sailed direct to Montreal from New York to pick up her transatlantic schedule. Calls at Quebec and Greenock were both dropped in 1970. The *Empress* made eleven round voyages on the Canadian service between April and October, and on 20 August carried a record 1,039 passengers on the westbound passage. There was more categorical assurance from Canadian Pacific that the ship was not for sale, in fact she was said to be operating at 82 per cent capacity throughout the summer of 1970.

On 29 January 1971 Mr Robert Edwards, director of the Port of Liverpool, said that the end of passenger trade at Liverpool was 'inevitable'. Some £3 million was required to bring back Princes Landing Stage to the standard required to operate large passenger ships. A month later the Riverside Railway Station, adjacent to Princes Landing Stage, was closed to all traffic.

Unfortunately the *Empress of Canada* was plagued with industrial unrest amongst her crew. Stewards persistently, and totally unacceptably, demanded the use of passenger facilities to be made available to them.

At 8.15 p.m. on 22 August 1971, when the *Empress of Canada* was one day out of Liverpool, she suffered a blowback in one of her boilers with a resulting fire in the boiler room. There was a full scale alert, with passengers being mustered at their lifeboat stations. However, the crew brought the fire under control within ten minutes.

Without any advance warning, on 9 November 1971 Canadian Pacific announced that the *Empress of Canada* would be withdrawn from service when she arrived back at Liverpool two weeks later on 23 November. Canadian Pacific stated that 'economic circumstances make it impossible to achieve a viable passenger ship operation'. This brought to an end over two years of rumour and counter-rumour.

The *Empress of Canada* left Montreal at 8 a.m. on 17 November 1971 with 300 passengers on board on her final voyage as a Canadian Pacific liner. In her ten and a half years in service, the ship had completed 121 round voyages across the North Atlantic, and had sailed on eighty-two cruises. The *Empress* was back at Liverpool on 23 November at the end of her last voyage and dock workers stood in silence as she moved slowly through the Gladstone river entrance. 'It was almost like the Cenotaph on Remembrance Day,' said her master Captain W.E. Williams. 'I feel sorry for the people who might have travelled with us as passengers, but who now never will. They will never know what they missed.'

With three long mournful blasts on her siren, the *Empress of Canada* said goodbye to the Mersey on 14 December 1971. With her lights blazing and her corridors and decks deserted, Liverpool's last transatlantic liner slipped her moorings at Gladstone Dock and got underway with a skeleton crew of less than 100. She was on her way to Tilbury, to be laid up until sold. Her master, Captain Richard Walgate, who had been with Canadian Pacific for forty-one years, said, 'We all feel very sad at leaving Liverpool. We will be thinking about all the people who have sailed with us, and all the people we will be leaving behind. I have served on all the Empress liners, but I've always had a soft spot for this one.' Captain Walgate supervised the final stages of the building of the ship on the Tyne, and sailed with her on the maiden voyage.

There was only a small group of dockers, company officials and relatives of crewmen on the quayside to say goodbye. As the *Empress of Canada* sailed past Crosby, she sounded the company signal, as had been done for years. Captain Walgate explained:

> We always used to give this signal – one long, two short and a long blast on the ship's whistle – as we sailed past the Blundellsands home of the late Captain R.V. Burns, the general manager. It was a habit we all got used to on the Empress boats and we keep it up because the people of the area expect it of us. Now the signal will be sounded for the last time.

Canadian Pacific commented: 'One of the difficulties is that, although the ship was built with cruising in mind, her design has since been overtaken by the specialised new liners now cruising in both the Mediterranean and the Caribbean'.

The *Empress of Canada* was quickly sold to Ted Arison to become the pioneer ship in the Carnival Cruise Lines fleet. She was renamed *Mardi Gras* on 14 February 1972. Her departure from Tilbury was delayed by the National Union of Seamen and Sam McCluskie, the NUS organiser, said, 'We are picketing this ship in order to combat the growing menace of crews of convenience. Their low pay undermines the hard-won wages and conditions which the NUS has fought for'. Tug crews and lock gate men at Tilbury 'blacked' the *Mardi Gras* and she did not sail for Miami until 26 February.

Carnival Cruise Lines was initially in a very weak financial position and it was essential that the *Mardi Gras* should earn money immediately. There was no time for a refit and on 11 March 1972 the *Mardi Gras* left Miami on her first cruise for Ted Arison. At that time she was the largest liner using the port and was too deep-drafted, with the result that in fully laden condition the *Mardi Gras* ran aground on departure. After twenty-four hours of fruitless effort to free her, the passengers were disembarked. She was eventually refloated and inspected and not found to be making water. The cruise continued.

The Carnival organisation was constantly just one step away from bankruptcy in its early days. Nevertheless, the *Mardi Gras* was rated as the 'Number One 7-Day Cruise Ship Sailing

The *Mardi Gras*, ex-*Empress of Canada*, the first cruise ship in the Carnival fleet. (Photo: Carnival Cruise Lines)

The Caribbean' by the travel trade in the United States. She was marketed as the 'Fun Ship'. By 1975 Ted Arison urgently needed a running mate for the *Mardi Gras* which he found in the *Queen Anna Maria*, the former *Empress of Britain*, then laid up at Piraeus.

In August 1979 the *Mardi Gras* sailed on a cruise to Canada and arrived at Montreal on the twenty-eighth of the month. She received a fireboat welcome on her first visit to the port for eight years. Another Canadian cruise was operated in 1980, but as it turned out, this was the last time that the *Mardi Gras* ever sailed in Canadian waters.

The attraction of brand new cruise liners in the now rapidly expanding Carnival fleet could not dim the enduring popularity of the *Mardi Gras*, and early in 1982 the ageing ship was given an extensive refurbishment. Even by 1989, after seventeen years with Carnival, the *Mardi Gras* was still recognisable as the *Empress of Canada*. By 1992 Carnival had eighteen ships and carried 1·1 million passengers during that year.

Towards the end of 1990 Carnival announced that it would transfer the *Mardi Gras* (ex-*Empress of Canada*) to join the *Carnivale* (ex-*Empress of Britain*) operating out of Port Canaveral. The two former Empresses sailed on an identical schedule to the Bahamas, in convoy and never out of sight of each other.

In 1993 the *Mardi Gras* was chartered to Gold Star Cruises, based in Galveston, Texas, and renamed *Star of Texas*. She would operate ten 'cruises to nowhere' each week consisting of four six-hour cruises, and six 'nightclub' cruises. On 30 October 1993 the *Star of Texas* sailed on her first cruise for Gold Star.

Gold Star Cruises rapidly found itself in financial difficulties, reportedly losing $4·5 million in just eleven months. On 9 November 1994 the *Star of Texas* was moved to Miami and renamed *Lucky Star*. She continued to operate short cruises, with one mid-week four-hour cruise costing just $19·95. The Gold Star operation was closed down on 30 December 1994 and the *Lucky Star* was laid up in the Bahamas for a while before sailing for Piraeus, where she arrived on 10 May 1995. Her name was changed to *Apollon* after Carnival had sold its pioneer cruise liner to Royal Olympic.

In 1997 a new British operator entered the UK cruise market, trading under the name of Direct Cruises. This was a subsidiary of the direct-sell package tour company, Direct Holidays, and was aimed primarily at the cruise market in the North of England, and in Scotland.

Direct Cruises secured a five-year charter on the *Apollon* from Royal Olympic which, after a reputed $20 million repair and refurbishment at the Skaramanga shipyard, sailed from Piraeus for Liverpool. However, the *Apollon* was diverted to Avonmouth for engine repairs and it was not until 30 May 1998 that she reached Liverpool just over twenty-six years after she last left the port. Apart from Liverpool, the *Apollon* operated cruises from Greenock and Newcastle upon Tyne.

The *Apollon* (ex-*Empress of Canada*) arriving at Liverpool on 31 July 1999. (Photo: John Shepherd)

On 21 July 1999 Direct Holidays, the parent company of Direct Cruises, was sold to Airtours, and a few months later came the news that the *Apollon*'s charter was to be cancelled and the cruise programme for 2000 was to be abandoned. Poor bookings were cited as the reason for winding-up Direct Cruises.

After a further period of lay-up, the *Apollon* operated a programme of short cruises to the Greek islands commencing in May 2001. In July 2001 the *Apollon* was chartered as an accommodation ship for delegates and press attending the G8 Summit being held at Genoa, after which she returned to her cruise programme. In February 2002 Royal Olympic claimed that the *Apollon* would need a complete refurbishment, and the now old ship was once again laid up.

The *Apollon* was sold for breaking up on 16 September 2003. Owners of redundant cruise ships were taking advantage of the higher prices which could be obtained for scrap metal. On 12 November the *Apollon* left Piraeus on her final voyage to the breaker's yard at Alang, India, where she arrived on 4 December. Initially she was anchored offshore, waiting to be hauled up on to the beach and reduced to a pile of scrap metal.

4

CUNARD LINE

In November 1838, prompted by the successful transatlantic voyages of the steamers *Sirius* and *Great Western* earlier in the year, the British Admiralty invited tenders for the conveyance of the mails by steamship between England and North America. A copy of this document reached Nova Scotian businessman Samuel Cunard. Born at Halifax, Nova Scotia, in 1787, Cunard had many shipping connections, as well as being the local agent of the Honourable East India Company.

In January 1839 Cunard sailed from Halifax to Falmouth on the Government sailing packet and after reaching London he submitted a tender for £55,000 per annum for a fortnightly steamer service from England to Halifax. The Lords of the Admiralty were interested in Cunard's proposal, and so he contacted Robert Napier of Glasgow with a view to ordering three steamers. A contract was signed between the Admiralty and Cunard on 4 May 1839 for a service to begin on 4 June 1840 and to run for seven years.

Robert Napier introduced Cunard to James Donaldson, George Burns and David MacIver, all with shipping interest in Glasgow, and these four men founded the British & North American Royal Mail Steam Packet Co. with a capital of £270,000. From its earliest days the company was popularly known as the Cunard Line. The company's first ship, the *Britannia*, was launched on 5 February 1840. This wooden paddle steamer, commanded by Captain Henry Woodruff RN, departed on the first mail sailing from Liverpool to Halifax and Boston on 4 July 1840, taking twelve days and ten hours on passage to Halifax. Samuel Cunard himself was on board.

The story of the Cunard Line is far too well known to be repeated in this synopsis, even if space permitted. Suffice it to say that, in the company's own words, it was 'over a century's conquest of the North Atlantic'. The company was the leader in passenger shipping on the North Atlantic using Liverpool as its principal UK port. Many of its ships were household names, such as the *Mauretania* and the *Lusitania* of 1907.

After the First World War, the Cunard Line's express passenger service to New York was transferred to Southampton.

During the war, the Cunard Line had lost twenty-two ships and in 1920 commenced a building programme of twelve new intermediate passenger liners for the Liverpool-based New York and Canadian services. Six of the new ships were intended for the New York service and were of 20,000 tons (except the *Lancastria*, which was of 16,000 tons); and six 14,000-ton liners were built for the Canadian service.

Four of these ships later became war losses: the *Andania*, *Carinthia*, *Laconia* and *Lancastria*. A further four were purchased by the Admiralty: the *Antonia*, *Ausonia*, *Aurania* and *Alaunia*. The four remaining liners, the *Ascania*, *Franconia*, *Scythia* and *Samaria*, were returned to Cunard in the late 1940s and operated the intermediate services until the advent of the new *Saxonia*-class in the mid-1950s.

SCYTHIA

Built by Vickers, Ltd, at Barrow in 1920.   **Yard No:** 493
Official No: 143730.   **Signal Letters:** G D Y P
Gross Tonnage: 19,930   **Nett:** 10,992   **Length:** 600·7ft   **Breadth:** 73·8ft
Owned by the Cunard Steamship Co. Ltd, registered at Liverpool.
6 steam turbines, double-reduction geared to two screw shafts.   **Service speed:** 16½ knots.

The *Scythia* was the first of the five 20,000-ton Cunard liners built after the First World War. She was built at Barrow-in-Furness by Vickers Ltd, having been designed by Mr L. Peskett, Cunard's naval architect, and launched on 23 March 1920 by Mrs Maxwell, the wife of one of the Cunard directors. The *Scythia* was something of a pioneer ship, intended to burn oil fuel and at the time of her launch the largest liner to be so designed. She was also of interest because of her double-reduction geared turbines. In her deck machinery, too, the *Scythia* departed from usual practice. Instead of being driven by steam, her winches and steering gear were electro-hydraulic.

Owing to a strike of joiners, the *Scythia* had to be transferred to Lorient in March 1921 for the completion of her accommodation. She eventually sailed from Liverpool on her maiden voyage to New York on 20 August 1921. Her original passenger accommodation was for 350 first class, 350 second class and 1,500 in third class. The large amount of emigrant accommodation was quickly rendered uneconomic on account of the severe restrictions imposed on U.S. immigration from 1922 onwards.

In March 1922 the *Scythia* reached Halifax, NS, at a greatly reduced speed having received damage to her turbine gearing, and later in the same year she was chartered to the Frank Tourist Co. to make a 'yachting cruise' from New York to the Mediterranean early in 1923. During October 1923 the *Scythia* collided with the White Star liner *Cedric* in dense fog off the Irish coast. Repairs proved to be extensive and took some three weeks, being carried out by David Rollo & Sons of Liverpool.

When King Amanulla of Afghanistan visited Liverpool in 1928 it was arranged that he would stay overnight on board the *Scythia* which was moved from her dock berth to Princes Landing Stage for the purpose. Also in 1928 the *Scythia* flew a special Welsh flag while acting

The Scythia (ahead) and Leyland's *Devonian* (astern) at Princes Landing Stage. Note the Cunard tender *Skirmisher* alongside the *Scythia*. (Photo: Cunard Line)

as 'Eisteddfod ship' bringing American passengers on a pilgrimage to Treorchy for the event. The *Scythia*, commanded by Captain William Prothero, disembarked her passengers at Cardiff. On 7 July 1934 the liner collided with the Isle of Man steamer *Viking* off Princes Landing Stage. The Manx steamer was outward bound to Douglas and the *Scythia* was approaching the stage prior to sailing to New York. There was slight damage to both ships.

In August 1939 the *Scythia* was taken over by the Government as a troopship and in August 1940 arrived at New York with over 700 passengers including some British child evacuees. She was converted to a troopship and on 23 November 1942 the *Scythia* was torpedoed by aircraft whilst at anchor off Algiers with a full complement of troops on board. Her master, Captain John Bertenshaw, secured a tow and the liner was taken across the Strait to Gibraltar for repairs, and was then sent to New York for overhaul.

On 21 February 1946 the *Scythia* had to put back to Bangor Bay, Northern Ireland, with turbo-feed pump trouble; the bedplate was cracked and a new rotor needed. She was bound for Halifax, NS, with 500 wives and 200 children of Canadian servicemen. Repairs were carried out by Harland & Wolff as she lay at anchor off White Head.

A few months later the *Scythia* arrived at Liverpool on 7 April 1946 with 2,500 returning German prisoners, including twenty-six stretcher cases. Also on board were 353 Royal Naval personnel. There was talk about the waste of shipping space when the *Scythia* sailed from Liverpool on 19 July 1946 bound for Bombay with only her crew on board. It was said that the ship was needed at Bombay for repatriation purposes, and that she could not be held to await outward bound passengers or service personnel.

In October 1948, under charter to the International Refugee Organisation and the Canadian Government, the *Scythia* commenced a series of voyages with 'displaced persons' from Cuxhaven and Le Havre to Quebec or Halifax.

The *Scythia* was de-requisitioned in November 1949. Following a refit by John Brown & Co. at Clydebank, she went back on North Atlantic service. On 17 August 1950 the *Scythia* left Liverpool on her first post-war commercial voyage for Quebec, returning to London. In 1951 she reopened the Southampton-Quebec passenger service, suspended since 1939. The *Scythia* had been designed for the New York service and was too deep drafted to proceed from Quebec to Montreal.

On 5 June 1952 the *Scythia* collided with the Canadian steamer *Wabana* in the Gulf of St Lawrence. At the inquiry which followed, both ships were held to blame for excessive speed in fog and the improper use of radar. The *Scythia* was holed on her starboard side and had temporary repairs carried out at Lauzon, Quebec.

In 1957 the *Scythia* returned to the Liverpool–Cobh–New York service and left Liverpool on 5 October on her last Cunard voyage. On her last two voyages across the Atlantic under charter, she carried Canadian servicemen and their families between Halifax, NS, and Rotterdam. The *Scythia* completed her last voyage at Southampton on 22 December 1957 and afterwards lay idle awaiting a decision as to her disposal. The old ship was sold to the British Iron & Steel Corporation (Salvage) Ltd of London. The *Scythia*, the first and last of her class, left Southampton on New Year's Day 1958, and followed the *Samaria* and the *Franconia* to the Inverkeithing shipbreaking yard of Thos. W. Ward Ltd.

The old *Scythia* was thirty-six years old and she certainly left behind a proud record and is, perhaps, especially remembered by Canadians. Her name was revived in 1965, the new *Scythia*, a cargo liner with engines aft, being a very different ship indeed from her famous predecessor. The new ship served Cunard for just four years before being sold to the Harrison Line in 1969 and renamed *Merchant*.

FRANCONIA

Built by John Brown & Co. Ltd, at Clydebank in 1923.   **Yard No:** 492
Official Number: 147216   **Signal Letters:** G B R Q
Gross Tonnage: 20,341   **Nett:** 11,145   **Length:** 601·3ft   **Breadth:** 73·7ft.
Owned by the Cunard Steamship Co. Ltd, Registered at Liverpool
Twin screws: 6 Brown–Curtis steam turbines, double-reduction gearing to two shafts.
Speed: 16 knots

The five ships of the *Scythia* class were the largest vessels ordered under the Cunard Line's immense building programme after the First World War. The first three, the *Scythia, Samaria* and *Laconia*, built between 1920 and 1921, were for the company's Liverpool–New York service. The later pair, the *Franconia* of 1923 and the *Carinthia* of 1925 were both intended for the transatlantic service in the summer, and were specially adapted to go cruising in the winter months. On this account the No.4 hold space was not used for cargo but was enlarged and fitted as a recreation area with swimming pool, racquets court and gymnasium.

The *Franconia* was designed by Mr L. Peskett, Cunard's naval architect, and she was launched on 21 October 1922 by Lady Royden, the wife of the Cunard chairman, Sir Thomas Royden. She left Liverpool on 8 June 1923 for a three-day 'shakedown' cruise and sailed on her maiden voyage to New York on 23 June. The new *Franconia* was almost continuously on the summer Liverpool–New York service and winter cruising until the outbreak of the Second World War.

The *Franconia's* first world-cruise left New York on 16 November 1922 and passed through the Panama Canal before calling at twenty-four ports. In December 1926 she ran aground at San Juan, Puerto Rico, in a particularly heavy swell. A charter to the Furness Bermuda Line took place in 1931 and for five months the *Franconia* operated the New York–Bermuda service in place of the burnt out *Bermuda*.

Initially the *Franconia* had accommodation for 221 in first class, 356 in second class and 1,266 in third class. Between 1930 and 1931 this was reduced and improved to 350 cabin class, 350 tourist class and 930 third class. At the same time the *Franconia's* hull was painted white, which was seen as a great improvement.

During 1934 the *Franconia* made two round voyages from London via Southampton to New York, resuming her Liverpool service and winter cruising in 1935. In 1938 she undertook a

The *Franconia* in the Clyde, 1949. (Photo: Cunard Line)

world cruise calling at thirty-seven ports and sailing 41,727 miles. The ship left New York on Christmas Eve 1937 and arrived back on 12 June 1938. She was away for a massive 170 days.

On the outbreak of war in September 1939, the *Franconia* was immediately converted for trooping and her first duty was to take 1,300 men to Malta. Whilst she was on passage she collided with Royal Mail Lines' *Alcantara*, but the damage was fairly slight. She then took 700 Polish troops to Marseille.

In June 1940 the *Franconia*, escorted by HMS *Vindictive*, was employed in evacuating troops from Narvik, following the Norway debacle. Later she evacuated troops from Brittany and embarked 8,000 at Quiberon Bay. The *Franconia* was badly damaged by near misses from bombs which severely shook her main engines and their seating. Extensive repairs were required when she got back to the UK.

Following the repairs to her engines in August 1940, the *Franconia* carried 2,935 troops from Gourock around the Cape of Good Hope to Suez, and in November took a further 2,000 to Gibraltar. She then made five voyages around the Cape to Suez or Durban, or to India during 1942. The following year the *Franconia* made seven round trips to North Africa and in July 1943 she took part in the Sicily operations, landing her troops in Augusta. From December 1943 to early in 1944 she was trooping from the USA to the Mediterranean, making one voyage to Taranto and one to Oran, and finally a transatlantic crossing to Italy.

On 17 January 1945 the *Franconia* left Liverpool under sealed orders for the Dardanelles and the Bosporus. She became the first British ship for four years to pass through the strait and all personnel were instructed to wear civilian clothing to appease Turkish neutrality. The *Franconia* entered the Black Sea to become the floating headquarters for the British delegation at the Yalta conference between Churchill, Roosevelt and Stalin. The *Franconia* then returned to Liverpool and a further spell of trooping, principally to Bombay and Karachi.

The *Franconia* was released from her war service in June 1948. Since being requisitioned almost nine years earlier, she had steamed 319,784 miles and had carried 189,239 passengers, mainly troops. The old ship was sent to John Brown's yard at Clydebank for a nine-month refit. Her machinery was overhauled, her hull and superstructure cleaned and repainted and her accommodation was refitted so that she could carry 250 first-class passengers and 600 in tourist class.

On 22 May 1949 the *Franconia* left the Clyde for dry docking at Liverpool and on 2 June sailed for Quebec on her first post-war commercial voyage. A year later, on 12 June, the *Franconia* ran aground on Orleans Island, shortly after leaving Quebec for Liverpool. Her 780 passengers were transferred to the *Stratheden* and the *Georgic* at Halifax, NS. The *Franconia* remained aground for five weeks before she was refloated on 16 July with the aid of six tugs and an icebreaker. She was found to be holed on her starboard side and to have sustained damage requiring dry docking and heavy repairs. As was the case with the *Scythia*, the *Franconia* had too deep a draft to proceed from Quebec to Montreal, and her masts were too tall for her to pass under the Quebec Bridge.

Following repairs the *Franconia* continued on the Canadian service, but her UK port was shifted to Southampton. On one voyage she suffered turbine trouble and repairs were carried out as far as possible at sea, but she had to turn back and reached Southampton at a speed of about 7-knots, escorted by the Cunard cargo vessel *Asia*. Her passengers were transferred to the *Queen Mary* and after two weeks of repairs the *Franconia* was back in service.

The *Franconia* left Liverpool for New York on 3 November 1956 on what was to be her final voyage. Her master, Captain D.M. Maclean, said that the *Franconia* ran into severe storms on her westbound passage and arrived at New York one and a half days late. The following day there was a longshoremen's strike and the *Franconia* was a day late leaving New York.

She sailed from New York on 16 November and in mid-Atlantic a message was received from the Greek steamer *Triton* to the effect that a seaman had fallen in heavy weather and urgently required medical assistance. The *Franconia* altered course and steamed 100 miles or so to the *Triton*, where the seaman was transferred in one of the liner's lifeboats. The *Franconia's* surgeon carried out two operations but the seaman died and was buried at sea.

The *Franconia* arrived at Cobh eighteen hours late and then, whilst on the last leg of the voyage to Liverpool, developed further turbine trouble. In appalling weather she anchored off Liverpool Bar and then made for an anchorage in Douglas Bay, Isle of Man.

The *Franconia* limped slowly into Liverpool in the morning of 30 November, five days late on what was her final transatlantic crossing. Four tugs met the ship at the Mersey Bar to escort her to the landing stage. The 129 passengers had been on board for two weeks instead of nine days. But few complained and agreed that the ship's company had done everything possible for their comfort. Some even enjoyed the extra days at sea, but there were several who, when the liner lay sheltering off the Isle of Man, wanted to be put ashore.

Captain MacLean commented, 'The Franconia has always been known as a happy ship, and in my opinion she is one of the finest ships on the North Atlantic service. It is very sad to say goodbye to her.'

Larger ships there have been, and faster ones, but the *Franconia* stood proudly amidst her peers for the restrained elegance of her accommodation. This had been fashioned to meet the requirements of people of wealth and leisure who had made the ship their home during world cruises. After the war, the *Franconia* retained her special niche in the Cunard fleet. And if her straight stem, two pole masts and counter stern looked oddly anachronistic when viewed against the raked stems, cruiser sterns and single tripod masts of the newer ships, there was much to admire in her exterior design which had a simple and serene dignity.

On 14 December 1956 the *Franconia* was sold to the British Iron & Steel Corporation (Salvage) Ltd and left Liverpool for Inverkeithing, arriving there on 19 December to be broken up. In view of the shortage of scrap metal, she commanded a high price. Now thirty-three years old, she had had a hard and varied life, nine years as a troopship and the rest of the time on the North Atlantic or world-cruising.

ASCANIA

Built by Armstrong, Whitworth & Co. Ltd, Newcastle, 1925.   **Yard No:** 971.
Official Number: 147307   **Signal Letters:** G K N J
Gross Tonnage: 14,440   **Nett:** 8,143   **Length:** 520ft   **Breadth:** 65·3ft.
Owned by the Cunard Steamship Co. Ltd. Registered at Liverpool.
Twin screws, 4 steam turbines, double reduction gearing.   **Speed:** 15 knots.

By the end of the First World War, the Cunard Line had lost all of its 'A' class of liners operating on the Canadian service: the *Albania, Ausonia, Andania, Aurania* and *Ascania*. The Canadian trade was of ever growing importance, and in the company's vast replacement building programme of the early post-war years, six new 'A' class liners were constructed for the Canadian routes.

The new *Ascania* was launched on 20 December 1923, but her building was then stopped for several months due to ever increasing costs and spiralling wage demands. It was not until 2 May 1925 that she was ready for her sea trials off the Tyne. These were successfully completed and she left for Southampton.

The original passenger numbers were 500 in cabin class, and 1,200 in third class, with a crew of 280. The *Ascania* left London on her maiden voyage on 22 May 1925 for Southampton, Quebec and Montreal. In 1927 the passenger accommodation was rearranged with 520 in cabin class, and third class reduced to 928.

In 1928 the *Ascania* took one Anchor Line sailing from Glasgow to Canada and made one voyage from Liverpool. The depression of the 1930s made very little difference to the *Ascania*

The *Ascania* at Liverpool. (Photo: *Shipbuilding and Shipping Record*)

and she carried on with her work on the Canadian routes, with an occasional voyage on the New York run.

The year 1934 proved to be a memorable one for the *Ascania*. In October she was one of the ships which went to the assistance of the *Millpool* which was sinking in a violent storm in mid-Atlantic. After searching the area for twenty-one hours, no trace of the ship was found.

A few weeks later, on 14 December, the *Ascania* was diverted to assist the steamer *Usworth*, whose grain cargo had shifted in severe weather. The *Usworth* had been taken in tow by the Belgian ship *Jean Jadot*, but the towline had carried away. One of the *Jean Jadot*'s lifeboats had managed to take off fourteen men, but it was overturned by the mountainous seas and twelve of the rescued men were lost.

The sea state was really unfit for boat work, but on the *Ascania*'s arrival her master, Captain L.C.P. Bisset, RNR, decided to make an attempt. After pumping out some fuel oil to leeward, he took the *Ascania* to within 100ft of the *Usworth*'s stern and sent away a 30ft lifeboat, manned by one officer and ten ABs. The boat managed to reach the *Usworth* and take off the remaining nine crew members.

The *Ascania* was making twice the leeway of the swamped *Usworth* and had to make a wide circle of the sinking vessel to get into a position suitable for recovering the lifeboat. The boat made it back alongside the *Ascania* but was rising and falling twenty feet in the heavy seas, and getting the men back on board was an extremely hazardous operation, but eventually they made it without loss.

This was one of the epic rescues of the North Atlantic, and on the *Ascania*'s return to the UK there were civic receptions. The boat's crew and Captain Bisset were all presented with Lloyd's Silver Medal for gallantry at sea and for the remarkable handling of the ship.

In November 1935 the *Ascania* was struck amidships by the steamer *Norwegian* and had a hole torn in her side, and in 1938 she ran aground near Bic Harbour in the St Lawrence, some 150 miles from Quebec, but was refloated without much difficulty. At the time the *Ascania* was carrying $3 million worth of gold bullion to Canada.

The *Ascania* arrived at Liverpool on 3 September 1939, the day war was declared. She was immediately converted into an armed merchant cruiser at Birkenhead and was commissioned on 16 October. For the next three years she patrolled the Atlantic, covering 147,000 miles in the process.

In October 1942 the *Ascania* was converted into a troopship and the following year she was further altered to become a L.S.I. (L) – Landing Ship Infantry (Large). With landing craft replacing her lifeboats, she was present at the Sicilian and Anzio landings. In 1945 the ship was converted back to a troopship and operated as such until she was released in December 1947.

By this time she was the only one of the six 'A'-class liners left to the Cunard Line. All six had started the war as armed merchant cruisers, and the *Andania* had been torpedoed and sunk in 1940. The other four were all bought by the Admiralty and converted into repair ships.

Following a very quick partial refit, and still with austerity accommodation, the *Ascania* reopened the Liverpool–Halifax service on 20 December 1947. She had accommodation for 257 first-class and 522 tourist-class passengers. At the end of 1949 the *Ascania* was sent to Alexander Stephen & Sons' yard at Linthouse for complete reconditioning. The *Ascania* returned to service on the Liverpool to Quebec and Montreal service on 21 April 1950 carrying a full complement of 198 first-class passengers and 498 in tourist class, plus a crew of 367.

The *Ascania* remained very much a Liverpool-based ship. In June 1952 she made a special call at Douglas, Isle of Man, with a party of Manx people from Canada on a homecoming visit. Two years later the new *Saxonia*, followed shortly by the *Ivernia*, made their appearance on the Canadian route from Liverpool, and at the end of September 1955 the *Ascania* was transferred to Southampton. She lasted a year at the southern port and completed her last Cunard voyage on 16 November 1956.

The *Ascania* made two trooping voyages to Cyprus, sailing on 23 November 1956, finally returning to Southampton on 20 December. Ten days later she sailed to Newport, Mon., where she was broken up by John Cashmore. Thirty-two years old, the *Ascania* was still a smart, sturdy-looking ship, but of course she was quite outclassed by the new quartet. She had spent almost her entire working life on the North Atlantic, and had come through it with flying colours.

H.M. ARMED MERCHANT CRUISER *ASCANIA*

by Guy Stafford

This is the story of a Cunard liner that went to war as an armed merchant cruiser in 1939. HMS *Ascania*, flying the White Ensign, played an important, if unspectacular, part in the early years of the war at sea.

It was 8 a.m. on a Saturday morning in late September 1939. The war was in its third week and the twenty naval ratings waiting outside the drafting office at HMS *Excellent* on Whale Island were wondering what the future held in store for them. Each had received a draft chit for AMC (Armed Merchant Cruiser) C5. They knew they were due to join her that day, but as to the name of the ship and where she was berthed, they had yet to learn.

Thirteen-and-a-half weary hours later they arrived at a blacked out Woodside Station at Birkenhead. There was a lorry to meet them and after a short trip through the darkened streets it entered Cammell Laird's yard and pulled up alongside a steamer in the dry dock.

That she was a Cunarder was obvious from her colours, but it was not until after the white-coated stewards had shown them to their accommodation that they knew her as the 14,500-ton *Ascania*. The chief and petty officers were accommodated on 'B' deck, the remainder on 'C' deck, cabins being an unheard of luxury to the naval men.

Three hectic weeks followed. Eight six-inch guns arrived on the quayside to be hoisted onboard and bolted down to the gun supports built in when the *Ascania* was constructed, four to port and four to starboard. A small director and range finder were fitted to the upper bridge and a height finder on a specially constructed platform abaft the single funnel. Two three-inch-high angle guns and twin Lewis guns on the wings of the bridge formed the anti-aircraft armament.

The magazines were constructed in the holds fore and aft. Small davits with electric winches served as shell and cordite hoists to each magazine. A coat of battleship grey was applied and the once-proud *Ascania* had become a warship.

During the busy three weeks at Cammell Lairds, a relationship had sprung up between the small naval party and those members of the merchant navy crew who were to remain with the ship on the T124 Articles of Agreement. The initial prejudices quickly gave way to curiosity and interest in each other's jobs. Many lasting friendships were formed in those early days.

At the end of the three weeks the main body of the naval crew arrived. It was a motley collection comprising of recalled pensioners, RNR, and RNVR ratings. The only active service ratings were the chief gunner's mate and the young ordnance artificer joining his first ship.

With the ship's company complete and under the command of Captain C.H. Ringrose-Wharton, RN, HMS *Ascania* went to sea for the first time – just for the day. Two days later, stored and fully armoured, she sailed for an unknown destination. Rumour was rife, the best bet being Scapa Flow for duties on the Northern Patrol, but once clear of Anglesey the *Ascania* turned to a southerly course and eventually steamed into Spithead. After some hours the ship entered Portsmouth Harbour and a unexpected weekend leave was granted to some of the crew. On Monday morning she sailed for Portland.

During the week that followed most days were spent at sea on gun trials. The six-inch Mk VII guns dated from between 1898 and 1904 and some problems were experienced with these elderly pieces and a great deal of glass was shattered during the firing, particularly on the promenade deck. The three-inch guns were 1917 vintage and caused no problems other than the lack of training for the crews.

On the Thursday evening of the *Ascania's* week at Portland two members of the ship's company were in a pub discussing the possibility of weekend leave again, only to be told by the barmaid that, 'if you're off that liner, you'll be on your way to Canada with a load of bullion come Saturday!' The men laughed, but strangely enough, on the Friday afternoon, a small coaster came alongside and some strange looking boxes were loaded under armed guard and stowed down below.

Saturday morning dawned bleak, grey and very wet. HMS *Ascania* left harbour with a two destroyer escort, and for several hours steamed up Channel until well out of sight of land, then she turned, left her escort, and headed out into the Atlantic.

The passage was rough and the weather still very wet when six days later Chebucto Head loomed out of the mist and the *Ascania* steamed into Halifax harbour and berthed at pier 22. The first ship of the 3rd Battle Squadron had arrived! Later she was joined by her sister Cunarders *Alaunia* and *Ausonia*, and later still by the *Jervis Bay*, *Montclare* and other AMCs.

After a few days in harbour the *Ascania* sailed as escort for one of the first convoys to leave Halifax. The weather was calm but foggy and with the ships unused to sailing in company, the inevitable happened. The *Oropesa* and the *Manchester Regiment* collided and the latter was reported sunk. This was the first of many such convoys, some fast but most desperately slow.

In January 1940 the pattern was altered. Up to then all the convoys had been handed over to the Local Escort Force off the coast of Ireland, but on this occasion the *Ascania* went all the way, right up the Clyde to refit in Glasgow. This gave the ship's company seven days' leave for each watch. It was during this period that the ship was fitted with depth charge throwers, but unfortunately no asdic, so the depth charges were of doubtful value – they were certainly never used in anger. An early type of radar was fitted with the enclosed aerial mounted on a small tower forward of the funnel.

With the refit completed the *Ascania* went back on station to Halifax, on the way forming part of a chain of ships covering the first 'secret' voyage of the *Queen Elizabeth* to New York. There were changes in the routine for the AMCs, with convoys to Bermuda and the West Indies where at least the weather was more kindly.

There was a not-so-welcome change in the routine for the Atlantic convoys. Where previously the handover to the local escort had meant a swift trip back to Halifax, the new idea was for the AMCs to put into Reykjavik to refuel and then to carry out at twelve day patrol of the Denmark Strait.

It was during this period that the *Ascania* was to demonstrate that she bore a charmed life. She had just returned to Halifax from a convoy and had secured alongside pier 36, ahead of the *Jervis Bay*, when word went round that the stay in port was going to be very brief. The ship was quickly stored and fuelled to sail with another convoy the following morning. The *Jervis Bay* remained alongside with engine trouble. Our convoy was an 'over and back' job so it was not so bad after all. The local escort appeared right on time and the *Ascania* headed back to Halifax.

On the evening of 5 November 1940, hands went to 'night action stations' as usual, checked all the equipment, and then reverted to 'cruising stations'. Half-an-hour later it was 'action stations' again and it was obvious that the *Ascania* had increased speed and was turning back. The word was quickly passed to all positions that the *Jervis Bay* was in action with a German pocket battleship and the *Ascania* was going to her assistance.

The ship's company prepared for the worst. Six-inch guns were no match for the eleven-inch guns of the *Admiral Scheer*. Two hours later the *Ascania* was ordered to resume her passage to Halifax and it was with very mixed feelings that this order was obeyed.

Meanwhile across the Western Ocean the drama was being played out. Against hopeless odds Captain Fogarty Fegen of the *Jervis Bay* turned his ship towards the enemy, her ancient guns blazing defiantly. For two hours the *Jervis Bay* fought on, giving valuable time for the convoy to scatter before she succumbed to her mighty opponent.

Much has been said about the ineffectualness of armed merchant cruisers, particularly by those who served in them. Too big, too slow, poorly armed, all of which was true; but in those two short hours the *Jervis Bay* justified the existence of them all.

The crew of the *Ascania* learnt the full story of the *Jervis Bay* when the ship arrived back in Halifax, and the unanimous feeling was that they should have gone on to assist their squadron mates. But orders, given by someone in a position to know the whole picture, are made to be obeyed, and so the *Ascania* survived to carry on her work.

The following April found the *Ascania* patrolling wearily in the Denmark Strait. On the twenty-second of the month her twelve days were up and she handed over the area to HMS *Rajputana*. As the *Ascania* steamed into Reykjavik a signal was received to say that the *Rajputana* had been torpedoed and sunk.

A month later the *Ascania* was back patrolling the Strait. The weather had, for several days, been sparklingly clear with the mountains of Iceland and Greenland standing out on the horizon. On the twelfth day, down came the fog. That afternoon, as she clawed her way through the murk, there was a sudden alarm – 'Hands to action stations!'

A dark shape loomed out of the fog. An aldis lamp flashed – it was HMS *Norfolk* shadowing the enemy. The *Ascania* was to remain on station while the scene was set for the coming battle. She might be needed, perhaps in a shadowing role if the enemy doubled-back, or perhaps even to sacrifice herself while the capital ships came up.

The following morning the *Ascania*'s captain broke the news to his ship's company: the mighty *Hood* had blown up, the *Prince of Wales* was damaged and the *Bismarck* was on the loose somewhere in the Atlantic. It was a frightening prospect. The *Ascania* remained on patrol until the *Bismarck* was found and destroyed.

In September 1941 the *Ascania* returned to the Clyde, and a few days later was despatched to Southampton for 'tropicalisation'. This entailed stripping out the cabins on 'C' deck and the construction of proper messdecks. An addition was made to the armament with two rocket projectors situated abaft the bridge. These were considered more dangerous to the ship than to the enemy!

Leaving Southampton for the Clyde the *Ascania* joined a large convoy heading south for Freetown. From there she sailed alone to Cape Town and Port Elizabeth. In the aftermath of the fall of Singapore she sailed for Melbourne and a week later left for Auckland to be attached to the Royal New Zealand Navy. She made many trips as a troopship until June 1942 when she sailed for the UK.

The *Ascania* passed through the Panama Canal and joined a convoy bound for Key West. This suffered numerous U-boat attacks, but because of the *Ascania*'s lack of asdic equipment, her depth charges were not used. From Key West the *Ascania* sailed north to New York, and a week later proceeded to Halifax to join an eastbound convoy to the Clyde.

The *Ascania*'s final voyage under the White Ensign was to Southampton to pay off and become a troop transport. During her three year commission she rendered sterling service with very little glory. The combination of Royal Navy and Merchant Navy worked very well, given the circumstances. The Merchant Navy might not like the Navy 'bull', and the Royal Navy may dislike the easy going way of the Merchant Navy, but in the *Ascania* and other armed merchant cruisers, they proved that together they made a wonderful team.

SAMARIA

Built by Cammell Laird (Shipbuilders & Engineers) at Birkenhead in 1921.   **Yard No:** 836
Official Number: 145923   **Signal Letters:** G J C F
Gross Tonnage: 19,848   **Nett:** 10,955   **Length:** 601·5ft   **Breadth:** 73·7ft
Owned by the Cunard Steamship Co. Ltd, registered at Liverpool.
6 steam turbines, double-reduction geared to twin screws.   **Speed:** 16 knots.

The *Samaria* was launched on 27 November 1920 and, at the time, was the largest passenger liner constructed on Merseyside. The launching ceremony was performed by Mrs J.H. Beazley, the wife of one of the Cunard Line directors, at a time when labour conditions were interfering considerably with shipbuilding output, and the *Samaria* was delayed for six months on the slipway and cost an additional quarter of a million pounds. The final cost of the *Samaria* was reputed to be just about as much as that of the first *Mauretania*, a ship of nearly twice her gross tonnage.

The *Samaria* as she appeared after her post-war refit. (Photo: Cunard Line)

The *Samaria* ran her trials in Liverpool Bay on 8 April 1922 and began her maiden voyage to Boston on 19 April. She was originally scheduled for the New York route, but owing to the delayed completion of the *Laconia* by a strike at Swan, Hunter & Wigham Richardson at Wallsend, the *Samaria* had her sailing date brought forward by a few days.

In June 1922, the *Samaria* was forced to return to Liverpool with engine trouble and her passengers were transferred to the *Laconia*. In July 1922 it was announced that the *Samaria* would make a round-the-world cruise (east-about), organised by Thomas Cook, sailing from New York on 20 January 1923. However, the *Samaria* was detained at Liverpool with gearing trouble and was not able to leave for New York until 24 January. She eventually sailed on the world cruise a fortnight later than scheduled, carrying 400 passengers. The cruise ended back at New York in June 1923, and a similar cruise was arranged for the following year. The *Samaria* had the distinction of being the first Cunard liner to transit the Panama Canal.

The next time the *Samaria* came into the news was in August 1926, when on a Saturday evening outside New York she narrowly missed being in collision with the Anchor Line vessel *Cameronia*. In dense fog the two ships came to within six feet of each other, and the *Cameronia*'s log line was carried away by the *Samaria*.

On 28 January 1928 the *Samaria* left New York for a thirty-day cruise to the Caribbean, the first of three such cruises. On 14 July of the same year she sailed from New York for Galway Bay with the Mayo Men's Association of New York on their annual pilgrimage to Croagh Patrick, Ireland's holy mountain. It was noted at the time that she was the first 20,000-ton liner to call at Galway, and while she was there she embarked pilgrims on their way to Lourdes.

During the years prior to the Second World War the *Samaria* established herself as a popular ship on the transatlantic run from Liverpool. After the outbreak of war she was taken over for service as a troopship. On 16 December 1939 the *Samaria* left Liverpool for New York, but had to put back after striking her escorting warship. Following the end of hostilities she carried many thousands of returning troops to Canada, accompanied by their wives and children. Her passengers during the immediate post-war years included many displaced persons. These voyages commenced in the main at Cuxhaven and sailed to Quebec or Halifax, often via Le

The *Samaria* in the course of demolition at Inverkeithing in December 1956. (Photo: *Shipbuilding and Shipping Record*)

Havre. In 1950 the *Samaria* made a series of voyages from London to Quebec, operating as a one-class ship. It was an innovation, although only short-lived, for passengers to board the ship at London.

In the autumn of 1950 the *Samaria* was given a long overdue refit by John Brown at Clydebank, and re-entered service when she sailed from Liverpool to Quebec on 14 June 1951 with accommodation for 250 first-class and 650 tourist-class passengers. In 1952 the Samaria grounded near Quebec. Her draft was almost that of the depth of St Lawrence, and it should be remembered that she was designed for the New York or Boston, not the Canadian service. The following year, in 1953, the *Samaria* represented Cunard among the 260 vessels at the Coronation Naval Review at Spithead.

The *Samaria* completed her last transatlantic voyage at Southampton on 3 December 1955. The British Iron & Steel Corporation bought her and she left Southampton on 26 January 1956, and arrived at Inverkeithing for demolition on the following day.

THE CUNARD–WHITE STAR MERGER OF 1934

The Cunard Line's great rival on the Atlantic express passenger service, the White Star Line, reported trading losses in each year from 1930 to 1933, and by the end of 1933 the company was bankrupt.

On 30 December 1933 the directors of the Cunard Line and the Oceanic Steam Navigation Co. (the White Star Line) met to put together the details of a merger.

On 28 March 1934, Royal assent was given to the North Atlantic Shipping Bill by which Cunard–White Star was formed and registered on 10 May. This was the Government's solution to two difficult problems. The Cunard Line required financial assistance to complete the *Queen Mary* and to build her consort, the *Queen Elizabeth*. The White Star Line was in a similar situation with three ageing liners operating on the same route as the Cunard Line. It, too, would need cash to replace its fleet.

The solution was to provide finance to complete the two Cunard Queens, and to amalgamate the two companies. A capital of £10 million was agreed, with Cunard holding 62 per cent. There were ten directors; six from Cunard and four from White Star.

Only two of the White Star Line's passenger ships were suitable for further service with the Cunard Line. These were the relatively new motorships *Britannic* and *Georgic*.

The *Britannic* (above) and the *Georgic* became part of the Cunard–White Star fleet in 1934. (Photo: *Shipbuilding and Shipping Record*)

BRITANNIC

Built by Harland & Wolff at Belfast in 1930.   **Yard No:** 807.
Official Number: 162316   **Signal Letters:** G D X F
Gross Tonnage: 27,666   **Nett:** 15,811   **Length:** 683·6ft   **Breadth:** 82·4ft
Built for the Oceanic Steam Navigation Co Ltd (White Star Line) and transferred to Cunard–White Star in 1934.
2 oil engines.   **Speed:** 18 knots.

In April 1928 the White Star Line ordered a new passenger liner from Harland & Wolff at Belfast. The new ship would be the first motorship in the fleet, the largest motorship under the British flag, and the second largest such ship in the world, only exceeded by the Italian liner *Augustus*.

The new ship was named *Britannic* and was designed for cabin and tourist-class service on the Liverpool to New York route in the summer months, plus extensive winter cruising. As usual for the White Star Line, the order went to Harland & Wolff at Belfast. The loss of the *Celtic* on rocks at Roches Point, at the entrance to Cobh harbour, in December 1928, caused the building of the *Britannic* to be speeded up.

The *Britannic* was launched on 6 August 1929 and she left Belfast for three days of trials in the Firth of Clyde on 26 May 1930. Following the successful completion of these trials, the new ship returned to Belfast, and left again on 21 June for Liverpool.

The *Britannic* had two funnels of the so-called 'motorship' design. In the opinion of many people, including myself, these low squat funnels detracted from her otherwise fine appearance. The forward funnel was a dummy and contained a smokeroom for the engineer officers, plus fresh water and hot water storage tanks. The *Britannic*'s oil engines reduced fuel consumption by 50 per cent when compared to the steamships, using 40 tons per day at 17½ knots. One comment was that her engine room was so cool it had to be fitted with radiators for winter warmth!

The *Britannic* manoeuvring in Gladstone Dock, Liverpool. (Photo: *Shipbuilding and Shipping Record*)

On 28 June 1930 the *Britannic* left Liverpool on her maiden voyage to New York, calling at Belfast and Greenock, and then settled down on her designed route with the *Cedric*, *Baltic* and *Adriatic*. The *Britannic's* passenger accommodation was originally designed for 504 cabin-class passengers, 551 in 'tourist-third-cabin' and 498 in third class. The naming of the first two classes could hardly have been more absurd – 'cabin' class obviously suggests that the other passengers did not have cabins, and 'tourist-third-cabin', a mixture of all three, would suggest that all the passengers, other than those travelling in the premier 'cabin class', were a third-rate crowd of tourists. These terms were chosen by the Atlantic Conference to set the passage rates in international liners of very varying luxury and comfort. 'Tourist-third-cabin' was normally shortened to 'tourist', and 'cabin class' was simply 'first class' without the extreme luxury of the large mail liners.

The *Britannic* was probably the largest and finest cabin-class liner in the world when she first came out and introduced new standards of accommodation on the Liverpool to New York route. In 1934 the final crash came for the White Star Line, when it was merged with the Cunard Line under the North Atlantic Shipping Bill to form Cunard–White Star Ltd. The White Star liners that remained after the merger, including the *Britannic*, retained their White Star colours and flew the White Star houseflag above that of Cunard.

Following the merger, the *Britannic* was transferred to a London–New York service, and she became the largest liner ever to have sailed up the Thames. The *Britannic* left London for the first time on 19 April 1935 and she remained on this route until the outbreak of war.

On 29 August 1939 the *Britannic* was requisitioned for service as a troopship. In the initial stages of the war she carried 3,000 men, but this was increased to over 5,000 troops by the time the war ended. In September 1939 the *Britannic* left the Clyde for Bombay and returned to the UK with British personnel. She operated principally carrying troops across the Atlantic, but made occasional trooping voyages round Africa to Suez.

In 1943 the *Britannic* carried American troops to the Sicilian landings, but her principal contribution to the war effort was in transporting over 20,000 US troops across the Atlantic in the build-up to the Normandy Landings. By the end of hostilities, the *Britannic* had carried 180,000 service personnel and she had steamed 367,000 miles.

Following repatriation work, the *Britannic* was released in March 1947 and sent to Harland & Wolff at Liverpool who gave her a complete refit before she re-entered service on the Liverpool – New York service. This work took almost a year and the accommodation was almost entirely rebuilt. Most cabins were provided with private facilities, and the passenger numbers became 429 in first class and 564 in tourist class.

On 22 May 1948 the *Britannic* left Liverpool on her first post-war commercial voyage to New York, and she continued on this route for the next twelve years. Winter cruising became an increasingly important part of her work and in January 1953 the *Britannic* sailed on a fifty-nine-day cruise to the Mediterranean with calls at twenty-two ports. This cruise was repeated in 1955.

In late 1959 and in 1960 the *Britannic's* machinery began to give trouble and on one occasion in 1960 crankshaft damage caused her to be held up in New York. She left Liverpool for New York, via Cobh, for the last time on 11 November 1960. Sailing from New York on 25 November, she was back in Liverpool on 4 December. The *Britannic* had completed 275 peacetime and wartime voyages.

The *Britannic* received a solemn reception as she sailed up to Princes Landing Stage to disembark her 353 passengers. No sirens sounded and there were no crowds waiting to say goodbye. Only the tugs which brought her in were dressed overall in honour of this last voyage.

John Prescott, a sixty-two-year-old liftman, had been on the maiden voyage. He said, 'She's a wonderful ship – so comfortable and so steady even in the worst seas.' The head waiter, Charles Leach, had been with Cunard for forty-two years and attended to the captain's table for the last time. 'Things are much less formal on ships these days,' he said, 'but the *Britannic* never changes. I'll be very sorry to see her go.' In the first-class restaurant, adjacent to the main doors, was a gaily decorated Christmas tree which would never see Christmas.

The *Britannic* was quickly sold for demolition and on 16 December 1960 she left the Mersey for the last time under her own steam for Thomas W. Ward's yard at Inverkeithing, Fife, where she arrived on 19 December. The *Britannic* was the last ship to fly the famous White Star Line houseflag, and she had been of immense value to her country in wartime, and to both her owners.

Breaking-up operations commenced in early February 1961, when the interior fittings were stripped out; many of these were sold at auction.

In 1957, Cunard announced that it had reserved a berth at John Brown's Clydebank yard to build a replacement for the *Britannic*. With sea travel rapidly being overtaken by the airlines in the late 1950s, this was cancelled and in 1961 the *Sylvania* took over the Liverpool–Cobh–New York service and remained on the route until the final sailing in November 1966.

The *Britannic's* bell and her steam operated triple-chime whistle are stored at the Merseyside Maritime Museum.

GEORGIC

Built by Harland & Wolff at Belfast in 1932
Official Number: 162365 **Call Sign:** L H R F **Yard No:** 896
Gross Tonnage: 27,759 **Nett:** 16,839 **Length:** 683·6ft **Breadth:** 82·4ft
Built for the Oceanic Steam Navigation Co. Ltd, (White Star Line), and transferred to Cunard–White Star in 1934
2 oil engines. **Speed:** 18 knots

The *Georgic* was launched at Belfast by Harland & Wolff for the White Star Line on 12 November 1931. She was the final ship built for the White Star fleet. She differed from her sister, the *Britannic*, completed two years earlier, in a number of respects. The *Georgic* was designed on ambitious lines with an almost straight stem, cruiser stern, and the then fashionable squat funnels with tops parallel to the deck. Unlike her sister, the *Georgic* had a rounded bridge front. Slightly larger than the *Britannic*, her original accommodation was for a total of 1,636 passengers: 479 in cabin class, 557 in tourist class and 600 in third class.

In April 1931 it was reported that construction work on the *Georgic* was to be speeded up so that she could enter service in May 1932 instead of June as was originally anticipated. Behind this idea was the fact that some 25,000 Americans were due to visit Dublin to attend the Eucharistic Conference that was to be held there from 22 until 29 June. As it turned out, the *Georgic* was not completed in time for the conference, and she began her maiden voyage on 25 June when she left Liverpool for New York.

The *Georgic's* forward funnel was a dummy and housed the radio room and the engineers' smokeroom. She was designed as a cabin-class ship but her passengers had surroundings and comfort equal to those provided in any deluxe liner of the day. The *Georgic's* trials took place in early June 1932 and a large party of guests was taken to join the ship in the Belfast Steamship Co.'s motorship *Ulster Monarch*, which was specially chartered for the occasion. The completion of the *Georgic* attracted great attention, and in welcoming her to the Mersey for the first time, the Lord Mayor of Liverpool offered his congratulations to the owners. The *Georgic* made the outward passage of her maiden voyage to New York in rough weather, but even so managed to arrive some twelve hours ahead of schedule.

In November 1932 the *Georgic's* sailing was brought forward two days in order that she could fit in with the postal arrangements for Christmas mail to the United States. On 11 January 1933

The *Georgic* with only one funnel, as she appeared after her post-war refit. (Photo: Skyfotos)

she made her first sailing from Southampton to New York, having moved south to replace the *Olympic* whilst that vessel underwent an extensive engine overhaul.

A record fruit cargo of 51,687 cartons, representing about 3,000 tons, was discharged by the *Georgic* at Liverpool in October 1933. On 10 May 1934 the vessel was amalgamated into the Cunard–White Star Line fleet. In June 1934 the *Georgic* was turned into a floating ballroom in aid of the David Lewis Northern Hospital's building fund. During January 1935 there was fire among some cotton bales in the ship's forward hold.

On 3 May 1935 the *Georgic* joined the *Britannic* on the London (King George V Dock)–Southampton–New York service, and was the largest vessel to use the Thames, being fractionally larger than the *Dominion Monarch*. In 1939 the *Georgic* reverted to the Liverpool–New York service and made five round transatlantic voyages on commercial service with cargo and passengers, although she was hampered by the fact that Americans had been ordered not to travel on her as she was a belligerent ship. While she was homeward bound on 11 March 1940, the Cunard–White Star Co. was informed that she would be taken off commercial service. After discharging a large cargo at Liverpool, the *Georgic* was ordered to the Clyde on 19 April where she was converted into a troopship for 3,000 men.

At the end of May 1940 the *Georgic* assisted in the evacuation of British troops from Andesfjord and Narvik, and as soon as she had landed these men at Greenock, she sailed south to assist in the withdrawal from Brest and St Nazaire. She was under repeated air attack and was indeed fortunate in not being hit. Between July and September 1940 the *Georgic* made a trooping voyage to Iceland and another to Halifax, NS, embarking Canadian troops after landing the evacuees she carried on the westbound passage. From September 1940 until January 1941 the *Georgic* was employed on a trooping voyage from Liverpool and Glasgow to the Middle East via the Cape, and afterwards trooped from Liverpool to New York and Halifax, then back to the Clyde.

On 22 May 1941 the *Georgic* left the Clyde under the command of Captain A.C. Greig, OBE, RNR, with the 50th Northumberland Division for Port Tewfik, Gulf of Suez. She was part of the convoy which had to be left almost unprotected during the hunt for the *Bismarck*. She arrived safely on 7 July 1941, but a week later on 14 July she was bombed by German aircraft operating from Crete while at anchor off Port Tewfik, with 800 Italian internees on board. Her fuel oil caught fire and the ammunition exploded in the stern area. The *Georgic* was gutted and the engine room flooded, but her crew managed to slip the anchor cable and beach the ship on 16 July, half submerged and burnt out. On 14 September 1941 it was decided to salvage the vessel and the hulk was raised on 27 October. The hull was plugged, and on 2 December the *Georgic* was taken in tow by the *Clan Campbell* and the *City of Sydney*. She reached Port Sudan on 14 December where she was made seaworthy. It had taken twelve days for the tow to cover 710 miles.

The *Georgic* left Port Sudan on 5 March 1942 and was towed by T. & J. Harrison's *Recorder*, with the tug *St Sampson* steering from astern. On the following day a strong north-westerly gale rendered the wallowing *Georgic* almost unmanageable. The southerly course had to be abandoned and the ships hove to. For five hours the *Recorder* battled to bring her charge head to wind, and in the process the tug *St Sampson* was damaged. The tug was rapidly filling with water and slipped her tow rope and drifted down wind. Shortly afterwards she foundered and her crew were picked up by the hospital ship *Dorsetshire*, which was passing at the time.

For twelve hours the *Recorder* and the *Georgic* rode out the gale and then, as the winds abated, cautiously swung back through 180-degrees to resume their course. Meanwhile they were joined by another tug, the *Pauline Moller* and the British India steamer *Haresfield*. Together they guided their labouring charge past Abu Ail and the islands of the southern Red Sea into the Gulf of Aden, and on to Karachi. The salvage crew responsible for the *Georgic* lived on board the *Recorder* and every few days boarded the liner from a motor launch in order to pump out a steady ingress of water.

On 31 March 1942, twenty-six days out of Port Sudan, the ships arrived off Karachi where the *Georgic* was taken in hand by eight harbour tugs. The *Recorder* and her consorts, having covered 2,100 miles with the *Georgic*, had completed one of the most successful salvage operations of the war. Captain W.B. Wilford of the *Recorder* was later invested with the OBE.

The *Georgic* remained at Karachi until 11 December whilst temporary repairs were carried out. She then sailed to Bombay, arriving on 13 December, where she was dry docked for hull cleaning and further repairs. Finally she loaded 5,000 tons of pig iron ballast and on 20 January 1943 the *Georgic* left Bombay under her own power for Liverpool where she arrived on 1 March, having made the passage at 16 knots. Shortly afterwards she sailed for Belfast, but had to anchor in Bangor Bay until 5 July awaiting a berth. After seventeen months the *Georgic* emerged on 12 December 1944 with one funnel and a stump foremast. She was now owned by the Ministry of Transport, with Cunard–White Star as managers. After trials, the *Georgic* left Belfast for Liverpool on 16 December 1944, three years and five months since she was bombed at Port Tewfik.

During 1945 the *Georgic* trooped to Italy, the Middle East and India. On Christmas Day she arrived at Liverpool with troops from the Far East, including General Sir William Slim, C-in-C of South East Asia. Early in 1946 the *Georgic* repatriated 5,000 Italian prisoners-of-war. In June 1946 on a homeward voyage from Bombay there was trouble between civilian women and service women, and this led to the barring of civilians on troopships unless no other transport was available.

In September 1948 the *Georgic* was refitted by Palmers & Co. at Hebburn for the Australian and New Zealand emigrant trade. She retained her White Star livery, and could accommodate 1,962 passengers in one class. In January 1949 the *Georgic* made her first sailing on the Liverpool–Suez–Fremantle–Melbourne–Sydney run with 1,200 'assisted passages'. However, as she was leaving Princes Landing Stage, a rope wrapped round one of her propellers and she had to re-dock. During the summers from 1950 to 1954, the *Georgic* was chartered back to Cunard and she made seven round voyages to New York each year as a one-class liner. In

1950 she was based at Liverpool, but Southampton was her terminal port from 1951 until 1954.

In the winter of 1954/55 the *Georgic* resumed 'assisted passage' voyages to Australia, and on 16 April 1955 she arrived at Liverpool with troops from Japan. She was then offered for sale, but the Australian government chartered her for the summer. The *Georgic's* final voyage was from Hong Kong to Liverpool with 800 troops, and she arrived on 19 November 1955.

On 11 December the *Georgic* was laid up at Kames Bay, Isle of Bute, pending disposal. In January 1956 the *Georgic* was sold for scrapping and on 1 February arrived at Faslane for demolition by Shipbreaking Industries Ltd.

MEDIA AND PARTHIA

The *Media* and the *Parthia* were the first new passenger ships to be built for the Cunard Line after the Second World War. The pair were unusual for Cunard in that, notwithstanding comfortable accommodation for 250 first-class passengers, they were basically large cargo carriers with a deadweight capacity of 7,000- ons. The two were cargo/passenger, rather than passenger/cargo ships, with a cargo capacity of 371,430 cubic feet, with 60,050 cubic feet of insulated space.

The problems of operating cargo/passenger ships were twofold. As passenger vessels the two ships had to keep to a strict schedule and this could be readily upset by stevedore strikes. Secondly, with accommodation for 250 first-class passengers, a large proportion of the crew was employed in the stewards' department. During the week-long layovers at New York and Liverpool, the members of the stewards' department had virtually nothing to do, but yet were maintained on full ship's pay.

The *Media* and the *Parthia* sailed on a four-weekly schedule from Liverpool to New York, providing a fortnightly departure on a Saturday afternoon. Very occasional calls were made at Greenock on the homeward passage, usually for the benefit of passengers wishing to attend the Edinburgh Festival.

At the time of their disposal in 1961, the Cunard chairman Sir John Brocklebank said that the two ships had been built in special circumstances and for special reasons after the war. He did not elaborate on exactly what these circumstances and reasons behind them were. Sir John went on to say that they had both served their designed purpose well but were now making a loss. It was the company's intention to replace them with smaller cargo ships which would make a profit.

Sir Humphrey de Trafford, a well-known race horse owner in the 1950s and early 1960s, and a regular Cunard passenger, named two of his horses after the *Media* and the *Parthia*.

MEDIA

Built by John Brown & Co. Ltd at Clydebank in 1946.   **Yard No:** 629.
Official Number: 181093   **Signal Letters:** G S W R
Gross Tonnage: 13,345   **Nett:** 7,480   **Length:** 518·4ft   **Breadth:** 70·3ft
Owned by the Cunard Steamship Co. Ltd, registered at Liverpool
4 steam turbines, double reduction gearing to twin screws.   **Speed:** 17 knots

The Media was the first of the two sister ships to be completed and was launched at Clydebank on 12 December 1946. She left Liverpool on her maiden voyage to New York on 20 August

The *Media* photographed on the occasion of her maiden voyage, 1947. (Photo: *Shipbuilding and Shipping Record*)

1947. In 1952 she became Cunard's first passenger ship to be fitted with Denny–Brown stabilisers.

During her annual overhaul in January 1961 there was a strike of Amalgamated Engineering Union members which caused her to be trapped in Liverpool's Gladstone Graving Dock for some months. Rumours began to circulate that the *Media* would be disposed of, mentioning as buyers the Cia Genovese d'Armamento SpA (the Cogedar Line), but as late as May 1961 Cunard was denying them. A fortnight later Sir John Brocklebank admitted to the press that contracts had in fact been drawn up for the sale of the *Media* at a price of £740,000.

The *Media* made her last sailing in Cunard service in September 1961, leaving Liverpool with just 145 passengers. On her homeward passage she answered a distress call from the German ship *Bornberg*, and took on board a crew member who was operated on for appendicitis by the *Media*'s surgeon. On 14 October 1961 the *Media* was officially handed over to her new owners with a short ceremony taking place mid-Mersey, when the Italian flag was replaced with the Blue Ensign.

The *Media* was very extensively refitted at Genoa by Officine Allestimento & Riparazioni Navia. In order to increase the space for passenger and crew arrangements, the two decks below the main deck, both originally used for cargo, were utilised and the superstructure enlarged by alterations to her lines, both forward and aft. The passenger capacity was increased from the original 250 to 1,224, accommodated in 377 cabins; 152 being two-berth, 220 four-berth and five eight-berth. A new style funnel completed the transformation and the changes raised her gross tonnage from 13,345 to 15,465. Under the new name of *Flavia*, she sailed from Genoa to Sydney in September 1962.

From 1968 the *Flavia* was used almost exclusively for cruising and the following year she was sold to Costa Armatori SpA of Naples for full-time cruising out of Miami. Somewhat unusually, the ship never received a Costa 'C' name. After thirteen years with Costa, the *Flavia* was sold to Flavian Shipping S.A. in 1982 and registered at Panama. Her name was changed to *Flavian* and she was laid up at Hong Kong.

The completely rebuilt *Media* as she appeared as the *Flavia*. (Photo: Shipbuilding & Shipping Record)

In 1986 the old *Media* was resold to Lavia Shipping, also of Panama, and the name once again changed, this time to *Lavia*. On 7 January 1989 fire broke out and the ship had to be beached. The ship, which had been laid up at Hong Kong since 1982 was apparently being renovated, and her crew misguidedly wasted time by trying to extinguish the blaze themselves before calling in the fire services. The *Lavia* became a total loss.

PARTHIA

> Built by Harland & Wolff at Belfast in 1948.   **Yard No:** 1331
> **Official Number:** 182417   **Signal Letters:** G S W Q
> **Gross Tonnage:** 13,362   **Nett:** 7,393   **Length:** 518·4ft   **Breadth:** 70·3ft
> Owned by the Cunard Steamship Co. Ltd, registered at Liverpool
> 4 steam turbines, double reduction gearing to twin screws.   **Speed:** 17 knots.

The *Media*'s sister ship, the *Parthia*, was built by Harland & Wolff at Belfast. She had the distinction of being the only passenger ship ever built by them for the Cunard Line. The new *Parthia* was launched on 25 February 1947 and left Liverpool on her maiden voyage to New York on 10 April 1948.

The success of the *Media*'s stabilisers led to the *Parthia* being similarly equipped in 1953. The *Parthia* became caught up in the same strike that had trapped the *Media* in dry dock in 1961, and it was not until 1 July of that year that she was back in service. At the Cunard Line's A.G.M the previous month, chairman Sir John Brocklebank had announced that the *Parthia*, along with the *Media*, would be disposed of, and on 1 November 1961 the New Zealand Shipping Co. completed the purchase of the *Parthia*.

The *Parthia* was sent to the Clyde to be converted to carry 350 passengers on a service from London to Auckland and Wellington via Curaçao, Panama and Tahiti; returning via Tahiti, Panama, Kingston, Miami and Bermuda. Her name was changed to *Remuera*.

The *Remuera* was reconditioned by Alexander Stephen & Sons at Linthouse. The dining saloon, galleys and all ancillary spaces were extended; a well-equipped laundry installed and a swimming pool was constructed on the after end of the promenade deck. Full air-conditioning was added and the *Remuera* sailed on her maiden voyage on 1 June 1962. Fares ranged from £155 for a berth in a six-berth cabin to £260 for a single-berth cabin with shower for the one-way passage. With the introduction of the *Remuera*, the New Zealand Shipping Co. withdrew the *Rangitata* and *Rangitiki* from service.

The *Parthia* preparing to board the Clyde pilot at Little Cumbrae. (Photo: *Shipbuilding and Shipping Record*)

After just two years on her new service, the New Zealand Shipping Co. announced in 1964 that it would be necessary to withdraw the *Remuera* towards the end of the year. The ship had made six round-voyages and several trans-Tasman passages and had been well supported by passengers. However, the cost of her conversion had proved greater than anticipated and there were increases in operating costs. Wool cargoes had been substantially reduced, and, as wool was to have provided the bulk of the cargoes, the *Remuera* suffered from loss of freight earnings.

The vessel was transferred to the Eastern & Australian Steamship Co. and renamed *Aramac*. On 8 February 1965 she inaugurated a Melbourne–Hong Kong–Japan service. Two years later the *Aramac* passed to the ownership of the Federal Steam Navigation Co. In November 1969 the end came when the old *Parthia* arrived at Kaohsiung for demolition.

THE *SAXONIA, IVERNIA, CARINTHIA* AND *SYLVANIA*

'A Brilliant Quartet'

Towards the end of 1951, the Cunard Line announced that it would build a completely new class of liner for the Liverpool–Montreal service. Initially the order was for two ships, but this was later increased to four. The new liners would be the largest Cunarders ever built for the Canadian service. However, even whilst the first two ships, the *Saxonia* and the *Ivernia*, were under construction, some airlines were formulating plans for transatlantic services. Nevertheless, the Cunard directors remained convinced that for the foreseeable future there would always be sufficient people who would wish to travel by sea and to keep its fleet of liners viable.

The basic design of these new ships combined a large passenger capacity with space for a substantial amount of cargo – all within the maximum dimensions which would permit safe navigation of the St Lawrence up to the terminal port of Montreal.

The ships could carry a complement of 125 passengers in first class, and 800 in tourist class. There was a cargo capacity of 300,000 cubic feet, including 15,000 cubic feet of refrigerated space. Denny–Brown stabilisers were fitted.

The *Carinthia* passing under the Quebec Bridge, July 1966. (Photo: John Shepherd)

All the first-class cabins had private facilities, but the vast majority of tourist-class passengers had to make do with shared toilet and bathroom facilities. For brand new ships in the 1950s, on a principal liner route, this showed a remarkable lack of forward thinking. Air conditioning in the new ships was very partial, extending only to the public rooms. Not one of the passenger cabins, and certainly nowhere in the crew's quarters, was air-conditioned.

However, as these new ships entered service between 1954 and 1957, they were hailed by the shipping press as 'a brilliant quartet'.

The principal shortcoming of the new ships was the large cargo capacity. It was far too large for liners designed to carry so many passengers – but it was too small to make them viable principally as cargo carriers. The time which is required to load and discharge cargo is very disruptive for ships trying to maintain a tight passenger liner schedule. To maintain the passenger schedule it was often necessary to refuse lucrative cargoes.

Long turn-rounds in port meant that the majority of the crew, who were employed in the stewards' department (some 300 out of a total crew of 425), had little or nothing to do, but during these periods of enforced idleness, they were maintained on ship's pay.

By the time the *Carinthia* and the *Sylvania* entered service in 1956 and 1957 the airlines were 'creaming off' the lucrative business traffic across the North Atlantic, and were making inroads into the tourist traffic.

However, speaking at Greenock on the eve of the *Sylvania*'s maiden voyage on 5 June 1957, Mr Frank H. Dawson, director and general manager of the Cunard Line, maintained that there was every indication of long and profitable careers for the four ships which formed the 'brilliant quartet' and which had been built to meet the requirements of Canada's rapidly growing population and the increasing volume of overseas trade.

SAXONIA AND IVERNIA

In the introduction to this book, I said that the principal criterion for including a ship was that it should be Liverpool-based. Some of the Cunard liners made only very rare appearances at Liverpool – such as the *Caronia* and the *Mauretania* undergoing winter overhaul in Gladstone Graving Dock – and these cannot be considered as 'Liverpool Liners'.

The *Saxonia* and *Ivernia* spent only a very short time based at Liverpool before they transferred to Southampton. In the case of the *Saxonia*, she was Liverpool-based from her maiden voyage on 2 September 1954 until she moved south on 19 June 1956. As for the *Ivernia*, she was based at Liverpool from July 1955 until April 1957.

However, it is perhaps appropriate to take a short look at the careers of the two elder sisters of Cunard's 'brilliant quartet':

THE MAIDEN VOYAGE OF THE SAXONIA

The issue of *Shipbuilding & Shipping Record* for 9 September 1954 reported:

> The wooing of the tourist-classes is continued in the new Cunarder, the *Saxonia*, which set off on her maiden voyage to Canada last Thursday. Not only do tourist-class passengers outnumber those travelling in first-class by six to one, but their present importance has been adequately recognised by the appointment, for the first time in a Cunard ship, of a head waiter in the tourist-class restaurant. This appointment is symbolic of the company's attitude throughout to tourist passengers. The head waiter's sole function, as always in the past in first-class dining saloons, is to see that the passenger is contented with his food. Similarly, in other public rooms and cabins the tourist passenger will find the company has gone out of its way to see that he is well catered for. Indeed, there are even some advantages over first class in travelling tourist on the *Saxonia*. As they serve so many more passengers, the tourist public rooms are much more numerous and spacious, whereas the first-class public apartments, while more extravagantly furnished, are naturally somewhat small by comparison.

Although no doubt the Cunard Line would disclaim any intention of setting up records, the fact that the *Saxonia* on her maiden eastbound crossing from Montreal to Liverpool completed the passage in the fastest time yet must have been gratifying to them. To accomplish the passage from the pilot station at Father Point, Quebec, to the Mersey Bar lightship in less than five days was an achievement worthy of congratulation to all associated with the ship.

On her record-breaking eastbound passage the *Saxonia* encountered continuous north-westerly gales. Her Denny–Brown stabilisers reduced the rolling to less than two degrees, a circumstance naturally appreciated by her passengers.

The *Saxonia* had one of the largest end-of-season passenger lists ever known and reached Liverpool at the end of her maiden voyage nearly nine hours ahead of her original schedule.

On the basis of an estimated speed of 19 knots the *Saxonia* was not expected to berth at Princes Landing Stage until Tuesday evening 21 September. Her master, Captain Andrew Mackellar, however, found that despite the rough seas and heavy swell encountered, his new ship was capable of almost another two knots. Consequently the *Saxonia* was off the Mersey Bar at 4.30 a.m. and alongside the landing stage by 9.00 a.m.

Passengers whom the Cunard Company had expected it would have to accommodate on board overnight to await trains the following day were instead in London in time for tea. The boat train from Riverside Railway Station, with 372 London-bound passengers, was the largest civilian train handled since the war.

The *Saxonia* leaving Liverpool on her maiden voyage, 2 September 1954. (Photo: John Shepherd Collection)

The *Saxonia* left Father Point, the St Lawrence pilot station, at 3.06 a.m. on 16 September and arrived at the Bar Light at 7.30 a.m. on 21 September. The new liner covered the 2,464 nautical miles at an average speed of 20.74 knots in four days, twenty-three hours and twenty-four minutes. Although the Cunard Line claim this crossing only as a record for its own ships, it is believed that the previous fastest time of a ship was five days and five hours.

Captain MacKellar was obviously delighted with his new command. 'She is a very fine ship in all ways,' he said. 'A particular asset for the St Lawrence river passage is her ready response to the helm. All her many mechanical devices worked according to plan, the stabilisers being particularly effective.'

The *Ivernia* followed the *Saxonia* down the slipway at John Brown's yard at Clydebank ten months later on 14 December 1954. Her short stay based at Liverpool was uneventful except for the fact that her maiden voyage commenced at Greenock on 1 July 1955, due to the fact that Liverpool was in the grip, once again, of a bout of industrial unrest.

Towards the end of the 1950s with air travel across the Atlantic on the increase, especially in the winter months, Cunard was having problems profitably employing four 20,000-ton liners which were basically emigrant carriers. Unlike the new Canadian–Pacific ships, the Cunarders were not suitable for cruising and so at the end of the 1962 St Lawrence season the *Saxonia* and the *Ivernia* were sent back to their builders for a major refit which would make them suitable for winter cruising.

On 1 January 1963 the *Saxonia* was renamed *Carmania*, and the *Ivernia* was given the new name of *Franconia*. A large lido deck with swimming pool was built on to the after end of each ship, the passenger accommodation was refurbished and the hulls painted a 'cruising-green', similar to Cunard's 'Green Goddess', the *Caronia*.

The *Ivernia* running her trials on the Arran Mile in June 1955. (Photo: *Shipbuilding and Shipping Record*)

The *Leonid Sobinov* (ex-*Carmania*, ex-*Saxonia*) retained her Cunard profile. (Photo: *Shipbuilding and Shipping Record*)

The *Carmania* and the *Franconia* rarely visited Liverpool in the next few years. However, the *Franconia* did operate two cruises from Liverpool over Christmas 1967 and New Year. Following these cruises she was overhauled in the port and on 30 January 1968 the *Franconia* had the dubious distinction of leaving Liverpool at 2 p.m. on Cunard's last ever scheduled transatlantic crossing to New York from the port, finally closing a service which had started 128 years previously with the departure of the *Britannia* on (American) Independence Day. The occasion was played down in the local press and only very few people were present on the landing stage to witness another significant event in the terminal decline of Liverpool as a passenger port.

The *Carmania* and the *Franconia* were both laid up in 1971 as a result of escalating operating costs, initially at Southampton and then in the River Fal. In August 1973 the two sisters were acquired by the Nikreis Maritime Corporation of Panama, acting as agents for the Russian Sovtorflot organisation. After a three-month overhaul, the *Carmania* was renamed *Leonid Sobinov*, and the *Franconia* became the *Fedor Shalyapin*. The ships retained their outward appearance and were instantly recognisable as the former Cunarders, right up to the end of their careers.

Both ships continued in operation for their Russian owners until the mid-1990s when stringent new SOLAS regulations would have required massive expenditure to bring them up to compliance. The *Leonid Sobinov* (ex-*Carmania*) left Odessa on 30 January 1999 under her own steam bound for the shipbreakers' yard at Alang, India. On passage she suffered the indignity of running out of fuel and was left drifting in the Indian Ocean until she was retrieved by two tugs. The former *Saxonia*, the eldest sister of Cunard's 'brilliant quartet', was dragged ashore at Alang on 1 October 1999 and demolition commenced.

The *Fedor Shalyapin* (ex-*Franconia*) remained laid up at Ilichevsk until she too made the passage to Alang where she was broken up in 2004. By a strange twist of fate the former *Ivernia* was demolished in the adjacent berth to her sister, the *Sylvania*, which as the *Albatros* had arrived at Alang on 19 January 2004.

CARINTHIA

Built by John Brown & Co. Ltd at Clydebank.   **Yard No**: 699
Official Number: 187137   **Signal Letters:** G V D Q
Gross Tonnage: 21,947   **Nett:** 11,630   **Length:** 608·3ft   **Breadth:** 80·4ft
Owned by the Cunard Steamship Co. Ltd, registered at Liverpool
4 steam turbines, double reduction gearing to twin screws

The order for the third ship of 'the brilliant quartet', which was to become the *Carinthia*, had been confirmed with John Brown at Clydebank in 1953. Princess Margaret agreed to launch the new ship and this took place on 14 December 1955, a rain swept day, but in Princess Margaret's own words, 'A happy and brilliant occasion'. Some 20,000 spectators braved the weather to watch the launch.

The *Saxonia* and the *Ivernia* had both been criticised for their interior modern décor, so the *Carinthia* returned to more traditional style. On 5 January 1956 a contributor to the *Architect and Building News* wrote: 'The Cunard Line has a wonderful record for seamanship, service and naval architecture, but an abysmal one for interior decoration'. The *Carinthia* had accommodation for 154 first-class and 714 tourist-class passengers, with some cabins being interchangeable. As was the case with her two elder sisters, the *Carinthia* was built with considerable cargo space and her five holds had a capacity of 290,000 cubic feet, plus 15,000 cubic feet for refrigerated cargo.

The new *Carinthia* left John Brown's yard on 12 June 1956 for her trials which were run on the Arran Mile. Whilst undertaking these speed trials she passed and exchanged greetings with the inward bound *Ivernia*. The master of the *Ivernia*, Captain McKellar transferred to the *Carinthia* for her maiden voyage. At a luncheon held on board the *Carinthia* at the time of her handover from her builders, Mr F.H. Dawson, the general manager of the Cunard Line, indicated that the *Saxonia* and the *Ivernia* would in future use Southampton as their terminal port in the UK.

The *Carinthia* left Liverpool on 27 June 1956 with over 800 passengers on her maiden voyage from Liverpool to Montreal. Shortly afterwards Cunard announced that the stalwarts of its Canadian service in post-war years, the *Franconia* and the *Ascania*, would be withdrawn from service in October 1956, to be followed by the *Scythia* a year later.

In January 1957 the *Carinthia* sailed on a cruise from New York to the Caribbean. It was not a success, due mainly to the very partial air-conditioning installed in the liner; just one feature which made her unsuitable for extensive cruising in her later years with the Cunard Line.

In April 1959 the *Carinthia* damaged her starboard propeller in the ice at Montreal, and she had to enter dry dock to have this changed at Liverpool at the end of the voyage.

The *Carinthia* passes under the Jacques Cartier Bridge on her maiden arrival at Montreal. (Photo: *Shipbuilding and Shipping Record*)

A post-war record of 115 transatlantic liner calls at Greenock was scheduled for 1960. Fifty-one of the visits were scheduled for Cunard liners, with the *Carinthia* and the *Sylvania* making a total of forty calls. The *Media* and the *Parthia* were also scheduled to anchor at the Tail of the Bank, and the *Ivernia* would be there on two occasions.

The Canadian Government chartered the *Carinthia* for six weeks commencing in November 1960 for trooping-voyages.

During her winter overhaul in January 1961, the *Carinthia* became caught up in the strike of Amalgamated Engineering Union members which trapped her in dry dock for some sixteen weeks. When this strike was settled the boilermakers who had been laid off the *Carinthia* commenced a threatened embargo of all Cunard vessels using Liverpool. This was the same industrial action which spelt the end of Cunard service for the *Media* and the *Parthia*. When the *Carinthia* eventually left the dry dock it was found that much of her interior woodwork had warped as a result of the unusual stress placed on the ship for so long, and joiners were hard-pressed to make her serviceable again as hundreds of doors had to be planed and re-hung.

It was not until 1 June 1961 that the *Carinthia* sailed from Liverpool on her first voyage of the year with 260 passengers bound for Quebec and Montreal.

Shortly after re-entering service the *Carinthia* collided with the Canadian vessel *Tadoussac* on 30 August, 1961 in thick fog some 30-miles upstream from Quebec, on passage to Montreal. A head-on collision was very narrowly averted. No casualties were reported.

The *Carinthia* was once again caught up in the turbulent industrial relations of the late 1950s and early 1960s, becoming strikebound from 19 April until 31 May, 1962.

In January 1964 the *Carinthia* left Liverpool for New York on a voyage which included a call at Bermuda. She had on board just 260 passengers and 1,800 tons of cargo. On her return eastbound voyage she carried 480 passengers and a mere 250 tons of cargo. Considering that the ship had a capacity for 868 passengers and 7,000 tons of cargo, these statistics must have been a sure indication to the Cunard Line of just how inappropriate was the design of these liners.

Towards the end of 1963 Cunard upgraded eighty tourist-class cabins on the *Carinthia* and provided them with private bathrooms. Considering that there were 250 tourist-class cabins in all, this was very much a token gesture and was too little too late. Given the success of the transformation of the *Saxonia* and the *Ivernia* into the *Carmania* and the *Franconia*, it seemed that Cunard was either unwilling or unable to rebuild the *Carinthia* and the *Sylvania*. They remained principally emigrant carriers.

In 1966 the *Carinthia* went cruising for the first time since January 1957. Two thirteen-night cruises to the Atlantic Isles from Liverpool were organised, the first leaving on 7 January. The *Carinthia* was laid up at Liverpool for the duration of the 1966 seamen's strike and for over six weeks there was no Cunard Line service across the North Atlantic. The strike itself proved to be the catalyst for the early withdrawal of the *Carinthia* from Cunard service, but it was by no means the only reason; the writing had been clearly on the wall almost since the ship's maiden voyage, and the 1966 strike only hastened the end.

The *Carinthia* was plagued by misfortune on her last round-trip of the year, to Canada in November 1966. Her outward sailing was delayed for forty-eight hours by severe gales in the Mersey, and on her return passage she was held up by fog in the St Lawrence. She then encountered storms in the Atlantic, described by her master, Captain H.L. de Legh, as the worst he had ever experienced. After being forced to heave-to off the Irish Coast, the *Carinthia* arrived back at Liverpool thirty-six hours late.

She had sustained rudder damage which necessitated dry docking, and it was touch and go as to whether she would be ready to undertake a fourteen-night Christmas and New Year cruise from Liverpool to the Atlantic Isles. In the event the *Carinthia* was ready, but the unscheduled dry docking meant that there hadn't been time to paint her hull white, and she completed her Cunard service in her original Cunard colours, whereas all her sisters were given white hulls early in 1967.

The *Carinthia* was taken off the Canadian service in July and August 1967 to operate two cruises from Liverpool to the Atlantic Isles, the first sailing on 20 July, and the second one on 31 July. Fares started at £60. A Cunard spokesman said, 'We expect these cruises at the height of the north country holiday season to be tremendously popular'. These were the first midsummer cruises by a Cunard ship from Liverpool since the *Lancastria* operated 'guinea-a-day' cruises in the 1930s.

Given the mammoth losses which Cunard incurred as a result of the 1966 seamen's strike, Cunard's new chairman, Sir Basil Smallpeice, finally 'grasped the nettle' in October 1967 and announced the withdrawal of the *Carinthia* from Cunard service. The *Carinthia*'s final voyage in Cunard colours left Southampton on 23 November 1967 for Halifax, NS, and she was back in Southampton on 9 December. After disembarking her passengers she was laid up alongside the *Caronia*. Her Cunard days were over.

Two of the Carinthia's well-known and popular masters.
Above: Captain D.M. MacLean. *Below:* Captain A. MacKellar.

The *Fairsea* (ex-*Carinthia*) passing through the Panama Canal. (Photo: Sitmar Line)

The *Carinthia* was quickly sold for a reported £1 million to the Sitmar Line on 31 January 1968. The contract of sale prevented the *Carinthia* from sailing on any of Cunard's regular routes, or from operating cruises from UK ports.

At the time of her sale, Sitmar held the Australian government contract for carrying emigrants from Southampton to the Dominion. Shortly after Sitmar's purchase of the *Carinthia* (and the *Sylvania*), the contract was awarded to the Greek Chandris Line. Sitmar therefore had a problem: what to do with its new purchases?

The *Carinthia*'s name was changed to *Fairland*, which at the time was thought to be appropriate for an emigrant carrier. However, she lay at Southampton for two years before sailing for Trieste on 9 February 1970, where she arrived on 21 February.

She was berthed adjacent to the *Sylvania* and both the Cunard sisters were given a massive conversion costing some $56 million to make them 'state of the art' cruising liners. This took almost two years and the *Carinthia* was the first to be completed. The name *Fairland* was now considered unsuitable and was changed to *Fairsea*.

On 3 November 1971, almost four years after her final Cunard voyage, the *Fairsea* sailed for Los Angeles where she commenced a cruise service to Mexico. In the summer months the *Fairsea* became Sitmar's Alaska ship, and her terminal port was moved to Vancouver. In the winter months the *Fairsea* operated a Los Angeles–Panama Canal–Curaçao service. The *Fairsea* and the *Fairwind* (ex-*Sylvania*), two outmoded transatlantic liners, had taken Sitmar Cruises to the very pinnacle of success.

On 28 July 1988, P&O took over Sitmar Cruises and the *Fairsea* was renamed *Fair Princess*. In 1993 P&O Princess Cruises issued a lavish brochure which enthused:

The intimate *Fair Princess* boasts a charming, private-club atmosphere that makes it easy to meet and mingle and make lasting friendships. Walnut-panelled walls, gleaming stainless steel rails, luxuriously thick carpet, butter-soft leather, reflective ceilings, etched glass doors and distinctive artwork all evoke seagoing traditions. This classic ship is packed from stem to stern with fabulous amenities – the *Fair Princess* is an uncommon delight.

Fancy! Could this really be the old *Carinthia*?

In early 1995 Princess Cruises sold the *Fair Princess* to Regency Cruises. Before the sale had been finalised, Regency Cruises had collapsed financially. The result was that P&O/Princess Cruises was left with a ship it did not want. The *Fair Princess* was laid up at Mazatlan, Mexico, and in the summer of 1996 P&O announced that she would replace the *Fairstar* (ex-*Oxfordshire*) cruises from Australia.

The *Fair Princess* sailed on her first cruise from Sydney on 7 February 1997, fully booked with 1,050 passengers on board. She was described as having 'a classic liner exterior and excellent sea-keeping qualities' suited to the South Seas. However, many of the *Fairstar*'s regular passengers were unhappy, referring to the *Fair Princess* as 'an old lady in her dotage'. There was a series of small mishaps on this first cruise – minor fires, burst pipes, defective lights etc. On 27 February 1998, with a full complement of passengers on board, all four of the *Fair Princess*'s generators failed, necessitating the cancellation of the cruise. In July 1999 bad publicity dogged the ship. Three of her passengers had gone down with typhoid fever. However, one travel writer enthused that 'the *Fair Princess* was Australia's most popular cruise ship'.

A surprise announcement came from P&O on 19 June 2000 to the effect that the sale of the *Fair Princess* had been negotiated earlier than expected, and that her entire cruise programme would be cancelled after November 2000.

The following day a press release was issued by The Great Canadian Gaming Corporation stating that it had acquired a 25 per cent interest in the *Fair Princess*. The ship would be based in the South China Sea to service the medium and short-haul cruise ship and entertainment market.

The *Fair Princess*'s final months of cruising for P&O were not without incident. In early August 2000 there were four cases of pneumonia on board, and there were rumours of Legionella bacteria onboard. Nevertheless, the *Fair Princess* received a clean bill of health when she arrived back at Sydney to take up duties as a hotel ship to provide accommodation for visitors to the Olympic Games.

The *Fair Princess* (ex-*Carinthia*) at Sydney. (Photo: P&O Princess Cruises)

The *China Sea Discovery* (ex-*Carinthia*) at Hong Kong. (Photo: John Shepherd Collection)

The *Fair Princess* left Sydney for the last time on 15 November 2000 following her last P&O cruise, and arrived at Hong Kong on 29 November. Following a survey by passenger safety inspectors, a list of defects, running to seven pages, was produced, all of which had to be made good.

In February 2001 the ship was renamed *China Sea Discovery*. The intention was to use her on gambling cruises out of Hong Kong at weekends, and to operate cruises between Haikou in Hainan and Halong Bay in Vietnam.

Having finally obtained her passenger safety certificate, the *China Sea Discovery* was far from successful. She often had less than twenty passengers on board for her overnight gambling cruises from Hong Kong. It was said that many of the Hong Kong based gambling ships had their names changed quite regularly because of the superstitious nature of their gambling passengers!

By June 2001 the *China Sea Discovery* was laid up at Kaohsiung, Taiwan, while her owners tried to find a way of breaking into the lucrative Asian cruise market. One rumour circulating at this time had it that the ship would be chartered to the German travel organisation Phoenix Reisen, and sail in tandem with the *Albatros* (ex-*Sylvania*). However, the managing director of Phoenix Reisen scotched this rumour and was quoted as saying, 'One *Albatros* is enough for us!'

In the event the *China Sea Discovery* returned to Hong Kong and by 2003 she was in near-derelict condition. After two more years of lay-up she was sold for scrap, and on 20 November 2005, now renamed *Sea Discovery*, she arrived at Alang, India, for demolition. That was not quite the end of the story of the Cunard liner *Carinthia*, for on 17 February 2006 a serious fire broke out in the engine room of the beached and partially dismantled ship, trapping nine demolition workers in the hull. The fire left the remains of the former *Carinthia* a charred hulk from stem to stern.

By way of conclusion, it is interesting to note that the four *Saxonia* sisters, Cunard's 'brilliant quartette' of the mid-1950s were all built by John Brown at Clydebank, and all met their end on the beach at Alang, India.

A YEAR WITH THE *CARINTHIA*

by John Shepherd

Part 1: Winter North Atlantic

The *Carinthia* remained on her designed route from Liverpool and Greenock to Quebec and Montreal all her working life in the Cunard fleet. In the winter months, from December to March, the terminal ports were Halifax, NS, and New York. She rarely called at Southampton, just very occasionally in the winter months. The *Carinthia* was the workhorse of the Cunard fleet in the early 1960s. When the other seven units of Cunard's passenger fleet went cruising, the *Carinthia* alone remained on the North Atlantic operating a skeleton service with, it has to be admitted, very few passengers.

The *Carinthia* was very much a Liverpool ship, with over 95 per cent of her crew living in the Merseyside area. After ten months on the *Queen Elizabeth*, I joined the *Carinthia* as a junior assistant purser in November 1963. I was promoted to crew purser (which carried the rank of second assistant purser) in March 1964, and remained in that capacity for the next fifteen months before moving to the tourist purser's office in July 1965, still as a second assistant purser, but in effect the deputy tourist purser. The year I am going to describe in this article is 1965. The *Carinthia* carried a purser's staff of nine. There was the chief purser, Peter Dawes. Next came the tourist purser and his deputy, the crew purser, three male junior assistant pursers and two lady assistant pursers. The ladies carried this rather grand title, rather than 'purserette', as preferred by the P. & O. and Union–Castle. The purser's department encompassed the three printers, a baggage master, an interpreter (who spoke four or five European languages) and the ship's orchestra. Also, the purser was responsible for the entertainers (of which more later).

The assistant pursers' accommodation was good on the *Carinthia*. Our cabins were on the boat deck, port side, forward, so we had fresh air and daylight. There was one two-berth cabin for the two junior lads; the rest of us enjoyed single-berth cabins which were comfortably furnished with settees and easy chairs. The lady pursers' cabins were rather more cramped, being down on 'A' deck. The entire purser's staff took their meals in the first-class dining saloon at their own table on the port side aft. We were allowed to choose anything we liked from the first-class menu, but the novelty of this wore off very rapidly, and we longed for some basic plain cooking. Fortunately, help was at hand, and first-class pantryman Stan Everett always produced a 'special' on each crossing for the purser's staff; either a pan of 'scouse' or a steak and kidney pie. We ate these specials in the crew purser's office as it was handy for the galley and avoided the embarrassment of passengers wanting a portion!

The *Carinthia* sailed from Liverpool on Saturday 19 December 1964 on a voyage to Halifax and New York. This would entail spending Christmas Day at sea and arriving at Halifax on Boxing Day morning. After a short stay of three hours in the Nova Scotian port, we sailed for New York where we berthed at Pier 92 on the evening of Sunday 27 December. Passenger numbers were low, the weather was foul, and there was not a lot for the purser's staff to do. Perhaps the most hard-worked member of the staff was the crew purser who had to deal with crew immigration procedures at New York. Before leaving Liverpool a complete manifest of the entire crew had to be lodged with the US Consul who would grant a visa. This visaed manifest was airmailed to New York where US Immigration would check every crew member's name against their black book. Remember, McCarthyism and communist witch hunts were still very recent back in 1964.

On arrival at New York, the *Carinthia* would slow down at the quarantine anchorage off Staten Island, just beyond the newly completed Verrazzano Narrows Bridge. Here the port officials would board by tender: these included the Port Health, US Immigration and US

Customs. Overseeing all this was Cunard's New York representative, one Tom Luby, who had the endearing habit of addressing everyone as 'Cuz', presumably short for 'cousin', or at least that's what I thought as a naïve twenty-year old. Everything was done to 'oil the wheels', so fillet steaks, salads and coffee were available for all the officials on their arrival onboard. This gave about ninety minutes of leeway whilst the *Carinthia* sailed across New York Bay, up the North River, and berthed at Cunard's time-honoured Pier 92. Passenger immigration procedures were generally just about complete as the *Carinthia* berthed alongside, and it only remained for the hold baggage to be discharged and cleared through Customs before the passengers could proceed on their way.

Not so the crew. US Immigration insisted on a complete muster. All officers and crew were required to present themselves at the crew purser's office with their Seaman's Identity Card and an identity document which had been typed by the crew purser on the voyage from Liverpool. I remember one young lad who appeared at the office with his documents being asked by the Immigration Officer, 'Are you a commy?' 'Yes', replied the lad, 'for the last two years.' It took some explaining to get it through to the officer that the lad in question was a commis waiter, and not a member of the communist party! Humour was in very short supply amongst the members of the US Immigration staff, or at least the ones I came into contact with. Eventually all the crew had been mustered, shore leave permits issued, and it was time to go off-duty.

The *Carinthia* lay at New York from Sunday evening 27 December 1964 until Saturday afternoon 2 January 1965. As far as ship's business went, there was very little to do apart from making a token appearance in the office for a couple of hours each morning. A boat drill was held, but as the dock was full of pack ice there was no chance of lowering the boats into the water. So, for six days, the 400+ members of the *Carinthia*'s crew were on full pay with virtually nothing to do. Our time was our own and with Broadway and 42nd Street just a five-minute, twenty-five cent bus ride away, we made the most of it. A visit to the world famous Radio City Music Hall to see the Christmas Show was a must, and there was an once-in-a-lifetime opportunity to be in Times Square to see in the New Year. The main problem was lack of money. As a crew purser, in 1965, I was paid just £45 a month. Although there were basic meals provided on board, many of us preferred to cross the dock road, which ran underneath the West Side Elevated Highway, to the Market Diner, that world famous haunt of Cunard crews whilst in New York. Excellent hamburgers, French fries and salads could be obtained at very reasonable prices.

As the *Carinthia* had been at sea on Christmas Day, on her passage from Liverpool, another Cunard tradition took place whilst we were in New York, namely crew Christmas dinner. The galley staff prepared roast turkey with all the trimmings, and this was served to the crew in the tourist restaurant, by the ship's officers who were also required, at their own expense, to provide seemingly endless pints of beer to the crew members they were serving. We also had a crew concert one evening in the tourist lounge, where various crew members displayed their previously unseen and unheard talents. From a host of applicants, I was selected, as crew purser, to compere this event, which was attended by most officers and crew, including the captain. We were indeed a happy crowd.

The return voyage to Liverpool left New York on Saturday 2 January 1965 and, following a call at Halifax the next day, we were back in Liverpool on Sunday 10 January. Once again the passenger numbers were very low, particularly in first-class where just twenty-two were carried.

After five days in our home port we were off to New York again on Friday 15 January, but this time Cobh was substituted for Greenock. The *Carinthia* was at anchor in Cobh harbour by ten the following morning and here again another Cunard tradition was played out. After boarding us from the pilot launch and bringing us to a safe anchorage, the Cobh Pilot had a chat with the *Carinthia*'s master and it was decided that it would not be safe, due to a rising sea, for him to disembark to the launch after taking the *Carinthia* to sea. The pilot would therefore

The first-class lounge on the *Carinthia*. (Photo: Cunard Line)

The first-class restaurant on the *Carinthia* (the chairs came from the *Aquitania*). (Photo: Cunard Line)

Passengers in both classes have the use of this splendid balconied cinema.

Cunard

The cinema on the *Carinthia*. (Photo: Cunard Line)

remain onboard and make the round-voyage to New York. After this decision had been taken, and it seemed to be taken on a very regular basis whether the seas were rising or not, the pilot would go ashore in his launch, collect a suitcase with clothes for the voyage and presents for all his friends and relations in the United States, and then return onboard in time to pilot the *Carinthia* out of the harbour. The Pilot was assigned a first-class cabin and was signed on the ship's articles as a 'supernumerary', at one shilling a month.

The *Carinthia* was back in New York on Friday 22 January after a call at Halifax on the previous day. Once again there was a full week in port. We were not scheduled to sail again for a full seven days. Just what the accountants of the twenty-first century who insist on six hour turnarounds of liners four times the size of the *Carinthia* would make of this leisurely approach, I don't know. Once again the entire crew was on board for a week on full pay with little or nothing to do. Without the New Year festivities the prospect of another week in New York had lost something of its attraction, and we were all a bit hard up after overspending three weeks earlier. Our week was broken up by the coming and going of other Cunard liners at New York: the *Caronia* setting out on her annual world cruise; the *Queen Elizabeth* on her series of five-day cruises to Nassau in the Bahamas; and the *Carmania* on her programme of West Indies cruises from New York. It was an opportunity for ship visiting and meeting old friends whom we saw only very rarely.

I think we were all pleased when sailing day arrived and we embarked passengers for Cobh and Liverpool on Friday 29 January. We called at Halifax the following day and were back in Cobh on 5 February. After piloting us in, our Pilot left the *Carinthia* following his round voyage as a guest of the company.

The one deviation which took the *Carinthia* to the sun occurred on the following voyage. Each year the Cunard Line scheduled one of its liners to call at Bermuda in early January on

The tourist-class smoking room on the *Carinthia* (the Beaver Club). (Photo: Cunard Line)

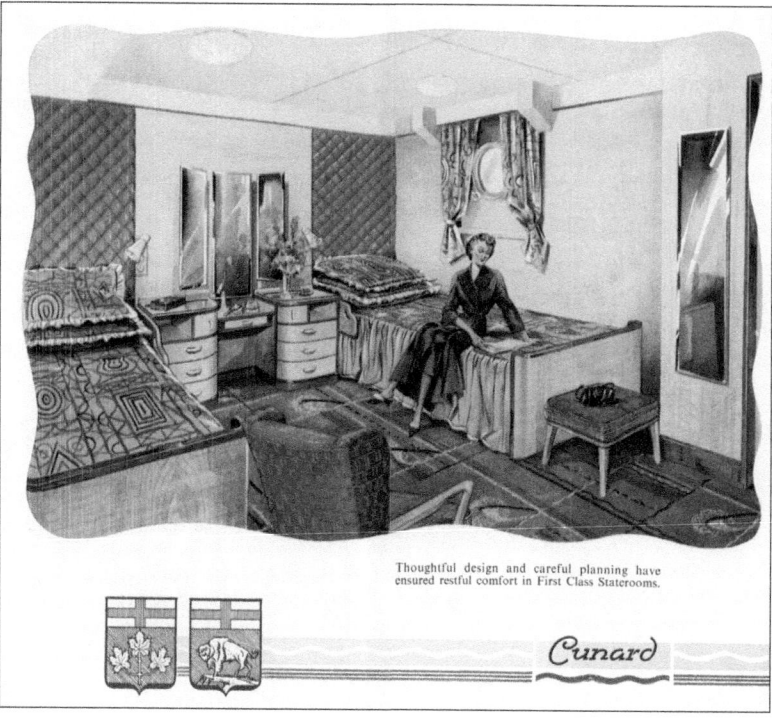

The first-class stateroom on the *Carinthia*. (Photo: Cunard Line)

The First Class Smoking Room recalls the days of Tudor England.

Cunard

The first-class smoking room on the *Carinthia*. (Photo: Cunard Line)

an outward sailing from the UK, and about six weeks later there would be another call by a homeward bound vessel. The purpose of these calls was to allow wealthy Brits to spend the worst of the winter in Bermuda and to travel home by Cunard. In 1965 the *Carinthia* was scheduled to make a call at Bermuda on Wednesday 24 February. We left New York on Monday 22 February and sailed into truly atrocious weather which delayed us by at least eighteen hours.

It was the practice for the transit passengers to be given six hours ashore on these Bermuda calls, but as the *Carinthia* was running a full twenty-four hours late, Cunard decided to abandon this arrangement and to anchor just long enough to embark the Liverpool passengers by tender, and then to sail immediately in an attempt to make up some lost time. Our transit passengers were told, and it was not well received. I happened to be in the tourist purser's office about midnight before we were due to arrive and a scrap of paper was pushed under the door. On it was written: 'We the tourist passengers expect shore leave, or there will be a riot'. I immediately took this to chief purser Peter Dawes, who in turn took it up to the master. The situation was taken very seriously and the arrangements were hastily revised to grant the shore leave to the passengers.

The approach to Bermuda is tricky and can only be attempted in daylight. The *Carinthia* arrived at the pilot station at the Five Fathom Hole at first light on Thursday 25 February and commenced the twenty-mile passage to the anchorage at Grassy Bay in the Great Sound. Here we were met by the ancient tender the *Chauncy M. Depew*, which took our Liverpool passengers to the quay at the capital Hamilton, where they enjoyed a few hours in the sun. The lady assistant pursers accompanied the tender and were on hand to greet our new passengers who would be joining us for passage to Liverpool.

The *Chauncy* was back alongside the *Carinthia* by 3.30 p.m. and we sailed immediately so as to be clear of the approach channel before nightfall. Our new passengers settled down and I remember some of the regulars amongst them who made this voyage every year. There was Sir Humphrey de Trafford and his wife. Sir Humphrey was a well-known race horse owner in the early 1960s and regularly named his horses after Cunard liners, such as *Media* and *Parthia*. Wilfrid Brambell, the star of *Steptoe & Son*, a popular 1960s' television comedy, was on board, as were the Graesser-Thomas family. Mr Graesser-Thomas was the chairman of the company which brewed Wrexham lager, the beer which was supplied to the *Carinthia* and the *Sylvania*. He always bought the entire crew a pint whenever he travelled. The crew were, in fact, not overly impressed with Wrexham lager, and the story goes that just before sailing from Liverpool one voyage they sent a sample ashore for an analysis. On arrival back in Liverpool the analyst's report was waiting. It read: 'This horse is unfit for further work!' Well, it's a good story.

After a final round-voyage to New York, the *Carinthia* arrived back in Liverpool on 23 March 1965, ready to commence her regular run to Quebec and Montreal.

Part 2: *Summer on the St Lawrence*

The *Carinthia*'s berth at Liverpool was in the Huskisson Branch Dock. After disembarking passengers at the Landing Stage, she would anchor in the Mersey awaiting the tide to enter the Sandon half-tide dock, and from there she would be towed to her berth. The schedule involved arriving at Liverpool on Fridays. The weekend in dock was a quiet time; with the ship shutdown there was no catering on board and any officers and crew on stand-by were paid a subsistence allowance to obtain their own meals.

The best point at which to start to describe a typical voyage is probably a Monday morning with the *Carinthia* alongside the Canadian berth on the south side of Huskisson Branch Dock. After a quiet Saturday and Sunday the ship came to life for paying-off the crew members who, for one reason or another, were leaving the ship at the end of the previous voyage. With the shipping master from Cornhill mercantile marine office, the Cunard paymaster Arnie Williams (who went on to become fleet personnel manager in the 1970s) and the crew purser in attendance, the forty or so crew members who were leaving the ship were signed off the Articles of Agreement and their balances of wages paid over to them. The *Carinthia* operated on a six-monthly running agreement, which meant that the Articles were closed only every six months. This avoided having to pay off and then to resign the entire crew of 420 every three weeks. All was usually complete by noon and then it was off to Cunard Building to visit various departments: Fred Waiting in the crew manning department in the basement who looked after the *Carinthia* (Les Ridyard was his opposite number who dealt with the *Sylvania*); and then upstairs to see Harry Roden or Blair Thornton, the superintendent pursers. With all the ship's business completed, the purser's staff retired to their favourite watering hole, the Corn Market, for a lengthy lunch.

The following day, a Tuesday, was busier. Normally there would be a crew boat drill with the lifeboats lowered to embarkation level. As much work as could be completed in preparation for the forthcoming voyage was done.

Sailing day on the Canadian service was always a Wednesday, with sailing time set for 8 p.m. Dependent on the time of high water, the *Carinthia* was moved from her berth into the Sandon half-tide dock by four Alexandra tugs. This was indeed an antiquated arrangement. The *Carinthia* was required to be in the half-tide dock about three hours before high water. Lock gates were then closed behind her and the level of the half-tide dock was run down to the level of the Mersey. With the aid of the four tugs she was then manoeuvred through the Sandon River entrance, which was a very tight fit indeed given the *Carinthia*'s 80ft beam. Once in the river the *Carinthia* would anchor until about 3.30 p.m., as she was required to be alongside the Landing Stage at 4 p.m., to commence loading the passengers' hold baggage – 'Not Wanted on Voyage'.

Winter in the North Atlantic. The view from the *Carinthia*'s bridge on 30 January 1965, whilst on passage from Greenock to Halifax, NS. (John Shepherd)

We were a happy group in the purser's department onboard the *Carinthia*. Chief purser was Peter Dawes, a very much respected Cunard Line senior officer. In charge of the tourist purser's office was John Williams or John Lecoustre, with Steve Gregson his deputy. I was crew purser. The two lady assistant pursers were Shirley Thomas in first-class and Mavis Burns in tourist-class, both of whom had been with the *Carinthia* for some considerable time. We carried three junior assistant pursers, but they tended to move around the Cunard fleet as required, and were not attached to the ship.

As soon as the gangways were in place things really got busy. In the crew office the shipping master, the official from the Shipping Federation and the Union representative arrived to sign on thirty or forty new crew. The senior first officer was a frequent visitor, checking up on the number of certificated lifeboatmen there were on board. Passenger embarkation would commence at 5 p.m. There were separate gangways for each class of passenger, and in tourist-class there would be up to 800 passengers to embark, about two thirds of them being emigrants to Canada. All this came to a head just before sailing time at 8 p.m., and the shore officials all made for the last shore gangway.

The regular master of the *Carinthia* in 1965 was Captain R.J.N. Nicholas who lived in Wallasey. One of his chief delights in life was blowing the ship's whistle. Promptly at 8 p.m. the last shore gangway was lowered and the tugs assisted the *Carinthia* away from the landing stage. As soon as the last tug had been let go, Captain Nicholas blew three prolonged blasts on the *Carinthia*'s steam whistle, which had a particularly majestic tone. This was followed by three long blasts from the tugs, and then one short final blast from the *Carinthia*. It was a very moving farewell, and its effect was never lost on our emigrant passengers or on their families waving from the landing stage.

The *Carinthia* moved slowly down the Mersey towards New Brighton, and here again there were three mighty blasts on the whistle, this time for the benefit of Mrs Nicholas, who lived in Elmpark Road, Wallasey.

After a twelve-hour passage, the *Carinthia* would be at anchor at the Tail of the Bank, off Greenock, by nine the next morning. The Greenock call made no economic sense as it added twelve hours to the passage to Quebec, just for the convenience of a few passengers. We also embarked mail, and I was once told that it was the mail contract that made it worthwhile. As soon as our anchor was down, a Clyde 'puffer' came alongside with the mail. About noon one of the Caledonian Steam Packet Co.'s fleet of Clyde steamers left the quay at Greenock and brought out the passengers and their baggage. As soon as all was onboard, the *Carinthia* sailed for Quebec at about 2 p.m. Once again Captain Nicholas blew three long blasts of farewell on the whistle.

The sail down the Firth of Clyde to the pilot station at Little Cumbrae Island is a delight, and I was usually despatched to the monkey island with a microphone connected to the ship's public address system to give a running commentary on places of interest as we passed them. After disembarking the Clyde pilot at Little Cumbrae and following three more blasts on the whistle, the announcement was made that all passengers were required to muster at their boat stations for boat drill.

Each member of the purser's staff was responsible for a boat station and was required to muster the passengers assigned to his station in two lines, with the women and children to the fore. He then checked that their lifejackets were properly donned and secured at the front with a reef knot. An inspection by the chief officer followed, and that in turn was followed by the safety announcement over the 'Tannoy' system advising the passengers what to do in the event of an emergency. I am still word perfect in this announcement although it is now forty years since I last heard it! As the *Carinthia* rounded the Mull of Kintyre, about four hours after leaving Greenock, she began to feel the effects of the swell rolling in from the Western Ocean. The *Carinthia* and her sisters were good, if a trifle lively, seaboats. The Denny–Brown stabilisers were extremely effective in reducing the ship's roll, but nothing could be done about

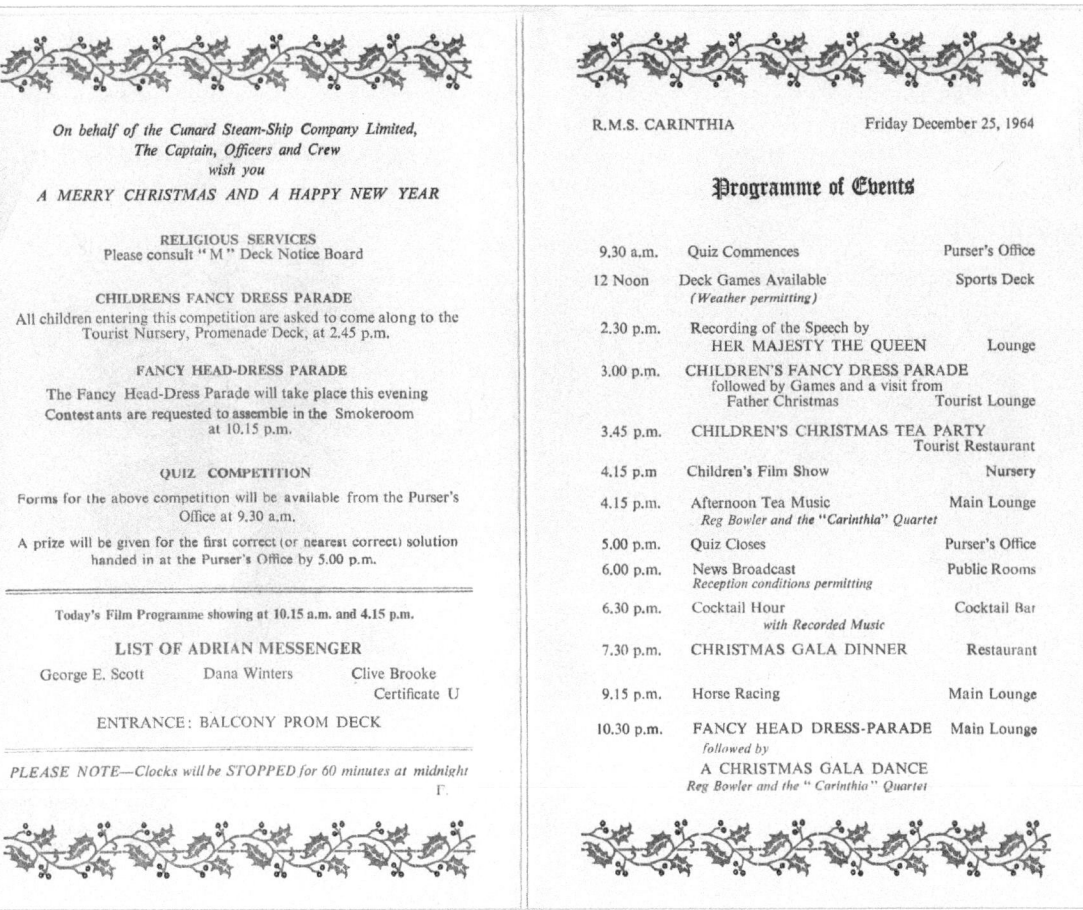

On behalf of the Cunard Steam-Ship Company Limited,
The Captain, Officers and Crew
wish you
A MERRY CHRISTMAS AND A HAPPY NEW YEAR

RELIGIOUS SERVICES
Please consult "M" Deck Notice Board

CHILDRENS FANCY DRESS PARADE
All children entering this competition are asked to come along to the
Tourist Nursery, Promenade Deck, at 2.45 p.m.

FANCY HEAD-DRESS PARADE
The Fancy Head-Dress Parade will take place this evening
Contestants are requested to assemble in the Smokeroom
at 10.15 p.m.

QUIZ COMPETITION
Forms for the above competition will be available from the Purser's
Office at 9.30 a.m.
A prize will be given for the first correct (or nearest correct) solution
handed in at the Purser's Office by 5.00 p.m.

Today's Film Programme showing at 10.15 a.m. and 4.15 p.m.

LIST OF ADRIAN MESSENGER

George E. Scott   Dana Winters   Clive Brooke
Certificate U

ENTRANCE: BALCONY PROM DECK

PLEASE NOTE—Clocks will be STOPPED for 60 minutes at midnight
Γ.

R.M.S. CARINTHIA   Friday December 25, 1964

Programme of Events

Time	Event	Location
9.30 a.m.	Quiz Commences	Purser's Office
12 Noon	Deck Games Available *(Weather permitting)*	Sports Deck
2.30 p.m.	Recording of the Speech by HER MAJESTY THE QUEEN	Lounge
3.00 p.m.	CHILDREN'S FANCY DRESS PARADE followed by Games and a visit from Father Christmas	Tourist Lounge
3.45 p.m.	CHILDREN'S CHRISTMAS TEA PARTY	Tourist Restaurant
4.15 p.m	Children's Film Show	Nursery
4.15 p.m.	Afternoon Tea Music *Reg Bowler and the "Carinthia" Quartet*	Main Lounge
5.00 p.m.	Quiz Closes	Purser's Office
6.00 p.m.	News Broadcast *Reception conditions permitting*	Public Rooms
6.30 p.m.	Cocktail Hour *with Recorded Music*	Cocktail Bar
7.30 p.m.	CHRISTMAS GALA DINNER	Restaurant
9.15 p.m.	Horse Racing	Main Lounge
10.30 p.m.	FANCY HEAD DRESS-PARADE *followed by* A CHRISTMAS GALA DANCE *Reg Bowler and the "Carinthia" Quartet*	Main Lounge

Christmas Day at sea on the *Carinthia*, 1964.

the pitching. If the swell was particularly heavy before dinner time then the *Carinthia* quickly became a battleground of human misery. One of the most common sights on the first evening at sea was to catch a glimpse of the ship's nursing sisters Joan Corfe and Ann Barbour scurrying around the passenger accommodation with trays of hypodermic needles containing a miracle injection to stave off seasickness. I never did find out what was in those needles, but it certainly worked and a seasick passenger at death's door at 6 p.m. could be seen tucking into a fine buffet supper by 10 p.m. It was, in the words of a popular song of the period, 'most efficacious in every way'.

The ship soon settled into sea routine. The first-class and tourist-class purser's offices were open each day at sea from 9 a.m. to 12 noon, and from 2 p.m. to 6 p.m. It was necessary to muster all the passengers and obtain details for the passenger manifests to be ready for arrival at Montreal, the port of entry into Canada. The purser's office also dealt with currency exchange, onward travel arrangements, in fact almost everything that a passenger might need during the voyage.

Down in the crew purser's office on 'R' deck forward, I worked my own hours. There were crew manifests and customs declarations to be prepared for arrival in Quebec. A running total of each crew member's wages had to be calculated in readiness for cash issues. Queries about income tax codes, allotment notes and overtime all came my way. The *Carinthia* carried a fiercely loyal crew and there were not many problems. This made my job quite easy. Occasionally someone stepped out of line, usually as a result of too much Wrexham lager, and I was called to the chart room where the 'logging match' took place. The offender was brought before Captain Nicholas and the charge read out. He was then fined a day's pay and maybe forfeited a day's pay – whatever punishment the master thought appropriate. It was my job to record the logging match in the ship's official log book, and to make the necessary deductions from the man's wages.

On the Canadian service the main weather problems were caused by fog and ice, not gales. We certainly had gales a-plenty, but they had high nuisance value only, unless they were particularly severe. The *Carinthia* and her sisters were well found, sturdy ships built for anything that the North Atlantic could throw at them.

The *Carinthia* proceeded to the south of Newfoundland, around Cape Race, for her first four Canadian round-voyages of 1965. By mid-June the Belle Isle strait between the northern tip of Newfoundland and southern Labrador was clear of ice, and using the strait as a short cut to the Gulf of St Lawrence, we saved about eight hours on the passage from Greenock to Quebec. We endured plenty of fog – whole days of it, in fact. During fog the ship's whistle was sounded according to collision regulations: one prolonged blast every two minutes, day and night. The ship's whistle was about 40ft above my cabin, and I developed the knack of sleeping through these intrusive blasts. If, on the other hand, the fog cleared and the whistle stopped sounding during the night, I woke immediately!

We carried three radio officers on board the *Carinthia*. A continuous radio watch was kept, with the radio officers working a three watch system. One of their main tasks was 'taking press' – sometimes hours of high speed Morse detailing world news which would be included in the *Carinthia*'s daily newspaper, the *Ocean Times*. The front page of the *Ocean Times* was laboriously hand set by chief printer Jack Newman from the news supplied from the radio office, and the first job each morning at sea for the junior purser in the first-class office was to proof-read the front page. After advising Jack of any errors, about 900 copies of the newspaper would be run off, depending on the number of passengers on board. Other than the front page, the remaining

---

Abstract of Log	**R.M.S. "CARINTHIA"**		Westbound
	Captain R. J. N. Nicholas, R.D., R.N.R.		

LIVERPOOL to MONTREAL (via Greenock & Quebec)   Wednesday, August 4, 1965

Date (1965)	Dist.	Lat. N.	Long. W.	Weather
Aug 4				At 20.06 B.S.T. (19.06 G.M.T.) left Princes Landing Stage, Liverpool
,, 4				At 21.12 B.S.T. (20.12 G.M.T.) Bar Light Vessel abeam—Departure
,, 5	188	To Kempock	Point	At 07.23 B.S.T. (06.23 G.M.T.) Kempock Point abeam—Arrival
,, 5				At 07.41 B.S.T. (06.41 G.M.T.) at Greenock Anchored
,, 5				At 14.19 B.S.T. (13.19 G.M.T.) Anchor Aweigh
,, 5				At 14.30 B.S.T. (13.30 G.M.T.) Kempock Point abeam—Departure
,, 6	430	56.16	16.31	Strong S'ly winds veering NW, mod'ating, cloudy & clear, showers
,, 7	509	56.22	31.42	Mod. NW'ly winds, mod. to slight sea, low swell, cloudy and clear
,, 8	458	54.35	44.50	Light breeze to WSW. gale later, slight sea, low swell to heavy swell
,, 9	445	51.37	56.07	Mod. W'ly gale to W'ly breeze, rough sea and swell, o'cast to clear
,, 10	506	48.46	68.05	Variable mod. breeze, slight sea, cloudy, fine, clear to o'cast, rain
,, 10	58	To Anse aux	Basques	At 14.39 E.D.S.T. (18.39 G.M.T.) Anse aux Basques abeam—Arrival
Total Distance	2406			
Aug 10				At 14.57 E.D.S.T. (18.57 G.M.T.) Anse aux Basques abeam—Dep.
,, 10	119			At 21.09 E.D.S.T. (01.09 G.M.T. 11th) West Point abeam—Arrival
,, 10		To	Quebec	Alongside Wolfe's Cove Q'bec, 10.08 E.D.S.T. (02.08 G.M.T.11th)
,, 11				Depart Wolfe's Cove, Quebec, 02.00 E.D.S.T. (06.00 G.M.T.)
,, 11				At 02.09 E.D.S.T. (06.09 G.M.T. 21st) Sillery Point abeam—Dep.
,, 11	133	To	Montreal	At 12.12 E.D.S.T. (16.12 G.M.T.) Tarte Pier abeam—Arr.
,, 11				At 12.59 E.D.S.T. (16.59 G.M.T.) alongside Shed No.3, MONTREAL

OCEAN PASSAGE : 5 days, 5 hours, 09 minutes   AVERAGE SPEED : 19.25 knots

Reduced Speed : 12 hours 34 minutes   Detention · 09 minutes

Abstract of Log				R.M.S. "CARINTHIA"	Eastbound
				Captain R. J. N. Nicholas, R.D., R.N.R.	

NEW YORK to LIVERPOOL (via Halifax and Greenock)   Monday, March 15, 1965

Date (1965)	Dist.	Lat. N.	Long. W.	Weather
March 15				At 10.54 E.S.T. (15.54 G.M.T.) left Pier 92, New York
" 15				At 12.30 E.S.T. (17.30 G.M.T.) Ambrose C.L.V. abeam Depart
" 16	454	42.50	65.02	Moderate sea, fine, clear
" 16	126	to Chebucto Head		At 18.06 A.S.T. (22.06 G.M.T.) Chebucto Head abeam Arrival
" 16	580			At 18.58 A.S.T. (22.58 G.M.T.) In Berth 21 Halifax
" 17				At 02.26 S.T. (05.26 G.M.T.) left Berth 21, Halifax
" 17				At 03.24 S.T. (06.24 G.M.T.) Chebucto Head Dept.
" 17	173	44.29	59.24	Slight sea, Cloudy and clear
" 18	464	45.58	48.52	Slight sea, low N'ly swell, o'cast, clear, o'ccnl snow flurries
" 19	448	49.53	39.23	Slight sea, low swell, cloudy, clear
" 20	409	52.42	29.27	Rough sea, very heavy NE'ly swell, cloudy, clear
" 21	362	54.32	19.50	Very rough sea, V. heavy E'ly swell, o'cast o'ccnl light rain, clear
" 22	435	55.30	07.11	Rough sea, low E'ly swell, overcast o'ccnl rain, clear
" 22	116	to Kempock Point		At 17.45 B.S.T. (16.45 G.M.T.) Kempock Point abeam—Arr.
Total Distance	2407			
March 22				At 18.03 B.S.T. (17.03 G.M.T.) Anchored Greenock.
" 22				At 20.35 B.S.T. (19.35 G.M.T.) Greenock Anchor Aweigh, Dept.
" 22				At 20.51 B.S.T. (19.51 G.M.T.) Kempock Point abeam—Dept.
" 23	184	to Bar Light Vessel		At 06.12 B.S.T. (05.12 G.M.T.) Bar Light Vessel—Arrival
" 23				At 07.43 B.S.T. (06.43 G.M.T.) Princes Landing Stage—L'pool

OCEAN PASSAGE: 5 days, 10 hours, 21 minutes   *AVERAGE SPEED*: 18.49 knots

Reduced Speed 30 hours, 35 mins.   *Detention*: 06 mins.

seven pages of the *Ocean Times* were prepared on shore before sailing and contained topical articles and advertisements.

Official messages from Cunard to the *Carinthia* at sea were sent in company code: groups of five letters. On receipt of one of these messages, and they could be received at any time of the day or night, one of the purser's staff was detailed to decode the message using the company code book, and to type the message in plain language at the bottom of the message. The use of code was a nightmare for the radio officers as just one incorrectly received letter in any one of the code groups could change the meaning of the message entirely. Similarly, all official messages from the *Carinthia* had to be coded by one of the purser's staff, and then checked for accuracy by one of his colleagues. It was a laborious and time-consuming process.

The second radio officer on the *Carinthia* in 1965 was Terry Maddrell, the son of the coxswain of the lifeboat at Port Erin, Isle of Man. One of Terry's jobs was to go down to the tourist purser's office for an hour each morning and collect any radio messages that passengers might wish to send. He recalls one old Irish lady who was upset that the *Carinthia* was running late due to persistent gales, and wanted to let her relations know that they need not meet her at Cobh until the following day. Terry explained to her at great length that she could, if she so wished, make a radio telephone call, but the old lady looked at him quizzically and said, 'Well, I better not do that, they might not be listening to the radio!'

The *Carinthia* spent Sunday at sea on every voyage. The Blue Ensign was flown on Sundays which the crew were delighted to see, not because of any particular religious sentiment, but because it meant an extra day's pay for working on a Sunday. A ship's divine service was organised in the tourist-class lounge for the passengers and any crew members who might wish to attend. There was usually a good turn out. The chief officer took the service, assisted by the senior first officer. Arthur Plant and the *Carinthia* orchestra provided music for the hymns. Their knowledge of hymn tunes was a bit limited (to about five, in fact) so that the same hymns turned up every voyage without fail. We never sang that sailors' hymn which has, at the end of each verse, the words: 'O hear us when we cry to thee, for those in peril on the sea'. I think that perhaps there was a Cunard management directive for it not to be used. However, 'The waves and storms of this uncertain world' were always mentioned at one point in the service!

The purser's staff was responsible for all passenger entertainment. This was pretty basic with a few games of bingo or a few horse races in the lounge after dinner. Bingo needs no explanation, but the horse racing involved moving wooden horses along a canvas track stretched across the dance floor. The horses were moved according to the throw of the dice, and one of the passengers was asked to shake the dice. The lounge steward actually moved the horses. All great fun!

In the early 1960s the Cunard Line was experimenting with professional entertainers on board to provide a cabaret show three times a voyage. We carried some past-their-sell-by-date cabaret artists to provide a song and dance routine to the music of Arthur Plant and the Orchestra. Names such as Boyer and Ravel, Flack and Lamar, the Trio Vitalites, and Brett Stevens spring to mind. In all fairness, I have to say that I never knew how the dancers kept their feet when the weather was bad and the dance floor was heaving around. The one exception to this rather motley collection was Adelaide Hall, who sailed with us regularly to entertain the passengers. She was magnificent.

There were many characters amongst the *Carinthia*'s crew. One was the chief barber Bill McAuliffe. Bill looked after the first-class passengers and had his small shop on 'A' Deck amidships. All the officers had their hair trimmed by Bill and his barber's chair became something of a confessional. I'm certain that Bill knew more about the *Carinthia*'s problems than anyone else on board. Then there was the ship's plumber John Kelly, known as 'Flush' Kelly, because after a few beers he would regale anyone within earshot about the intimate workings of a flush valve. There were many other great characters on board, but with the passage of time their names have slipped my memory.

As the voyage wore on the *Carinthia* entered the calm waters of the Gulf of St Lawrence and proceeded to the pilot station at Father Point. The shipping channel hugged the north shore of the gulf, and it was a highly scenic passage close in to the Laurentian Mountains. We passed the spectacular Montmorency Falls (higher than Niagara) and shortly afterwards berthed at Quebec City. Here the port officials boarded us and the normal procedure was for them to join the *Carinthia* for the passage to Montreal and to clear the passengers through immigration on the way. Passengers were not allowed to leave the ship at Quebec: Montreal was the port of entry into Canada.

However much they had enjoyed the ocean crossing, the passengers were always anxious to get ashore at Montreal and as soon as the hold baggage had been discharged they were allowed ashore. Some of the passengers were not even halfway into their journey. Those bound for Western Canada had another five days on the train to endure.

The *Carinthia* always had a full day in Montreal (a Thursday) before embarkation for the eastbound passage on Friday. A full crew boat drill was held with lifeboats manned and sent away around the dock. It should be remembered that apart from two motor lifeboats, the remainder were fitted with 'Fleming Gear'. This gear consisted of a series of handles which the occupants of the boat pushed and pulled in order to turn the propeller.

Passenger numbers for the eastbound crossing were usually low in the early part of the St Lawrence season, but picked up in June, July and August, with tourists wishing to visit Europe. Sailing time from Montreal was twelve noon and the *Carinthia* would be off Quebec by seven in the evening, helped along by the river current. Here, a tender came out to meet us, perhaps bringing another dozen or so passengers.

The routine for the eastbound crossing was similar to the westbound with the exception that instead of stopping the ship's clocks for an hour each evening, they were advanced one hour at 2 a.m. – in effect making a twenty-three-hour day.

There was the usual call at Greenock where the Liverpool pilot and the British immigration officer boarded. After clearing the Greenock passengers, he would screen the Liverpool passengers on the passage from the Clyde to the Mersey, in order to save time on arrival at Liverpool. Having the Liverpool pilot onboard meant that we did not have to stop to board a pilot at the Bar, but proceeded directly up the Mersey where we would berth at the Landing Stage at 6 a.m.

The hold baggage was immediately discharged and most passengers were ashore by 9 a.m. A special train for London would be waiting at the Riverside Railway Station if numbers warranted it, but more often than not passengers were conveyed by bus to Liverpool's Lime Street Station.

Then there was the rigmarole of docking. The *Carinthia* moved off the stage to an anchorage in the Mersey to await the tide at Sandon River entrance. She was then manoeuvred into the half-tide dock, and finally through to her berth in Huskisson Dock.

The years 1964 and 1965 had been poor ones for the Cunard Line and its passenger operations had all lost money. Economies were effected, but it was all too little too late. The age of the jet aircraft had arrived. I remember going on the boat deck one morning in 1965 and seeing one of the *Carinthia's* sailors painting the brasswork (of which there was plenty) with white paint. The time consuming and therefore expensive routine of polishing the ship's brass was to be abandoned. It was very sad and the writing was on the wall.

The *Carinthia's* schedule in 1966 was badly disrupted by the forty-two-day seamen's strike from 23 May until 2 July. This was a catalyst, but by no means the only reason, for the *Carinthia's* early withdrawal from service in 1967. The Cunard Line had a new chairman, Sir Basil Smallpiece, and it was he who grasped the nettle and ordered the withdrawal of the Queens, the *Mauretania*, the *Caronia*, the *Carinthia* and the *Sylvania*. The once mighty Cunard passenger fleet was down to just three ships: the *Carmania*, the *Franconia* and the new *QE2*.

SYLVANIA

Built by John Brown & Co. Ltd at Clydebank in 1957.   **Yard No:** 700
Official Number: 187164   **Signal Letters:** G V T F
Gross Tonnage: 21,989   **Nett:** 11,665   **Length:** 608·3ft   **Breadth:** 80·4ft.
Owned by the Cunard Steamship Co. Ltd. Registered at Liverpool
4 steam turbines, double-reduction gearing to twin screws.

In March 1955 the Cunard Line gave John Brown of Clydebank the confirmation of its order for the final ship in what the shipping press was describing as 'a brilliant quartet'. This was to be the *Sylvania*, and she was launched by Mrs Norman Robertson, wife of the Canadian High Commissioner in London, on 22 November 1956. The Cunard directors remained convinced that for another decade at least there would always be sufficient passengers who would wish to travel in a certain degree of luxury and style which would keep the new liners viable.

The new *Sylvania* was ready for her trials on the Arran Mile on 27 May 1957, and two runs were made, at 5 a.m. and 9.30 a.m. The Cunard Line took the opportunity to announce that following the successful completion of its building programme for the Canadian service, a berth had been reserved at Clydebank for a further passenger liner to replace the ageing *Britannic*.

The new ship left Greenock on 5 June 1957 on her maiden voyage to Quebec and Montreal. Industrial troubles at Liverpool had prevented the new liner visiting her home port prior to the maiden voyage.

Mr Frank H. Dawson, director and general manager of the Cunard Line, speaking at a luncheon held on board the *Sylvania* prior to her maiden voyage, commented: 'The last fifteen months have probably been the most difficult of my 45 years' service with the company. In that time, up to March 1957, we suffered from trials and tribulations, mostly from labour.' In spite of this, Mr Dawson spoke mainly of achievement and hope and said:

We may go on and build other ships in the future because we have a great and abiding affection for our Canadian cousins. Canada has developed and is going to be increasingly

AE2   PUBLISHED ON BOARD CUNARD LINERS

Ocean Times

R.M.S. "SYLVANIA"   Tuesday, 15th February, 1966   Mediterranean Cruise Edition

VIETCONG MINE LONELY ROAD: 54 KILLED

Bus Carrying Civilians, Enlisted by U.S., Blown into Canal

SAIGON.—Vietcong mines brought fresh horror to the battlefields of South Vietnam, killing 54 Vietnamese civilians, a number of American troops and a camera man. Three mines, planted by guerillas along a lonely road, north of Saigon, claimed the civilian dead, in the worst incident of its kind in the Vietnam war, reports the "Daily Telegraph."

Two mines exploded at the same spot, blowing into a canal a bus carrying farmers enlisted by the Americans to gather rice to prevent it falling into Vietcong hands. A few hours later, a motor scooter touched off the third mine, killing seven more Vietnamese.

The last major mine incident was in Saigon, last June, when 42 people were killed and 80 injured, when a Claymore mine exploded in the dining room on a floating restaurant.

Fifteen on Trial

PARIS.—Fifteen men went on trial here for the abortive plan to blow up President de Gaulle in August 1964, reports Reuter.

Early Election Forecast in Britain

LONDON.—Informed sources said that Prime Minister Wilson was not expected to decide, for certain, the timing of a General Election until after his trip to Moscow next week.

Observers believed that a major diplomatic success there might well send him to the country, probably in April, in an attempt to increase the Labour Party's three-vote majority in Parliament.

A clear majority of Wilson's Cabinet now favours an early election and the Prime Minister himself is leaning toward one.

AUSTRALIA CHANGES TO DECIMAL CURRENCY

SYDNEY.—Australians switched to decimal currency with comparative ease, though some people were not quite sure how many cents are in the new dollar, reports Wireless Press.

Some old people were perplexed by the new notes and coins, and one elderly lady who received a dollar note and a mixture of new coins in her change sighed and

From All Quarters

LONDON. — Prime Minister Seretse Khama, of Bechuanaland, begins talks here, today, with Colonial Secretary Lord Longford on independence for the British Protectorate in Southern Africa's Kalahari Desert.

LONDON.— The editor of the "Daily Mail," Michael Randell, has won the "Hannen Swaffer Award" as the Journalist of the Year for 1965, he receives £500 and a gold quill pen.

WASHINGTON.—The Joint Economic Committee has made public a staff study on the methods used in various countries for moving unemployed workers to areas with labour shortages.

SEOUL.—The funeral altar was wrecked by a seething crowd of over 100,000 people who packed the streets of Eastern Seoul at the traditional Royal funeral rites for Queen Yun who died ten days ago.

CASABLANCA.— Over 4,000 people were left homeless by a fire that swept through a shanty town here and destroyed nearly 600 homes.

The ship's daily newspaper, the *Ocean Times*, 15 February 1966.

important to our daily life. There is an enormous potential there and we, as a Company, have tried to be of service to it. Cunard's total share of the Canadian passenger trade since 1947, both westbound and eastbound, has totalled 614,000 passengers.

The *Sylvania* operated the Canadian service from Liverpool in company with her sister the *Carinthia* during the summer and autumn of 1957 until the end of the St Lawrence season. Her maiden arrival at New York was on 17 December 1957 and she then sailed on a Christmas cruise to the West Indies. This was purely a token gesture. On 10 January 1958 she resumed transatlantic service, and on 5 April returned to the Canadian run.

In the *Sylvania*'s first full year in service (1958) some 1,036,000 passengers crossed the Atlantic by sea. However, this was also the year when the first commercial jet service was introduced between Europe and New York and there was immediate effect, in 1959, on the number of passengers who chose to cross by sea. For the *Sylvania* and her sisters, built without a real thought toward even occasional use as cruise ships, this was bad news indeed.

The *Sylvania* served the Canadian run for only a relatively short time. In November 1960 it was announced that she would replace the *Britannic* on the Liverpool–New York service. Any thoughts about building a proposed replacement for the *Britannic* had been abandoned due to increasingly poor results from Cunard's passenger liners, and the general manager's gung-ho comments on the eve of the *Sylvania*'s maiden voyage just three years earlier now sounded rather hollow.

The *Sylvania* on her sea trials, 27 May 1957. (Photo: John Brown & Co., Clydebank)

During her annual refit in January 1964, eighty of the *Sylvania*'s tourist-class cabins were refitted and equipped with private bathrooms. Whilst this was a welcome move, it was far from enough to make her competitive with other liners then in service. It was a token gesture – after all, there were in total 250 tourist-class cabins.

It was becoming clear to the Cunard Line directors that the demand for transatlantic passages during midwinter was in terminal and rapid decline, and on 10 February 1965 the *Sylvania* made a twenty-seven-day cruise from Liverpool to the Mediterranean. The following winter saw the *Sylvania* more extensively employed on cruising until 20 April 1966. Hardly had she settled back on the Atlantic than the six-week seamen's strike commenced in mid-May and the *Sylvania* got caught up in the dispute when she docked in Liverpool.

Three weeks after the end of the strike, on 22 July 1966, Cunard's chairman Sir Basil Smallpiece informed the company's employees, both afloat and ashore, just how serious the financial situation had become. The seamen's strike had cost Cunard £3 million. Sir Basil commented: 'This is the bottom of the barrel. There is enough left in the kitty for eighteen months, perhaps a couple of years, and that's it. In the past five years the passenger liners have bled Cunard to the extent of £14 million in total losses.'

The Cunard Line closed the Liverpool–New York route at the end of 1966 and the *Sylvania* made the final crossings in November. The Mersey Docks & Harbour Board shed no sentimental tears: it had always been more interested in long-stay cargo ships rather than quick turnaround passenger liners.

The *Sylvania* had her hull painted white during her 1966/67 overhaul, and on 13 January 1967 she sailed from Southampton on a thirty-six-day cruise to the Caribbean. Only the public rooms had air-conditioning; the passenger cabins had to make do with forced draught and fans, and it became intolerably hot at times. On her return from the West Indies, the *Sylvania* was based on Gibraltar for a series of five Mediterranean cruises. The passengers were flown from Gatwick to Gibraltar, introducing the concept of fly/cruise-holidays.

During these cruises the *Sylvania* carried a SRN-6 hovercraft on her foredeck. The British Hovercraft Corporation was trying to interest the governments of various countries bordering the Mediterranean in purchasing hovercraft, and to give government officials a practical demonstration of the hovercraft's capabilities it was put into the water, using the ship's gear,

Date	Dist.	Lat.	Long.	Weather etc.
February 11		N	W	At 1147 GMT left Berth 106, Southampton
„ 11				At 1339 GMT Nab Tower abeam
„ 11	74			At 1757 GMT Le Havre Light Vessel DEPARTURE
„ 11				At 1938 GMT alongside berth Joannes Couvert Arrival
„ 11				At 2039 GMT left berth Joannes Couvert
„ 11				At 2115 GMT Le Havre Light Vessel Departure
„ 12	271	48.02	05.53	Moderate sea, heavy W'ly swell, overcast and clear
„ 13	470	40.51	09.42	Very rough sea, heavy W'ly swell, cloudy, occassional rain
„ 14	416			At 1036 ST [0936 GMT] Europa Point, Gibraltar, abeam Arrival
„ 14	1157			At 1117 ST [1017 GMT] Anchored off Gibraltar

Passage: 2 days, 12 hours, 21 mins.   Average Speed 18.44 knots
Total reduced speed: 1 hour, 56 mins.

„ 15				At 0152 ST [0052 GMT] left anchorage
„ 15				At 0200 ST [0100 GMT] Europa Point, Gibraltar, abeam Departure
„ 15		36.50	01.09	Rippled sea, fine and clear
„ 16	212	38.46	8.23 E	Rough sea, low SE'ly swell overcast and clear
„ 17	467			At 0600ST [0500 GMT] Breakwater Light, Naples abeam Arrival
„ 17	300			At 0703 ST [0603 GMT] alongside Stazione Maritima
	979			

Passage: 2 days, 4 hours   Average speed 18.98 knots
Total reduced speed: 1 day, 21 hours

„ 18				At 1852 ST [1752 GMT] left Stazione Maritima
„ 18			E	At 1909 ST [1809 GMT] Breakwater Light, Naples abeam Departure
„ 19		37.18	18.13	Rippled sea, cloudless and clear
„ 20	318			At 0448 ST [0648 GMT] Psittalia Lighthouse, Piraeus, abeam Arrival
„ 20	343			At 0754 ST [0554 GMT] alongside King Constantine Quay
	661			

Passage: 1 day, 10 hours, 39 mins.   Average speed 19.08 knots
Total reduced speed: 18 hours, 48 mins.

„ 21				At 0156 ST [2356 GMT] left King Constantine Quay
„ 21				At 0224 ST [0024 GMT] Psittalia Light, Piraeus, abeam Departure
„ 21		35.32	26.05	Slight sea, low W'ly swell, cloudy and clear
„ 22	197			At 0603 ST [0403 GMT] Ras El Tin, Alexandria, abeam Arrival
„ 22	315			At 0805 ST [0605 GMT] alongside Maritime Terminal
	512			

Passage: 1 day, 3 hours, 39 mins.   Average speed 18.81 knots
Total reduced speed: 18 hours, 3 mins.

„ 24				At ... ST [1013 GMT] left Maritime Terminal
„ 24				At 1306 ST [1106 GMT] Ras El Tin, Alexandria abeam Departure
„ 25				At 0651 ST [0451 GMT] Beirut Lighthouse abeam Arrival
„ 25	340			At 0750 ST [0550 GMT] alongside Eastern Mole Quay

Passage: 17 hours, 45 mins.   Average speed 19.38 knots
Total rduced speed: 11 hours, 35 mins.

„ 27				At 0157 ST [2357 GMT 26th] left Eastern Mole Quay
„ 27				At 0... ST [0018 GMT] Beirut Lighthouse abeam Departure
„ 27				At 0618 ST [0418 GMT] Haifa Breakwater Light abeam Arrival
„ 27	72			At 0816 ST [0618 GMT] moored at Breakwater

Passage: 4 hours.   Average speed 18.75 knots
Total reduced speed: 4 hours

„ 28				At 1814 ST [1615 GMT] left moorings
„ 28				At 1836 ST [1636 GMT] Haifa Breakwater Light abeam Departure
March 1	326	33.52	28.44	Rippled sea, low NW'ly swell, cloudy and clear
„ 2	390	35.54	21.09	Rough sea, low SE'ly swell, cloudy and clear
„ 3	294			At 0654 ST [0554 GMT] Pt. San Raineri, Messina, abeam Arrival
„ 3	1010			At 0815 ST [0715 GMT] alongside Colapesce Quay

Passage: 2 days, 13 hours 18 mins.   Average speed 16.77 knots
Total reduced speed: 61 hours, 18 mins.

„ 3				At 2011 ST [1911 GMT] left Colapesce Quay
„ 3				At 2033 ST [1933 GMT] Pt. San Raineri, Messina, abeam Departure
„ 4	309	37.57	09.24	Calm sea, cloudy and clear
„ 5	464	36.46	0.11 W	Rough sea, low N'y swell, cloudy and clear, occasional showers
„ 6	273			At 0615 GMT Breakwater, Tangier, abeam Arrival
„ 6	1046			At 0817 GMT alongside Quai de Paquebots

Passage: 2 days, 10 hours, 42 mins.   Average speed 17.97 knots
Total reduced speed: 43 hours, 15 mins.

„ 6				At 1400 GMT left Quai de Paquebots
„ 6				At 1421 GMT Breakwater, Tangier, abeam Departure
„ 7	272			At 0454 GMT St. Marta Lighthouse Lisbon, abeam Arrival
„ 7				At 0740 GMT alongside Alcantara Quay

Passage: 14 hours, 33 mins.   Average speed 18.90 knots
Total reduced speed: 5 hours, 54 mins.

„ 8			W	At 1608 GMT left Alcantara Quay
„ 8				At 1730 GMT St. Marta Lighthouse Departure
„ 9	346	44.12	08.49	Moderate sea, low W'ly swell, cloudy and clear
„ 10	475	49.51	1.31	Moderate sea, low swell, overcast and clear
„ 10	60			At 1600 ST [1500GMT] Le Havre Light Vessel abeam Arrival
„ 10	881			At 1724 ST [1624 GMT] alonside berth Joannes Couvert

Passage: 1 day, 21 hours, 30 mins.   Average speed 19.30 knots
Total reduced speed: 14 hours, 00 mins.

„ 10				At 2251 ST [2151 GMT] left berth Joannes Couvert
„ 10				At 2200 ST [2100] GMT Le Havre Light Vessel abeam Departure
„ 11	74			At 0509 GMT Nab Tower abeam ARRIVAL
„ 11				At 0800 GMT alongside Berth 106, Southampton
	7078	Total miles		

Average speed 11.00 knots

Tuesday, February 15, 1966

Dinner

JUICES	Tomato	Grapefruit	Pineapple

Chilled Crabflake Cocktail

HORS D'ŒUVRE

Salade Italienne	Tomatoes Orientale	Gendarme Herrings
Antipasto	Oeufs Farcie Anchoise	Portugaise Sardines
Smoked Salmon with Capers		Tunafish Salad
Chilled Table Celery	Queen Olives	Mixed Nuts

SOUPS Petite Marmite Creme Sevigne

Cold : Consomme

FISH

Fried Fillet of Whiting, Gribiche Sauce
Supreme of Barbue, Duglere

ENTREES

Frankfurter Sausage and Braised Sauerkraut
Riz de Veau Braise, Demi Deuil

**CONTINENTAL
SPECIALITY**

Ropa Veja, Espanola
Small slices of Beef, Lamb and Pork fried in Butter with Chopped Onions, Pimentoes and
Quarters of Tomatoes served with Fried Bread Croutons

JOINT

Roast Leg and Shoulder of Lamb, Mint Sauce and Jelly

**GRILL (to order)
10 mins.**

Pork Chop, Glazed Fruit
Brochette of Veal Kidney, Berichonne

RELEVE

Roast Bedfordshire Chicken, Farcie, Bread Sauce

VEGETABLES Broccoli Hollandaise Fried Parsnips

Garden Peas au Menthe
Macaroni Bolognaise

POTATOES	Boiled	Rissolees	Macaire	French Fried
SORBET	Raspberry			Lemon

COLD BUFFET

Roast Ribs and Sirloin of Beef, Horseradish Cream	Pressed Brisket of Beef
Roast Duckling, Mimosa Salad	Galantine of Chicken
Roast Leg and Shoulder of Lamb, Mint Sauce	Rolled Ox Tongue

SALADS	Hearts of Lettuce	Beetroot and Onion	Mixed Bowl	Parmentier
DRESSINGS	Mayonnaise	Lemon	French	Thousand Islands

SWEETS

Souffle Suchard	Pears Helene	Coupe Royale
Compote of Peaches and Pineapple, Chantilly Cream		Gateau Battenburg

ICE CREAM Vanilla Coffee Neapolitan

CHEESES Assorted Cheese Board

SAVOURY Croute Indian

FRESH FRUIT

Apples	Oranges	Tangerines	Plums	Pears
Dates		Raisins		Figs
Crystallised Ginger				Almonds

Tea and Coffee (Hot or Iced)

Left: Abstract of log: *Sylvania* Mediterranean Cruise, 1966. *Above*: The dinner menu on a Cunard cruise, *Sylvania*, 1966.

at various ports and sent on demonstration runs. The hovercraft was not there to provide sightseeing trips for cruise passengers, although an occasional short trip for passengers was made around the bay between official trips. Lowering and recovering the hovercraft was a time-consuming business for the deck crew involving considerable overtime, but fortunately British Hovercraft was picking up the tab for this.

After completing her cruise programme, the *Sylvania* returned to the Canadian service, alternating between Liverpool and Southampton as her terminal port. It was Expo 67 (the World Fair) at Montreal and Cunard hoped to attract passengers who wished to visit the fair. After leaving Montreal on 15 June 1967, the *Sylvania* ran aground just below Trois Rivières, and all efforts to refloat her failed. She had on board almost a full complement of passengers, and two days later they were taken off by tender and offered an air passage or a berth on the next Canadian–Pacific sailing.

The *Sylvania* stubbornly refused to be refloated, and it was only when her bunkers and fresh water ballast had been pumped out, and the crew sent away in the lifeboats, that she reluctantly came off the St Lawrence mud. She was towed back to Montreal and entered Canadian Vickers' floating dock on 26 June and remained there for three days whilst damage to her propellers was made good. Her entire crew was living aboard during this time, which was extremely trying for all concerned as the ship was virtually shut down with no forced draught in the heat of a Canadian summer. After leaving the floating dock, the *Sylvania* remained at Montreal until her next scheduled sailing on 4 July.

In October 1967 the Cunard chairman Sir Basil Smallpiece announced that the *Sylvania* would be withdrawn, along with the *Carinthia* and the *Caronia*. In a masterstroke of public relations, Sir Basil said that the *Sylvania* was unsuitable for cruising, and then wondered why passenger numbers were so low on the extensive cruising programme which lasted until 7 May 1968.

The *Sylvania* sailed from New York on 11 December 1967 for Europe with 462 passengers; the only Cunard liner to be making a North Atlantic Christmas crossing. She called at Halifax, NS, for seventy-seven more passengers.

The *Sylvania* completed her Cunard service almost eleven years to the day after she had left Greenock on her maiden voyage on 5 June 1957. She was laid up at berth 101 Southampton alongside her sister, the *Carinthia*. They were redundant and outmoded, yet, ironically, their most successful years were still to come.

The *Sylvania* with her white hull, introduced in January 1967. (Photo: Cunard Line)

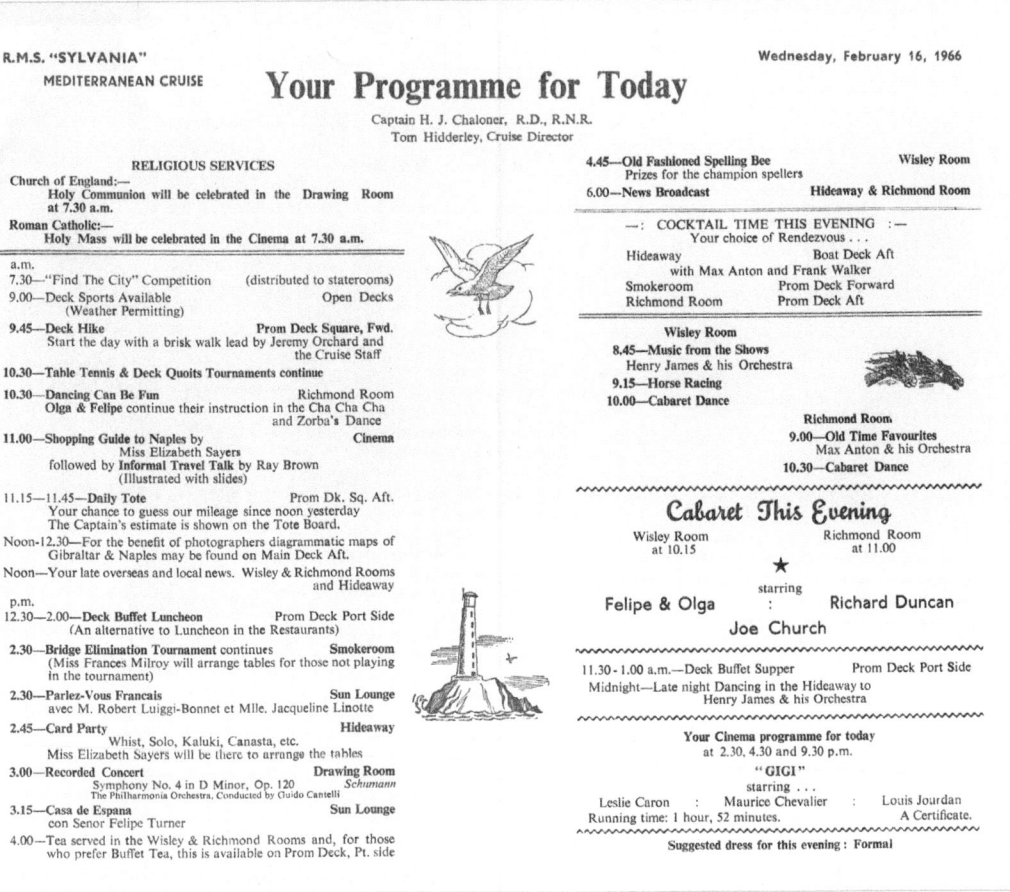

R.M.S. "SYLVANIA"
MEDITERRANEAN CRUISE

Your Programme for Today

Wednesday, February 16, 1966

Captain H. J. Chaloner, R.D., R.N.R.
Tom Hidderley, Cruise Director

RELIGIOUS SERVICES

Church of England:—
Holy Communion will be celebrated in the Drawing Room at 7.30 a.m.
Roman Catholic:—
Holy Mass will be celebrated in the Cinema at 7.30 a.m.

a.m.
7.30—"Find The City" Competition (distributed to staterooms)
9.00—Deck Sports Available Open Decks
(Weather Permitting)
9.45—Deck Hike Prom Deck Square, Fwd.
Start the day with a brisk walk lead by Jeremy Orchard and the Cruise Staff
10.30—Table Tennis & Deck Quoits Tournaments continue
10.30—Dancing Can Be Fun Richmond Room
Olga & Felipe continue their instruction in the Cha Cha Cha and Zorba's Dance
11.00—Shopping Guide to Naples by Cinema
Miss Elizabeth Sayers
followed by Informal Travel Talk by Ray Brown
(Illustrated with slides)
11.15—11.45—Daily Tote Prom Dk. Sq. Aft.
Your chance to guess our mileage since noon yesterday
The Captain's estimate is shown on the Tote Board.
Noon-12.30—For the benefit of photographers diagrammatic maps of Gibraltar & Naples may be found on Main Deck Aft.
Noon—Your late overseas and local news. Wisley & Richmond Rooms and Hideaway
p.m.
12.30—2.00—Deck Buffet Luncheon Prom Deck Port Side
(An alternative to Luncheon in the Restaurants)
2.30—Bridge Elimination Tournament continues Smokeroom
(Miss Frances Milroy will arrange tables for those not playing in the tournament)
2.30—Parlez-Vous Francais Sun Lounge
avec M. Robert Luiggi-Bonnet et Mlle. Jacqueline Linotte
2.45—Card Party Hideaway
Whist, Solo, Kaluki, Canasta, etc.
Miss Elizabeth Sayers will be there to arrange the tables
3.00—Recorded Concert Drawing Room
Symphony No. 4 in D Minor, Op. 120 Schumann
The Philharmonia Orchestra, Conducted by Guido Cantelli
3.15—Casa de Espana Sun Lounge
con Senor Felipe Turner
4.00—Tea served in the Wisley & Richmond Rooms and, for those who prefer Buffet Tea, this is available on Prom Deck, Pt. side

4.45—Old Fashioned Spelling Bee Wisley Room
Prizes for the champion spellers
6.00—News Broadcast Hideaway & Richmond Room

—: COCKTAIL TIME THIS EVENING :—
Your choice of Rendezvous . . .
Hideaway Boat Deck Aft
with Max Anton and Frank Walker
Smokeroom Prom Deck Forward
Richmond Room Prom Deck Aft

Wisley Room
8.45—Music from the Shows
Henry James & his Orchestra
9.15—Horse Racing
10.00—Cabaret Dance

Richmond Room
9.00—Old Time Favourites
Max Anton & his Orchestra
10.30—Cabaret Dance

Cabaret This Evening

Wisley Room Richmond Room
at 10.15 at 11.00

★
starring
Felipe & Olga : Richard Duncan
Joe Church

11.30 - 1.00 a.m.—Deck Buffet Supper Prom Deck Port Side
Midnight—Late night Dancing in the Hideaway to
Henry James & his Orchestra

Your Cinema programme for today
at 2.30, 4.30 and 9.30 p.m.
"GIGI"
starring . . .
Leslie Caron : Maurice Chevalier : Louis Jourdan
Running time: 1 hour, 52 minutes. A Certificate.

Suggested dress for this evening : Formal

A day at sea on a cruise, Cunard-style, 1966.

The *Carinthia* and the *Sylvania* were both sold quickly to the Società Italiana Trasporti Marittimi SpA (the Sitmar Line) at a price of £1 million each. Sitmar intended operating the two ships on the Australian immigrant service, but then lost the contract with the Australian government. As a result, the two ex-Cunarders remained laid up for almost two years. The *Sylvania*'s name was changed to *Fairwind*.

On 6 January 1970 the *Fairwind* left Southampton under tow and arrived at Trieste on 18 January. The ship was completely rebuilt and on completion was totally unrecognisable as the former *Sylvania*. Every one of her passenger cabins had been redesigned and all of them had private bathrooms. It was not until 14 June 1972 that the work was complete and she sailed on a positioning voyage to Los Angeles. Sitmar advertised the *Fairwind* as 'the most luxurious cruise ship ever seen in most parts of the world'. The *Fairwind*'s usual route involved transits of the Panama Canal on voyages from San Juan to Acapulco, and from Los Angeles to Mexico.

The reputation of Sitmar Cruises continued to grow. The *Fairwind* with her sturdy North Atlantic hull, and strong bows built to withstand any seas, ensured her passengers a far more comfortable voyage than any new purpose-built cruise ship could offer.

After twelve years of successful cruising the *Fairwind* was completely refurbished in 1984. In 1988 she made two cruises up the Amazon as far as Manaus. Later in the year one of her propeller shafts fractured and she had to be towed to a San Francisco shipyard for repairs. When

The *Sylvania* in Canadian Vickers' floating dock at Montreal, 27 June 1967. (Photo: John Shepherd)

The *Albatros* (ex-*Sylvania*) at anchor off Liverpool, 13 May 1997. (Photo: John Shepherd)

she reappeared it was with the extended name *Sitmar Fairwind*. As if to show her disapproval for this new name, the ship broke down again a few weeks later off Nassau and had to be towed to New York for lengthy repairs.

On 28 July 1988, P&O acquired the entire share capital of Sitmar Cruises. The price paid was $210 million. This meant that the *Fairwind* returned to British ownership. She was given a new name *Dawn Princess*. Her first cruises for P&O took her from New York to Halifax, Quebec and Montreal. It was indeed ironic that she should return to the old familiar waters of her Cunard days.

During a dry docking at Portland, Oregon, in 1991, asbestos was discovered in the *Dawn Princess*, with the result that the vessel was out of service for three months whilst it was removed. In 1992 P&O Princess Cruises stated that the *Dawn Princess* (ex-*Sylvania*) 'no longer fits into the Company's modern fleet', and in 1993 she was withdrawn from service. She was purchased

ABSTRACT OF THE LOG OF THE
Cunard R.M.S. "SYLVANIA"
Captain L. K. Goodier
NEW YORK TO LIVERPOOL (via BOSTON, Mass. & COBH)

Date (1966)	Dist.	Lat. N.	Long. W.	Weather, etc.
April 29				At 1057 EDST (1457 GMT) left Pier 92, New York
,, 29				At 1248 EDST (1648 GMT) Ambrose Ch. L.V. DEPARTURE
,, 30	349			At 0630 EDST (1030 GMT) Boston L.V. abeam ARRIVAL
,, 30				At 1231 EDST (1631 GMT) alongside C'wealth Pier No. 5, Boston
,, 30				At 1500 EDST (1900 GMT) left C'wealth Pier No. 5, Boston
,, 30				At 1624 EDST (2024 GMT) Boston L.V. abeam DEPARTURE
May 1	392	44.07	62.12	Slight sea and low S'ly swell, overcast and clear, continuous rain
,, 2	463	46.54	51.58	Mod sea and low S'ly swell, overcast with misty patches
,, 3	452	49.36	41.25	Rough sea and mod confused swell, overcast and clear, drizzle
,, 4	463	51.52	29.48	Rough sea and mod variable swell, overcast and clear, showers
,, 5	466	51.36	17.14	Very rough sea, heavy WNW'ly swell, cloudy and clear, showers
,, 6	346	To Daunt	L.V.	At 0630 BST (0530 GMT) Roche Pt. abeam ARRIVAL
Total	2582	Miles		
,, 6				At 0707 BST (0607 GMT) Anchored Cobh
,, 6				At 1400 BST (1300 GMT) left Anchorage Cobh
,, 7				At 1415 BST (1315 GMT) Roche Point abeam DEPARTURE
,, 7	229	TO LIVERPOOL		At 0136 BST (0036 GMT) Bar Light Vessel abeam ARRIVAL
				At 0545 BST (0445 GMT) alongside Princes L'ding Stage, Liverpool

OCEAN PASSAGE : 5 days, 9 hours, 6 minutes   *Average Speed :* 20.00 knots
Reduced Speed : 0 hr. 9 mins.   *Detention :* Nil

A typical eastbound transatlantic crossing in 1966.

by Happy Days Shipping and on 18 August 1993 she was renamed *Albatros*, on charter to the German tour operator Phoenix Reisen.

An ambitious program was planned for the *Albatros* which included an annual 100-day world cruise. On 30 May 1995, when the vessel was sixty miles off Yanbu in the Red Sea, a flash fire broke out in the engine room. The blaze was quickly extinguished but the boilers were shut down as a precaution. The *Albatros* eventually reached Jeddah where her passengers were landed and flown home on chartered flights. The ageing liner was towed to Marseille for repairs which took until 26 July 1995.

A couple of years later the *Albatros* sailed from Bremerhaven on a two-week cruise around the British Isles. She called at Liverpool on 13 May 1997 and three days later was at anchor off St Mary's in the Scilly Isles. Shortly after sailing the *Albatros* struck the well-charted North Bartholomew Rock in St Mary's Sound. Her 504 passengers remained onboard until a chartered ferry took them to Penzance a day later.

The *Albatros* sailed to Southampton under her own steam on 25 May and was dry docked. It had been the most serious incident of her long life. What saved her from becoming a total loss was the extra strength built into the ship to help her withstand the ice of the St Lawrence on her designed route in her Cunard days.

The *Albatros* returned to service with Phoenix Reisen and completed another six years of ambitious cruises, which included an amazing 130-day world cruise in 2001. The end came in November 2003 when the forty-six-year-old former *Sylvania* was taken out of service allegedly due to technical problems, and a planned world cruise was cancelled.

The old ship was laid up at Genoa for several weeks, but then sailed for Alang where she arrived on 19 January 2004 to meet her end at the hands of shipbreakers. Demolition was complete just as she reached the 47th anniversary of her maiden voyage. By any standards, the former Cunard liner *Sylvania* had had an amazing career!

5

ELDER DEMPSTER

lder Dempster, as we knew it, can be traced back to 1852 and was formed by a group of six businessmen of the day, one of whom was Mr MacGregor Laird. It was, however, some twenty years earlier that the first seeds were sown to establish the greatest shipping line ever to link the West Coast of Africa with the United Kingdom.

In 1832 Laird felt that there was real scope for legitimate and regular trade with the Niger River, and organised an expedition to West Africa using the steamers *Quorra* and *Alburkkah*. The venture was a commercial failure and Laird returned to Liverpool in 1834, a broken, disheartened and very sick man.

It would seem, however, that MacGregor Laird had been bitten by the bug of Africa in more ways than one. Following talks with the British Government, Laird set up the African Steamship Co., incorporated by Royal Charter in 1852. On the staff of the Liverpool agency of the new company were two Scots: Alexander Elder, who was superintendent engineer, and John Dempster. Both these men were fired-up by Laird's enthusiasm.

At the end of 1868 a number of Glasgow businessmen had noted the growing trade to the West African coast and announced their intention of setting up a new company to be known as the British and African Steam Navigation Co. John Dempster was approached to act as Liverpool agent for the new venture, and accepted. Dempster realised that he would require an

Elder Dempster's last passenger ship, the beautiful *Aureol*, built in 1951. (Photo: Elder Dempster)

active partner in his agency and thought of his old colleague Alexander Elder, who was now working as a surveyor with the Board of Trade. Following talks, Elder resigned from the Board of Trade, and the firm of Elder Dempster & Co. was born on Merseyside.

A year passed with fierce competition between the African Steamship Co. and British and African S.N. Co. before they both got together and came to terms and arrangements whereby all their future sailings to West Africa would be on a divided basis.

In 1884, both Mr Elder and Mr Dempster retired from the Board of Elder Dempster, although they retained their directorships of the British and African Steam Navigation Co. Their retirement from the Board brought about the appointment of Alfred Jones as the controlling partner in Elder Dempster. Jones started to purchase shares in the rival African Steamship Co. until he had obtained control, at which time he placed the company under Elder Dempster management.

Not content with the West Africa market, Alfred Jones branched out into other parts of the world. Firstly, he turned his attention to the North Atlantic, where Elder Dempster took over the Dominion Line's extensive cargo and cattle trade, which had been operating out of the Bristol Channel to Canada. A little while after this acquisition, the Canadian Beaver Line (Canada Shipping Co. Ltd) fell on hard times and was acquired as a going concern by Elder Dempster in 1898, operating regular services from Liverpool to Canada. The Beaver Line was soon back on a sound footing, with newer and larger vessels being added to its fleet.

Elder Dempster's main area of business remained its West African services. To meet the increasing demand for passenger accommodation, Elder Dempster built five passenger/cargo liners between the wars. The first was the *Aba* of 1918, followed by the *Adda* of 1922, the sister ships *Accra* and *Apapa* of 1926 and the *Abosso* of 1935. At the end of hostilities the *Aba* was returned to Elder Dempster but was not worth reconditioning. The other four newer passenger ships were all war losses.

If the passenger service from Liverpool to West Africa was to continue, new ships would be an urgent priority after the war, and in February 1945 two new ships were ordered from Vickers–Armstrong Ltd at Barrow-in-Furness. These were the *Accra* and the *Apapa*, both launched in 1947. These two ships were larger developments of the pre-war Elder Dempster mail liners of the same name. Four years later the graceful *Aureol* entered service, remembered by many on Merseyside as the most beautifully proportioned passenger liner ever to use the port.

ACCRA

Built by Vickers Armstrongs Ltd at Barrow in 1947.   **Yard No:** 948
Official Number: 181100   **Signal Letters:** G J S W
Gross Tonnage: 11,600   **Nett:** 6,448   **Length:** 452·9ft   **Breadth:** 66·2ft
Owned by Elder Dempster Lines, Ltd
2 Doxford diesel engines, twin screws.   **Speed:** 15.5 knots.

The *Accra* was ordered in February 1945 as the first of Elder Dempster's new passenger ships to reintroduce the thrice-weekly passenger service from Liverpool to Lagos. The new *Accra* was launched at Barrow on 25 February 1947 by Mrs Creech-Jones. She left Liverpool on her maiden voyage on 24 September, under the command of Captain C.C. Cave. Initially the ship carried a black hull.

Just over two years later, in November 1949, the *Accra* suffered a broken crankshaft, and she arrived back at Liverpool on one engine, five days late. She was returned to her builders at Barrow for repairs, and during this period she was repainted with the familiar grey hull and green boot-topping. In 1960 much needed air-conditioning was installed in the passenger decks.

The *Accra* leaving Liverpool on her maiden voyage, 24 September 1947. (Photo: Elder Dempster)

The *Accra*'s service in the Elder Dempster fleet was brief and on 8 November 1967, having completed 171 voyages, she sailed from Liverpool for Cartagena, Spain, where she was demolished by J. Navarro Frances. Disturbed conditions in West Africa, which affected Elder Dempster's traditional trade, played a part in the relatively short career of the *Accra*.

A VOYAGE TO WEST AFRICA IN THE *ACCRA*

by Fred Thompson

Liverpool, on a grey September day in 1952, did not present a particularly auspicious start to life in Africa. I had travelled from Euston on the boat train that, on arrival at Liverpool, had snaked its way across the streets, under the overhead railway, and alongside the Mersey to Riverside Station. I was allowed forty-cubic-feet of baggage as a newly appointed Colonial Education Officer and I had two large wooden crates of household goods, a tin trunk that was intended to deter the voracious insects of forest or desert, and suitcases for my cabin. Each piece carried the Elder Dempster logo and a big letter 'T', this being my initial, to aid identification in the baggage hall. Customs and Immigration had to be cleared, currency regulations were strictly enforced and only ten pounds sterling could be taken out of the country in cash. Baggage handlers were busy trundling trolleys on to the ship and I walked along a gangway into the entrance hall on 'B' deck. My previous voyages to sea had been in the cramped quarters of wartime troopers, this was very different, and it was First Class!

Cabin stewards came to meet passengers and I was taken in hand by a stocky Liverpudlian who led me to 'D' deck where I was to share a two-berth cabin. It was quite basic; there was a wash basin, two chairs, a tall cupboard and storage space below two bunks, one of which was below a porthole. Bathrooms and toilets were situated nearby. My cabin mate was already installed; like me he was bound for Nigeria on first appointment as an education officer.

There was a little time to explore the *Accra*. The boat deck was damp and windswept. There was a generous allocation of space for public rooms which included a library, card room, smoke room and lounge. The entrance hall, still busy with embarking passengers, contained the purser's office, a shop and hairdressing salons for both ladies and gentlemen.

Passengers were directed to the first class dining saloon on 'E' deck to meet the Purser and make their table bookings for meals. The saloon was panelled in African hard woods and the floor was covered with thick linoleum that could easily be washed down if need be should spillages occur in rough weather. One end of the saloon was dominated by the captain's table, an elongated oval which seated nine guests. It was flanked by tables for senior officers. Crisp white table linen, sparkling cutlery and glassware shone in the subdued lighting. Tables seated four, six or eight passengers; senior colonial officers and company directors were guests at the captain's table and those of his senior officers. First-tour young men like myself were placed where the purser thought fit, usually close to the doors to and from the galley.

Prior to departure all passengers had been asked to provide details of rank, title, decorations and branch of service or company, to Elder Dempster. Each us received a passenger list and it was a formidable document. It included all the hierarchy of the colonial service; company directors of banks or the United Africa Company and bishops of African dioceses. There was a fair number of nursing sisters, women education officers and a handful of unaccompanied wives travelling out to join their husbands. There were very few children on board as it was government policy at that time to discourage parents from taking them to West Africa. Indeed, before the Second World War the reputation of the West Coast had been so bad that wives of colonial officers were allowed to accompany their husbands only with the greatest reluctance and had to pay their own passages. The development of anti-malarial prophylactics and the tremendous contribution made by wives in West Africa to the war effort had done much to relax the attitude of the British Government from the 1950s onward.

The second-class passengers were accommodated aft in four-berth cabins. They had their own lounge and dining saloon, as well as a small area of deck space. The list included missionary families and a few Africans returning home from studies in Britain.

As the *Accra* was tied up at the landing stage, dinner on the first night was informal. The ship's bars were closed and the open decks were deserted. Liverpool was wet, cold and dismal. However, the dining saloon was warm and inviting, and for those of us newly qualified from universities and used to the spartan diets of post-war Britain, the menu was staggering! Soup, hors d'oeuvres, fish, choice of entrée, sweets, cheese, biscuits and coffee were served deftly and efficiently by stewards immaculate in bow ties and white jackets.

After dinner I wandered up to the boat deck to find a force 10 gale howling up the Mersey. Departure was postponed for twenty-four hours. The bars remained closed and the crew was taking unexpected shore leave, but the passengers could not go ashore because of immigration restrictions. Worse was the knowledge that Liverpool FC was playing at home, and our cabin steward went ashore to watch them.

The following morning, a Sunday, the *Accra's* engines were throbbing and she eased off the landing stage with the assistance of two tugs. At breakfast we could see the Irish Sea foaming past the portholes and there was a pronounced motion on the ship, dip and roll, as the Welsh hills slipped past to port and the dining saloon emptied rapidly as many passengers suddenly felt an aversion to bacon and eggs or fresh grilled kippers. Fiddles were rigged and the stewards swayed sure-footed with laden trays.

The Bay of Biscay was quite benign after the Irish Sea, and soon the dining saloon was full, the deck chairs were busy with passengers wrapped in rugs, whilst others were walking brisk circuits of the boat deck. The bars were open and everything was duty-free. Life was good!

Shipboard routine was quickly established. Early morning tea with heavy white china bearing the Elder Dempster crest came on a silver tray with a selection of fruit. Breakfast was available from 08.00–09.30. The menu was huge: fruit juices, all cereals known to man, fresh fruit, fish such as grilled sole, bacon, eggs, mushrooms and American hash with fried potatoes, bread in variety and Danish pastries.

Passengers staggered away to walk the deck, search out library books, plan deck games or just slump into deck chairs in sheltered corners. In the card room the bridge fanatics had established themselves. They played all morning, most afternoons and every evening. The children on board were actively discouraged from entering the room and only the bar stewards were really welcome to replenish pink gins or brandy gingers at frequent intervals.

At around 10.30 a.m. hot bouillon was served; this would be replaced by ice cream once the *Accra* was in the tropics. At 11.30 the lounge bar and the smoke room bar opened; the beer was popular but seasoned colonial officers preferred a pink gin! Luncheon was served from 12.30.

After lunch was a quiet time; many passengers took a siesta either in their cabins or on deck where the weather was becoming ever warmer. At 3.30 p.m. tea – cucumber and salmon sandwiches with cream cakes to follow – would be served by the stewards, or it was available on a 'help yourself' basis in the lounge.

Dinner was now a formal occasion for all on the captain's table and those of the senior officers. The gentlemen wore stiff shirts, bow ties and mess jackets and the ladies were in long frocks, some with elbow length gloves.

The *Accra*'s first port of call was Las Palmas in the Canaries. This was anticipated with great excitement for, in 1952, it was a 'free' port. Goods not available in England, or available but subject to heavy import duty, were to be had virtually 'at cost' in Las Palmas. Our stay would be short because of late departure from Liverpool. Many local traders came on board and set out their wares on the boat deck.

As the passengers returned to the *Accra* for an evening departure, they found changes much in evidence. The swimming pool had been filled; the ship's officers had exchanged blue serge for white drill shirts, shorts and long white socks. We were now only a few days from Africa and flying fish as well as dolphins reminded us that we were in tropical waters.

The *Accra*'s dawn arrival at Freetown evoked memories of my wartime visit some nine years earlier. On that occasion the harbour was filled with a southbound convoy and two frigates rushed out into the Atlantic to ambush a wolfpack that had shadowed us for much of the voyage. Then, as now, the bumboats came out to meet us. There was no deep-sea wharf at Freetown in 1952 so lighters came out for the cargo, and disembarking passengers went ashore by launch.

Once the *Accra* was underway again news came that the onward postings had been received. Colonial officers going to the Gold Coast or to Nigeria had to wait until the ship left Freetown to learn their final destinations. All postings were advised to the ship in Morse code and against my name I found 'Kathina'. I looked at the map near the notice board and could not find it. An old hand soon put me right: 'That should be Katsina, the radio officer got his Morse wrong and read four dots instead of three. I hope you play polo – the Emir is dead keen!'

The voyage continued around the bulge of Africa and into the Bight of Benin. The *Accra* was never far off the land and by day the high cumulus could be seen building up over the coast, heralding the heavy rain of an equatorial afternoon. Takoradi was our next port; a new creation to serve what was then the Gold Coast, within a few years to be Ghana. Here there was a deep water quay with berths for six vessels; yet only a few years before Elder Dempster ships had anchored offshore and surf boats, paddled by Kroo boys, had carried passengers and cargo ashore through the surf. It was the Kroo boys' proud boast that the passengers were safely landed without even a splash on their topees.

The *Accra* could carry 150 deck passengers and a large number boarded at Takoradi. Many were semi-itinerant labour seeking work in the boom city of Lagos. Some came with their families, laden with cooking pots, charcoal, yams and bedding rolls. The forward deck was a mass of busy, vociferous, colourful people. Working space was restricted and this did little to improve the tempers of officers and deckhands working the ship.

The following day found the *Accra* steaming slowly into the harbour at Lagos. To starboard was Lagos Island, the old Colonial capital. Apapa wharf was on the port side where the *Accra* would berth. This was the end of the voyage with customs and immigration formalities to be cleared. In the early 1950s these presented no great problems, although old hands said that to wear a King's College Lagos tie ensured a speedy passage through, as all the officers claimed to have relatives at K.C.!

It was all exciting; Lagos was noisy, and noisome, colourful, brash and already alive with nationalism, although the goal was still nine years away. I spent one night in the house of the Inspector General of Education. My onward journey north was to be by train, but the track had been washed out so I spent the next fortnight fuming at the Ikoyi Rest House, a former RAF camp that had little to recommend it. It was ill lit, damp, humid, infested with mosquitoes by night and lacking basic facilities. It was an inauspicious beginning to what became, in the end, five very happy years up country in Katsina, where I never played polo but enjoyed my cricket!

A PA PA

Built by Vickers Armstrongs, Ltd, at Barrow in 1948.　**Yard No:** 949
Official Number: 182411　**Signal Letters:** M A C E
Gross Tonnage: 11,607　**Nett:** 6,453　**Length:** 452·9ft　**Breadth:** 66·2ft.
Owned by Elder Dempster Lines, Ltd
2 Doxford diesel engines, twin screws.　**Speed:** 15.5 knots.

The *Apapa* was ordered from Vickers Armstrong at Barrow at the same time as the *Accra*, in February 1945. The sister ships cost £900,000 each to build. The *Apapa* was launched on 1 September 1947 by Mrs A.C. Tod, and left Liverpool on her maiden voyage to Apapa on 11 March 1948, under the command of Captain J.J. Smith. As with her slightly older sister, the *Apapa*'s hull was painted grey with green boot-topping, during her annual overhaul in 1949. Air-conditioning was installed in 1960.

In 1949 three members of the *Apapa*'s catering department broke into the ship's strongroom whilst on passage from Freetown to Takoradi. They opened a case containing £10,000 of West African currency notes, and replaced them with kitchen paper. The case was landed at Takoradi

The *Apapa* at Liverpool. (Photo: Elder Dempster)

and signed for as intact by the authorities. It was only when the case was opened in the bank at Sekondi that the theft was discovered! The culprits were apprehended and eventually brought to trial at Liverpool.

In 1955 the first Archbishop of West Africa, Leslie Gordon Vining, died on board the *Apapa* whilst travelling home to the UK on sick leave.

Somewhat unusually, the *Apapa* was caught up in strike action by seventy-five Nigerian members of her crew in June 1959. They had been staging a sit-in, alleging racial discrimination, and walked off the ship on 25 June, just twenty-four hours before sailing time. They were classed as 'deserters' by Elder Dempster, and the 275 passengers booked for the *Apapa* were reassured that the liner would sail from the Mersey on time, manned by the 101 European members of the crew.

The Nigerians were demanding the removal from the *Apapa* of the chief steward, second steward and chief storekeeper – all Europeans. They maintained that these three were responsible for discrimination between African and European crew men over the distribution of food, drink and cigarettes. They claimed that Europeans got better food, the beer for the African men was diluted, and that they were not allowed to buy certain brands of cigarettes! A spokesman for Elder Dempster said that the Europeans on the *Apapa* lived at a rather higher standard than the African men, but that this would apply to any ship. He commented, 'As regards the allegation that the beer is watered down, it's just unthinkable!'

The *Apapa* sailed from Liverpool on 26 June 1959, with her passengers serving themselves to meals and making their own beds on the fourteen-day voyage. As they embarked they were told that they would receive £1 a day as recompense for these inconveniences. The majority of the passengers regarded the whole affair as a joke, and there was only one cancellation.

The Nigerian crew who walked off the *Apapa* were accommodated in Stanley House, a colonial welfare centre in Liverpool, while the Home Office considered their position. They were eventually flown back to Lagos in a chartered BOAC Stratocruiser, paid for by Elder Dempster.

The *Apapa* remained in service for one year longer than the *Accra*, and on 20 September 1968 completed her 177th and final round voyage to West Africa for Elder Dempster. She too had become a victim of the competition from the airlines.

Unlike the *Accra*, the *Apapa* was sold for further trading, and in November 1968 she sailed for the Far East under the name of *Taipoosham*. She had been sold to the Shun Cheong Steam Navigation Co. of Hong Kong and was placed on the Hong Kong–Singapore–Penang service. The *Taipoosham* was given a white hull, but her port of registry remained Liverpool.

The former *Apapa* lasted for just over six years in her new guise, and was scrapped at Kaohsiung in February 1975.

AUREOL

Built by Alexander Stephen & Sons Ltd at Glasgow in 1951.   **Yard No:** 629
Official Number: 183819   **Signal Letters:** G M G J
Gross Tonnage: 14,083   **Nett:** 7,715   **Length:** 502ft   **Breadth:** 70·2ft
Owned by Elder Dempster Lines, Ltd
2 Doxford diesel engines, twin screws.

In March 1949 Elder Dempster ordered the third and final passenger ship to enable a fortnightly service from Liverpool to West Africa to be maintained. The new *Aureol* (named after a mountain in Sierra Leone) was launched on 28 March 1951 by Mrs E. Tansley. Just over seven months later she left Liverpool on her maiden voyage, on 8 November, under the command of Captain J.J. Smith.

The *Aureol* alongside Princes Landing Stage under a blanket of snow, 2 February 1969. (Photo: Elder Dempster)

The new ship was larger than her earlier sisters and had cost twice as much to build as the *Accra* and the *Apapa* combined! The *Aureol* had accommodation for 253 first-class passengers, with another 100 in cabin class. A crew of 145 was required to man her.

By the mid-1960s the West African passenger service was becoming less and less profitable. After the sale of the *Accra* and the *Apapa*, the *Aureol* was left to carry on the service on her own, and was converted to a one-class liner with 451 berths. Although the southbound voyage usually carried a near full complement of passengers, berth occupancy northbound had been little more than 60 per cent for several years. More significant than the decline in passenger numbers was the increase in operating costs in a ship which necessarily carried a large crew. Speaking at a trade mission to Nigeria in November 1971, Mr Peter F. Erlam, a director of Elder Dempster, commented: 'The *Aureol* is now an old ship and is expensive to operate, maintain and repair.'

On 16 March 1972 the *Aureol* made the final West African passenger sailing out of Liverpool. Her departure was held up by thick fog which prevented the liner leaving her berth in Brocklebank Dock for the landing stage. More than 400 passengers were on board – almost a full complement. Chief barkeeper on the *Aureol*, Malcolm Hanlon, summed up the feelings of regret when he said: 'Liverpool is such a great port. To see a ship like this leaving for the last time really does hurt.'

The Mersey Docks & Harbour Co. commented: 'We are pleased to note that the *Aureol* will be replaced by an express cargo service to West Africa from Liverpool.' Not much sentiment there!

The *Aureol* returned to Southampton at the end of this voyage as the Mersey Docks & Harbour Co. had closed the passenger facilities at Princes Landing Stage. Southampton

A special postal cover marking the final voyage of the *Aureol*.

remained the UK terminal for the *Aureol* for the next two and a half years until 21 October 1974 when the ship was laid up in the southern port after completing 203 round voyages in the West African passenger trade.

Mr G.J. Ellerton, the chairman of Elder Dempster Lines, said that the withdrawal of the *Aureol* was a matter of deep regret. It would mean the end of a service begun in the 1860s, and for that reason they had hoped it would be possible to find a replacement ship which would enable a viable passenger service to be continued.

The *Aureol* was quickly sold to the Marianna Shipping & Trading Co. of Panama, and in January 1975 she was renamed *Marianna VI*. In March she arrived at Jeddah to be used as an accommodation hostel. Four years later, in 1979, the former *Aureol* was towed to Piraeus to be overhauled and refurbished.

The following year the *Marianna VI* was back in the Red Sea at Rabegh, some 125 miles north of Jeddah, once again in use as an accommodation ship. Ten years later, in 1990, she was returned to Piraeus where Elder Dempster's last passenger ship was laid up in good condition.

The lay up continued for eleven years until, in 2001, the old *Aureol* was towed to the breakers' yard at Alang, India. The ship had spent more than half her fifty years in a static role, either as an accommodation ship or in lay up.

THE LEAVING OF LIVERPOOL

From the *Liverpool Echo* – 16 March 1972

Today the graceful liner *Aureol*, the flagship of the Elder Dempster fleet and last of the great liners of ply from Princes Landing Stage, says farewell to the Mersey and writes 'finis' to a proud era in Liverpool's maritime history.

Echo readers will have watched with sadness over the past decade as our columns have chronicled the passing of some of the most illustrious names in Lloyd's Register of Ships. And, on each occasion we have said goodbye, we have wondered what there could be left to write about.

Yet, as the last echoes of the sirens fade, the ghosts of other great ships will slip by in the wake of the *Aureol* as she passes into the hazy distance beyond Perch Rock.

Ships like the *Britannic*, the *Georgic*, the *Mauretania*, the *Scythia*, the *Circassia*, the *Reina del Mar*, the *Nova Scotia*, the *Voltaire* and the *Hubert*, and the utterly magnificent *Empress of Scotland*.

It was in Liverpool that the age of luxury afloat came into being with the introduction of steamships on the North Atlantic.

We can truly claim to have seen it all.

Elder Dempster cannot be blamed for taking their great white ship to Southampton. Circumstances have dictated the decision for them. It would have hardly have been an economic proposition to have provided a landing stage for a passenger sailing just once every six weeks.

The Port of Liverpool has today said goodbye to some of the glamour that contributed to its greatness.

The *Aureol* and the *Accra* laid up at Liverpool for the duration of the 1966 seamen's strike. (Photo: Elder Dempster)

6

THE PACIFIC STEAM NAVIGATION CO. LTD

The Pacific Steam Navigation Co. Ltd came into being on 27 September 1838 and fifteen months later, in January 1840, it was granted its Royal Charter. The prime mover behind the new company was William Wheelwright, who was born at Newbury Port, Massachusetts in March 1798.

The new company's first two ships were the *Chile* and the *Peru*, the former leaving Falmouth on 27 June 1840 and the latter sailing on 15 July from Plymouth. Both ships arrived at Valparaiso on the same day, 16 October 1840, after a voyage of 8,600 miles via the Strait of Magellan.

By 1873 the Pacific Steam Navigation Co. (PSNC), with a fleet of nineteen ships, was the largest steamship owner in the world. However, massive overexploitation of the trade to Chile led to as many as eleven of the PSNC ships being laid up.

In 1910 PSNC was acquired by the Royal Mail group of companies. Royal Mail had a strong presence in the Caribbean with services to Brazilian and Argentinean ports.

The trans-Panama isthmus railways were making inroads into PSNC's business to Peru, and coupled with the opening of the Argentine–Chile railway in 1910, PSNC started to reduce its fleet.

On 15 August 1914 the Panama Canal was opened for shipping and the effect on the Pacific Steam Navigation Co. was profound. The canal changed the commercial balance of the western Atlantic as the industrial north-east of the United States was now as close to Valparaiso as it was to Rio de Janeiro. From Liverpool the only practical route to Valparaiso was now through the canal, and PSNC's investment in building up the Strait of Magellan service was obsolescent. Indeed, the amalgamation of PSNC and Royal Mail was the company's salvation.

Two new passenger liners were built at Belfast by Harland & Wolff in 1914. These were the *Orduña* and the *Orbita*. They both came through the First World War unscathed and from 1926 until the outbreak of the Second World War sailed on PSNC's service from Liverpool to Callao and Valparaiso via the Panama Canal. Both ships survived the Second War but never returned to PSNC service; the *Orduña* being broken up at Dalmuir in 1951, and the *Orbita* at Newport, Mon. in 1950.

A third passenger liner joined the PSNC fleet in 1931. She was the *Reina del Pacifico*.

REINA DEL PACIFICO

Built by Harland & Wolff at Belfast in 1931.   **Yard No:** 852
Official Number: 162339   **Signal Letters:** G M P S
Gross Tonnage: 17,872   **Nett:** 10,402   **Length:** 551·3ft   **Breadth:** 76·3ft
Owned by the Pacific Steam Navigation Co. Ltd, registered at Liverpool
Quadruple Screw Motor Vessel

There was widespread regret on Merseyside at the end of 1958 about the news of the final disposal for demolition of the familiar *Reina del Pacifico*, even though her later years were marred by a series of unfortunate incidents which brought her into the popular press with uncanny regularity.

Throughout her pre-war career she gave excellent service and the same could be said of her war role as a troopship.

Completed in 1931 by Harland & Wolff at Belfast, the *Reina del Pacifico* quickly made a great name for herself for comfort and reliability. On her completion she was of considerable interest due to her method of propulsion: she had quadruple screws each driven by trunked piston 12-cylinder oil engines working on the single-acting four-stroke principle. She had four auxiliary engines besides, each driving a dynamo and accommodated in a separate engine room, divided from the main one by a watertight door.

The *Reina del Pacifico* was launched on 23 September 1930, and she became the largest vessel to date in the fleet of the Pacific Steam Navigation Co. She was the first of the company's ships

An artist's impression of the *Reina del Pacifico* passing the Mersey Bar lightship *Alarm* in the 1930s.

to be given a white hull, and the first of its passenger ships to be given a name that did not begin with 'O'. The new liner's two funnels added to her appearance, but the forward one was a dummy.

As far as the passenger accommodation was concerned, the *Reina del Pacifico* provided a new standard of luxury in the South American trade. On completion she could carry 800 passengers in first, second and third-class accommodation. The public rooms were decorated in Spanish designs of the Moresque and Colonial periods.

Before commencing her maiden voyage to South America, the new *Reina del Pacifico* made a three-day shakedown cruise to the North Sea with company guests on board. Her maiden voyage on her intended route left Liverpool on 9 April 1931, calling at La Rochelle, Vigo, Bermuda, Bahamas, Havana, Jamaica, Panama Canal, Guayaquil, Callao (nineteen days), continuing to Antofagasta and Valparaiso (twenty-five and a half days). On 19 January 1932 she commenced her first annual 'Round South America' voyage. Her record passage from Liverpool to Valparaiso in just under twenty-five days was made in 1936. In 1937 Mr Ramsay MacDonald died on board the *Reina del Pacifico* whilst on a holiday voyage to South America.

The *Reina del Pacifico* was taken up for trooping service just before the outbreak of the Second World War and her first voyage in this capacity was in the rearrangement of overseas garrisons: she sailed from the Clyde for Singapore, and afterwards brought the first Canadian troops to Britain.

On more than one occasion the enemy claimed to have sunk her, but these reports, like the premature report of Mark Twain's death, were greatly exaggerated and she continued her trooping service mainly on long distance routes. The *Reina del Pacifico* rushed troops to Norway in April, 1940, and as quickly evacuated them a few weeks later. On her arrival at Bygden Fjord she steamed around in circles at full speed for two hours whilst the fjord was depth-charged by her escorts, HMS *Fearless* and HMS *Brazen*, forcing *U49* to the surface.

After that she was employed mainly in the Middle East, and escaped damage in the Red Sea under attack from Italian aircraft. On occasions she averaged well over 20-knots for twenty-four-hour periods. In 1941 the *Reina* was taking troops from Halifax, NS, to Singapore by the westabout route, but the following year she was converted into an assault ship to take part in the French North African and Sicilian landings.

At one stage in her wartime career the *Reina del Pacifico* was at Avonmouth when that port was subjected to a heavy air attack. She was straddled with high explosive and incendiary bombs but again escaped without damage. On another occasion whilst lying at anchor in Walton Bay she was bombed, and had a similar experience at Liverpool, where a delayed-action missile exploded in the dock alongside, but her luck held and the only damage she suffered was to crockery.

On 21 October 1942 the *Reina del Pacifico* embarked troops for the 'Z' landing at Oran. She was flagship to the Senior Naval Officer Landing. The Algiers force had to be twenty-four hours ahead of the Oran force, so that at one stage the *Reina* had to steam back on her tracks for eight hours in order to pass through the Strait of Gibraltar in darkness. At 3.30 p.m. on 7 November 1942, the *Reina del Pacifico* met up with the equipment ships off Oran. She was on time to the minute, and at 7.00 the following morning her landing craft took her troops ashore. Later the ship berthed in Oran harbour.

In 1943 the liner was off Gibraltar when she was attacked by German aircraft on two successive days but no hits were scored. German radio reported that the *Reina* was 'torn to pieces and disappeared in a few seconds'.

After the Sicily landings the *Reina del Pacifico* took King Peter of Jugoslavia and his staff to Port Said, and then sailed on to Taranto with troops. Following the Italian campaign she was once more used on long distance hauls carrying troops of all nationalities. The *Reina* was then placed on repatriation duties to and from the Middle East. The ship's astonishing good luck during her wartime voyaging might very well be said to have given the lie to the stories that went around in her final years that she was a 'hoodoo' ship.

The *Reina del Pacifico*'s sinister record began in 1947 when she was the subject of a serious crankcase explosion on 11 September whilst on trials off Copeland Island in the North Channel, after being refitted at her builders' yard at Belfast, before re-entering commercial service. This explosion caused the deaths of twenty-eight members of her crew and the PSNC's technical staff. The vessel returned to Harland & Wolff's Belfast yard and was eventually put back on her peacetime service to the West Coast of South America about a year later. She opened the first British operated express liner service between Britain and Colombia by introducing regular calls at Cartagena into her schedule.

A Court of Inquiry was held at Belfast in April and May 1948 to investigate the cause of the explosion, and its findings were published on 5 June 1948. The primary cause was found to be the piston of No.2 port outer engine overheating and igniting an inflammable mixture present in the crank chamber of the said engine. It was stated that nine days prior to the explosion, a previous sea trial on 2 September was abandoned because of serious overheating of the port outer cylinder liner.

There then followed a series of minor incidents – engine trouble and the like – which culminated in the grounding of the ship on Devil's Flat, Bermuda, on 9 July 1957. With 400 Liverpool-bound passengers on board, the *Reina del Pacifico* was aground on sand, listing some twelve degrees to starboard. A spokesman for the PSNC said in Liverpool: 'We have received no message that would in any way suggest the ship is in danger. Captain E.C. Hicks has reported

The first-class lounge on the *Reina del Pacifico*. (Photo: Pacific Steam Navigation Co.)

The first-class dining saloon on the *Reina del Pacifico*. (Photo: Pacific Steam Navigation Co.)

that the liner is not taking on any water. It is expected that the *Reina del Pacifico* will be refloated on the next high tide.'

However, this was not to be. The US Coastguard cutter *Castlerock* joined two local tugs in refloating attempts. The passengers were retained on board because it was considered too risky to land them ashore by tender, and because of difficulty in finding hotel accommodation for them.

Two days after the grounding, cargo and fuel oil were being discharged from the stranded liner, and ground tackle was laid down to assist in a further refloating attempt. Over 22 tons of salvage equipment was air-freighted to Bermuda.

The *Reina del Pacifico* was successfully refloated in the early hours of 12 July. Steel hawsers were passed under the hull and attached to ballast tanks on either side of the vessel. The tanks were then filled with compressed air. The list had been reduced to just four degrees by the removal of cargo and fuel oil. Three lines attached to anchors were dropped near the stern and connected to capstans on the vessel's stern. Each of these lines, according to salvage experts, supplied leverage equal to the pulling power of four tugs. Heavy steel rollers, flown in from England, were placed on the reef. The local tugs *Justice* and *Bermuda* took the strain of pulling the *Reina del Pacifico* into deeper water.

After being successfully refloated, the Reina moved to an anchorage in Grassy Bay, in the Great Sound at Bermuda, so that 700 tons of cargo could be reloaded. The *Reina del Pacifico* resumed her passage to Liverpool on 14 July and arrived back in Liverpool on 24 July 1957.

On her next voyage after leaving Liverpool, on 15 August 1957, the *Reina del Pacifico* had to put into Milford Haven with generator trouble and it soon became clear that she could not be repaired in time to complete the voyage, which was cancelled. The *Reina* returned to Liverpool for major repairs to her generating plant.

On 10 November 1957 the *Reina del Pacifico* dropped her starboard inner propeller whilst manoeuvring in Havana harbour (Cuba). The liner continued her voyage at reduced speed on the remaining three propellers, calling at Kingston, La Guaira, Cartagena and Cristobal, before passing through the Panama Canal to Balboa where she was eventually dry docked to have a spare fitted. This spare had been shipped out to Panama in the motorship *Salinas*, another PSNC vessel.

At the end of March 1958 it became clear that when the *Reina del Pacifico* reached Liverpool at the completion of her voyage she would be withdrawn from service. At that stage it was not clear what was intended as far as the ship's future was concerned, although it was obvious that she would be offered for sale. The *Reina* arrived at Princes Landing Stage at the end of her final voyage on 28 April 1958, and the Pacific Steam Navigation Co.'s managing director, Mr H. Leslie Bowes, commented: 'This ship has been a great asset to the Company, and despite all these 'Jinx Ship' stories, has been exceedingly well liked'.

Whilst lying at Liverpool awaiting disposal, negotiations were taking place for the old ship's sale to Japanese shipbreakers, but this deal fell through and the *Reina del Pacifico* was eventually sold to the British Iron and Steel Corporation (Salvage) Ltd, London. When she left the Mersey for the last time, the *Reina* was bound for Newport, Mon., to be scrapped by the shipbreaking firm of John Cashmore Ltd, the same company that had broken up her former consort, the *Orbita*, in 1950.

THREE WEEKS TO COLOMBO IN 1945

by Peter Clowes

The war in Europe had only a few weeks to run when I joined the *Reina del Pacifico* at Liverpool. I was a humble writer in the Royal Navy at the time and I was in the habit of scribbling daily entries into a spiral-backed notebook that I kept in my kitbag.

With several hundred other officers and ratings I had travelled through the night from Devonport barracks by special train. As our coaches were shunted down to Riverside Station at about 10.30 a.m., railway and dockside workers waved us 'farewell'. Then we saw our home for the next few weeks – the *Reina del Pacifico* looming over the landing stage, her hull painted a dull grey and streaked with rust after five years of war.

Our quarters, on the waterline, were rather overcrowded as the *Reina* was carrying 2,500 passengers this trip. There was little sign of the charming Spanish and Moorish interiors which had graced tourist travel in pre-war days.

At 7.45 p.m. on 15 April 1945 we pulled away from the landing stage and then lay in mid-Mersey overnight. I joined in an informal football match on the after end of 'E'-deck before going below, queuing with a tin mug for a special ration of grog from the rum bosun, and then slinging my hammock over a linoleum-topped mess table.

There were 'emergency stations' the next morning, each man wearing a blue lifebelt and red safety light, and at 1 p.m. we steamed down the Mersey with other ships, including several American tankers, before anchoring off New Brighton for another night.

On 17 April the *Reina del Pacifico* hoisted pennants and steamed out of the Mersey, past the protruding masts of the *Ullapool* and the *Tacoma City* which had been sunk by mines earlier in the war. With us was a mixed batch of tankers, cargo steamers, troopships, a destroyer and two frigates, all proceeding in line ahead with the Rock lighthouse abeam, and then forming two columns when clear of the swept channel. Several more vessels were waiting to join us at the Mersey Bar.

The *Reina del Pacifico* formed part of convoy KMF43, which turned out to be one of the last escorted convoys to leave the shores of Britain in the Second World War. We were guarded by the destroyers *Escapade* and *Icarus*, the frigates *Loch Katrine* and *Ness* and the corvette *Oxford Castle*.

We steamed at about 13-knots. Morning mist was followed by afternoon sunshine. There was a long steady swell and I swiftly succumbed to a short, sharp bout of seasickness. I obtained a couple of tablets from the sick bay and retired early to my swinging hammock.

The fourteen ships being escorted towards the southern Irish coast, and then south to Gibraltar, were in columns with a gap of three cables between each ship. The *Reina del Pacifico* ploughed through calm seas, immediately astern of the *Capetown Castle*, carrying 3,200 men to India. To starboard was the *Georgic* with 3,850 troops for Malta and Egypt, followed by the *Samaria* with 3,450 men for Italy and India. The third column was led by the *Alcantara* (3,700 troops and airmen for Algeria and Italy), and HMS *Princess Beatrix*, a former Harwich–Hook ferry and a veteran of the North African landings, astern. The convoy commodore, Sir Arthur J. Baxter, was onboard the liner *Orion*.

On 19 April several of the ships in the convoy held a thirty minute exercise for their gun crews, the 40mm Bofors guns on the *Begum* providing the most impressive show. There was some excitement in the early hours of 22 April when the 'river'-class frigate, *Ness*, dropped a pattern of depth charges at a suspected submarine contact.

The Clyde based *Escapade* and *Ness* were relieved by two escorts from Gibraltar on 20 April as our convoy neared the Mediterranean. When the Rock of Gibraltar hove into view throughout a blanket of haze, all the ships in the convoy steamed into the roadstead. After an exchange of signals, Captain J.V. Longford of the *Reina del Pacifico* ordered speed to be increased to 15-knots and we headed east, alone, through the Mediterranean.

Sun awnings and canvas air chutes for the engine room were erected. Many of the Navy passengers lolled in the sunshine on 'D'-deck, reading tattered books and magazines from the ship's limited library. We had a medical examination and then washed our uniforms with rubbery soap in buckets of sea water, and fitted white covers to our caps. I leaned over the bow to watch graceful porpoises keeping pace with the ship which was vibrating considerably as she increased speed.

On 25 April we passed the island of Pantelleria with its high cliffs. There was tombola on 'E'-Deck - £15 for a full house – but I was unsuccessful. A ship's concert was held in the evening.

Captain Longford steamed a smoke float the following morning and gave the RN gunners an hour's practice. The *Reina* zigzagged to let the Bofors gunners aft have a fair share. Our biggest gun, in the stern, proved the most accurate, hitting the target several times at ranges of up to two miles. Then rocket-fired crimson parachutes floated in the blue sky as the midships Oerlikon cannons blazed away. Everyone on board was delighted, not least a party of Wrens leaning over the rails on the upper deck.

Later in the week I had to queue for a haircut from a leading stoker in the next mess. Another concert was held, but the noise of the *Reina's* overworked ventilation plant made it difficult to hear what was going on. The concert ended with the massed singing of *Just a Song at Twilight* as a silvery moon floated over the distant coast of Egypt.

There was a commotion on 27 April when fire broke out in the stern galley. Smoke and fumes spread for nearly an hour before everything was brought under control. When I went on deck the next morning we were steaming slowly past the waterfront at Port Said, taking our place in a convoy of vessels making its way through the Suez Canal. Water and fuel boats came alongside when we reached Suez. Egyptian feluccas with high lateen sails arrived to conduct business with fezzes, handbags, wallets and belts. Baskets were used to haul the goods to the *Reina*'s decks and the lissom, brown merchants, climbed their masts to bargain with us. At 6 p.m. we weighed anchor and set off down the Red Sea. Blackout restrictions were lifted and everyone was ordered into white tropical rig. I was appointed mess cook and had to scrub the deck and scrape clean the garbage bins in the sweltering conditions below. There was more laundry work, using sea water not very successfully; but there were fresh oranges for supper and these made a welcome change from our almost unchanging diet of tinned pilchards.

We were soon in the Arabian Sea and had our first sight of flying fish skimming over the smooth water. I went to a 16mm film show on 'E'-Deck – seeing *The Wicked Lady* for the third time – while the officers and wrens danced on the floodlit boat deck.

There was another ship's concert on 7 May and at the end Captain Longford informed everyone to rousing cheers that the end of the war in Europe had just been announced. We sang *Land of Hope and Glory* lustily as the *Reina del Pacifico* sped on across the Indian Ocean.

I was scrubbing the messdeck when the *Reina* passed the breakwaters at the entrance to Colombo Harbour at 9 a.m. on 8 May, VE-Day. The town of white, red-roofed buildings seemed to be celebrating. The officers, Wrens and Royal Marines disembarked but most of us were confined to the ship and bought pineapples and coconuts from the Sinhalese traders who came alongside in droves. A supply of beer – one bottle per man – was brought on board.

As darkness fell at 7.45 p.m., Winston Churchill's voice came over the loudspeakers. The *Reina del Pacifico*'s deep siren joined the shrieks and screams of every other ship in the harbour. Throughout the night searchlights blazed, rockets were fired and flares ignited. The cruiser *Cleopatra*, moored close by, hoisted a mass of fairy lights across her forecastle.

I disembarked the following day and went to the Royal Navy's transit camp, HMS *Mayina*, which lay in dense forest a few miles outside Colombo. I never saw the *Reina del Pacifico* again, but her name cropped up in the news from time to time. Although the liner has now vanished from the seas, she still retains a place in my heart. I was only eighteen when I sailed in her and it was the first time I had been to sea. My old tattered diary brought back many memories.

REINA DEL MAR

Built by Harland & Wolff at Belfast in 1955.   **Yard No:** 1533
Official Number: 187132   **Signal Letters:** G T Y N
Owned by the Pacific Steam Navigation Co. Ltd; registered at Liverpool
Gross Tonnage: 20,225   **Nett:** 11,234   **Length:** 600·9ft   **Breadth:** 78·4ft
6 Steam Turbines, double reduction gearing to 2 shafts

This 20,255-ton turbine steamer, with accommodation for 766 passengers in three classes, was built at Belfast by Harland & Wolff, and launched on 7 June 1955 by Mrs H. Leslie Bowes, the wife of PSNC's then managing director. Watching the launching ceremony were the ambassadors of Colombia, Peru and Ecuador, and the Minister of State for Chile. Also present was Mr C. Warwick, the chairman of Royal Mail Lines, PSNC's sister company, who turned to Mr Bowes and commented, 'You know Leslie, she'll never pay'. Nor did she! In his after luncheon speech, Mr Bowes said that he and his colleagues profoundly believed that, whatever might be the future developments in the air, there would always be a steady demand for accommodation in beautiful and comfortable ships of which, he said, the *Reina del Mar* was an outstanding example.

The new *Reina del Mar* took shape as a replacement for the ageing diesel liner, *Reina del Pacifico*, on the service between Europe and the West Coast of South America. The two-funnelled *Reina del Pacifico* did not have an enviable reputation as a seaboat, but in spite of her nickname 'the Rolling Reina', many were sad to see her go.

The *Reina del Mar* on her sea trials in the Firth of Clyde in March 1956. (Photo: *Shipbuilding and Shipping Record*)

The new ship was designed to sail from Liverpool, via European ports and the West Indies, through the Panama Canal to Ecuador, Peru and Chile. The accommodation was air-conditioned, and she had Denny–Brown stabilisers. Her public rooms were pleasant if unremarkable; her speed was a moderate 18 knots and her early career followed a routine pattern. She seemed all set for a quietly successful life on the Valparaiso run.

The *Reina del Mar* arrived at Liverpool for the first time on 9 April 1956 and eleven days later sailed on a pre-maiden voyage three-day cruise to the Western Isles of Scotland. By coincidence, on that same day, Friday 20 April, the new *Empress of Britain* left Liverpool on her maiden voyage to Quebec and Montreal.

The new *Reina del Mar* left Liverpool on Thursday 3 May 1956 on her sixty-five-day maiden voyage to the West Coast of South America, calling at some thirty-eight ports en route. On her arrival back in Liverpool on 7 July her master, Captain George Rice, reported that, 'she handles beautifully and steers like a yacht'. At that time the Reina's chief engineer was Mr A. Currie, so it was inevitable that the new ship quickly became known as the 'Curry and Rice' liner! The new ship operated with the *Reina del Pacifico* as her consort until the latter was sold for scrap in 1958.

The 1950s boom filtered away towards the end of the decade as long-range airliners grabbed ever higher percentages of the passenger trade. Political troubles in Cuba, for many years a major stopover and an important source of revenue, added to the difficulties. With the missile crisis of John Kennedy's presidency, the end of the West Coast passenger run was in sight. PSNC Archivist John Lingwood aptly summed it up: 'the sonic boom of jet travel sounded the death-knell of passage by sea'.

The *Reina del Mar* leaving Liverpool on her maiden voyage, 3 May 1956. (Photo: *Shipbuilding and Shipping Record*)

During these early years, the new 'Queen of the Sea' rarely found herself in the news. An interesting group of passengers travelled in her in 1962: half a dozen young climbers heading for some of the great Patagonian peaks. The group included Chris Bonnington and Don Williams.

In 1962 a call at Port of Spain, Trinidad, was added to the Reina's schedule to provide a fast passenger service (eleven days) between the UK and the southern Caribbean island.

Rumours circulated in the spring of 1963 that the *Reina del Mar* would leave the South American service for a time and go cruising. A single cruise from Liverpool had already been arranged for August of that year, with the staggering result that every one of her berths was filled after the booking had been open for only a matter of hours. Half of the 570 passengers on the cruise had paid between £50 and £60 for the fortnight's voyage to the sun, which worked out at 2½d (1p) per sea mile!

On 2 May 1963 confirmation was received of a five-month charter in the summer of 1964 to Travel Savings Ltd, a cheap cruise scheme owned jointly by the South African businessman Max Wilson, the Union–Castle Line and Canadian Pacific. Members of the Travel Savings Association (TSA) could join an eighteen-day cruise to New York for just £45.

In October 1963 Mr J.J. Gawne, a director of PSNC at Liverpool, gave details of the long battle his company had fought in an attempt to retain the *Reina del Mar*. The Government was asked on several occasions for a grant to save her on the Mersey to South America passenger run 'as a symbol of British craftsmanship'. 'The *Reina del Mar* has been running at a loss,' explained Mr Gawne, 'and we felt we must stop the drain. Representatives of the Foreign Office and Ambassadors pleaded with us not to take the Reina off the South America run.'

In her early years, the *Reina del Mar* was dubbed the 'Curry and Rice' ship after Mr Alexander Currie, the chief engineer, and Captain G.H. Rice, the master.

Few liners have been involved in as complex a situation as the *Reina del Mar* during 1963 and 1964. There was a change of plan in September 1963, and the Reina found herself sailing into stormy waters. Max Wilson and his TSA were to buy her as their first ship; when she came into their hands in the spring of 1964 for a little over £3 million, the first task was an expensive conversion. At this juncture, Royal Mail Lines, PSNC's parent company, acquired 25 per cent of TSA shares, an equal holding with the other members. TSA's first cruise, employing the *Empress of Britain*, took place in the autumn of 1963, and a notable feature was the low average age of the passengers. When Max Wilson announced his intended purchase of the *Reina del Mar*, he spoke enthusiastically of the progress made by his scheme: 'This is only the beginning,' he promised; 'to date we have sold 26,000 berths – roughly twenty-six shiploads of passengers. Bookings are coming in at a minimum of 1,000 a week. Our membership in Britain is over 30,000.'

In November 1963 a powerful controversy sprang up over the decision to resell the *Reina del Mar* to the Greek shipowner A.J. Chandris. Flying the Greek flag and manned by a Greek crew she would be chartered back to TSA for her lifetime. Chandris would become a fifth equal shareholder. Sir Nicholas Cayzer, the then chairman of TSA, pointed out that the organisation was primarily a sales concern and not a shipping company, and was not geared to operating a cruise ship on a complicated itinerary.

Ambitious plans were announced. With an increase from 770 to 1,150 in her passenger capacity, and with new public rooms and facilities, the *Reina del Mar* would be well equipped for her new role as a fulltime cruise liner. A sixty-day voyage from Durban to Japan for the Olympics was scheduled as a curtain raiser.

In many quarters the projected sale of the *Reina* to the Greeks was severely criticised. The Merchant Navy and Airline Officers' Association described it as 'appalling', and stated:

British seafarers, who have served this country well in both peace and war, will be dismayed to learn that a Greek company is apparently regarded as better suited to the operation of cruising ships because, according to TSA, it has demonstrated its ability to provide an altogether satisfactory standard of service at very competitive rates.

The National Union of Seamen was equally vocal. NUS General Secretary William Hogarth said: 'Here is a clear case for government action to halt such sales of British ships abroad for use in competition with our own ships. At first glance, this is tantamount to condoning flags of convenience.' The TSA Board, contentedly watching their enterprise through rose-coloured glasses, were more than a little taken aback by the angry and persistent attack upon them. Just when the unions were putting great pressure on the Max Wilson group to keep the *Reina del Mar* under British flag, the Greek liner *Lakonia* caught fire and sank with heavy loss of life. At the end of February 1964, while the Reina herself was making a farewell voyage to Peru and Chile via the West Indies, Florida and Panama, the decision was taken not to sell her to Chandris.

A new consortium, comprising PSNC (with a holding of 25 per cent), Canadian Pacific, British & Commonwealth Shipping (Clan Line and Union–Castle), and Max Wilson's TSA became the new owners of the *Reina del Mar*. The liner had been incurring losses, on the West Coast of South America service, running at between £200,000 and £300,000 a year, and in her eight years at sea she had never made a profit.

With Captain D. Idris Jones in command, the *Reina del Mar* left Liverpool on 2 January 1964 on her last scheduled voyage on the service for which she had been designed. On 10 March the *Reina* arrived at Belfast for conversion into a one-class cruise liner at a reported cost of £500,000. Her cargo space was converted into additional passenger accommodation and she was ready for sea again on 10 June when she sailed on an eighteen-day cruise from Liverpool to New York. Some 700 TSA members were onboard, with tourist fares ranging from £45 to £75. The *Reina del Mar* retained her familiar yellow funnel but carried the initials TSA in blue, inside a blue circle, upon it. However, the Travel Savings Association was foundering and in July 1964 Max Wilson's scheme for cheap cruises was dropped. In October of that year Union–Castle acquired all the TSA shares and the *Reina del Mar* reverted to PSNC ownership.

For the next nine years the *Reina del Mar* operated as a full-time cruise ship on charter to the Union–Castle Line. The charter was due to expire in September 1974, but in November 1973 it was announced that Union–Castle had purchased the Reina outright from Royal Mail Lines, the parent company of PSNC.

In mid-June 1974 there came a surprise announcement from Union–Castle to the effect that the *Reina del Mar* would be withdrawn from service in April 1975 because of greatly

The *Reina del Mar* following her 1964 rebuild. (Photo: *Shipbuilding and Shipping Record*)

increased operating costs. The tremendous increase in the cost of fuel oil played a major part in this decision, though no doubt crew wages and the cost of maintenance and repairs also contributed. The fact remained that this fine ship, only eighteen years old and very popular with the British cruising public, was unable to pay her way.

The *Reina del Mar* completed her 1974 UK cruising programme and then sailed for Cape Town where she operated her 1974/75 series of cruises from South Africa to South America. Following her return to Southampton the *Reina del Mar* was laid up on 1 April 1975 and eight weeks later she sailed for the shipbreakers at Kaohsiung, Taiwan.

THE TRAVEL SAVINGS ASSOCIATION

Max Wilson and his Travel Savings Association have been directly involved in the careers of three Liverpool liners – the *Empress of Britain*, the *Empress of England* and, perhaps most notably, the *Reina del Mar*. In early 1964 Mr Wilson gave an interview to the special correspondent of *The Journal of Commerce*.

Max Wilson, founder of the rapidly growing Travel Savings Association, would surely have been the choice of the panel if a competition had been held in 1963 for the 'Man of the Year' in the British travel industry. A year ago eyebrows were being raised when he launched an advertising campaign, with full-page advertisements in the national press, announcing the formation of the Travel Savings Association (TSA) and its plans for 'pay-now-travel-later' cut price cruises. Shipping circles appeared at this stage to be unimpressed by this appeal to the mass market for cruise passengers. Travel agents were for the most part up in arms against a plan which provided for direct calls being made on people who had filled in coupons clipped from the Max Wilson adverts. But all this seems like a bit of history now. With some 35,000 coupon replies within two weeks of the launching of his publicity campaign, Max Wilson was much too busy getting on with the job of selling holidays at sea to pay much heed to his critics. Max Wilson commented:

> I believe that most people would like to try a sea holiday. The right type of cruise at a realistic price will sell hundreds of thousands of sea holidays. I work on the assumption that there is a mass market to be created.
>
> Our present, 1964, programme is a test period and the ships, in their present form are test ships. I do believe our requirements for ships will grow beyond even my present anticipation.

The Journal of Commerce interviewer went on: 'Now we come to the $64,000 question. How is it possible to make profits on cheap fares when shipping companies have been struggling to make ends meet on relatively high fares?'

Max Wilson replied: 'This is, as you say, the $64,000 question. You will understand when I say, with the best will in the world, I have no intention of answering it!'

Maybe Max Wilson himself had no idea about the answer to that question. The Travel Savings Association 'bubble' burst and Max Wilson and his TSA sank without trace.

7

UNION CASTLE

THE *WINDSOR CASTLE* REMEMBERED

by Peter Elson, senior features writer, *Liverpool Daily Post*

The final ship to be included in this book about Liverpool's last passenger liners never embarked or landed a passenger in the port – though she was built by Cammell Laird at Birkenhead. The *Windsor Castle*, at 37,640 gross tons, became the largest passenger liner ever to be built on the Mersey and was part of the Union–Castle Line's plan to reduce the passage time from Southampton to Cape Town to just eleven days. The new ship joined the rest of the fleet in the tradition of the Cape mail service, with a liner departing from Southampton on the stroke of four every Thursday afternoon.

The new *Windsor Castle* represented the ultimate development of the South African mailship and she could carry 237 passengers in first class, and 585 in tourist class. The *Windsor Castle* was destined to become the last of Union–Castle's passenger ships when in 1965 her running mates, the *Pendennis Castle* of 1958, and the *Transvaal Castle* of 1962, were transferred to the Safmarine fleet and flew the South African flag. As on the North Atlantic, passenger traffic in the South African trade was falling off due to competition from the airlines, and the final blow came in 1977 with the containerisation of the cargo services. The large passenger liners were no longer viable and the *Windsor Castle* closed the Cape mail and passenger service with her departure from Cape Town on 6 September 1977.

When the *Windsor Castle* sailed on her maiden voyage in 1960, it was said that every passenger travelling in first class was titled. Costing £10 million, the Royal Mail Steamer was the last great South African mail ship and the finest vessel that Cammell Laird's Birkenhead workforce could turn out. As the new flagship of the Union–Castle Line, she slashed two days off the schedule of the 6,000-mile voyage to Cape Town from the previous thirteen and a half days.

The Queen Mother launched the *Windsor Castle* in brilliant sunshine on 23 June 1959, before a crowd of 50,000, and watched by millions more on television. What should have been an unadulterated celebration of the country's maritime supremacy was marred by a nine-week dispute which had started on the ship. Dubbed by the press as the 'who twangs the twine war', striking boilersmiths argued with shipwrights about who should draw chalk lines on the ship's plates. As a result thousands of workers were laid off, the launch postponed and the lavish ceremonial luncheon cancelled.

Yet the launch proved so popular that the traffic gridlocked in Birkenhead and police shut the shipyard gates thirty minutes before the launch, fearing a crush. This caused uproar amongst the crowd, with hundreds of ticket-holders excluded from the yard. Whether through stress or atmospherics, the Queen Mother suffered a severe nose bleed which jeopardised the event, timed for the vital high tide. Fortunately she recomposed herself and christened the ship just one minute after its scheduled time of 1.30 p.m. She alluded to the shipyard row in her speech later, saying: 'I am so glad to be here and to launch the *Windsor Castle* in spite of the difficulties which I know you have had to contend with.'

Bob Hunt, from Prenton, Birkenhead, was a charge-hand supervisor on the launch day, working in a 5ft high space beneath the ship. He recalls:

> Using a seven pound hammer I had to split out the supporting keel blocks so the *Windsor Castle* would settle on to the heavily greased launching ways. When we had finished the foreman alerted the launch platform and the Queen Mother smashed the bottle on the bows. Simultaneously a bell was rung telling the men to trigger the release on the hydraulic rams which were holding the ship in place.
>
> Immediately the ship's weight started carrying her down the slipway. It was a fantastic sight seeing this massive ship sliding into the water. It wasn't noisy, just the sound of grease cracking under the hull and a few crashes and bangs.
>
> With so much water displaced, there was a big backwash onto the slipway, so the shipyard stewards had to keep the surging crowds well back.

Mr Hunt retired from Cammell Lairds in 1993 as steel construction manager.

Bob Jones, another Prenton man, says:

> I remember the day we laid the first keel plate. Cammell Laird was delighted to have won such a prestigious contract. This was in the days before prefabrication and the workforce could adapt to building anything, having completed the aircraft carrier *Ark Royal* a few years earlier. We could build tankers or tugs, in fact anything that was required of us.

Mr Jones, who started as a shipwright, later becoming manager for accuracy control on steel welding, and in charge of the mould loft, went on, 'The *Windsor Castle* is a beautiful ship and the fact that she has lasted so long is a great tribute to Lairds.'

David Smith from Birkenhead was indentured as an apprentice shipfitter at Cammell Lairds in 1957 when he was sixteen. He said:

> The 11,000-man workforce built outstanding ships in the harshest of conditions. Labour relations were appalling and there were genuine grievances that highly-skilled craftsmen weren't respected by management or paid appropriately. Yet out of this chaos came the *Windsor Castle*. It was amazing to see the way that things went together and the beauty of the craftsmanship in the lounges, bars, cinema and ballroom. Wonderful woodwork, no expense spared. There had been nothing like this since the building of the *Mauretania* before the war.

On completion of fitting out at Birkenhead, Union–Castle cancelled the *Windsor Castle*'s shakedown cruise from Liverpool to the Western Isles, and the new liner sailed early for Southampton on 13 July 1960. The fear of further industrial action in which the new liner might be caught up prompted this decision.

The *Windsor Castle*'s maiden voyage was from Southampton on 18 August 1960 when she sailed for Cape Town, Port Elizabeth, East London and Durban with a full passenger list. Just over seven years later she celebrated her 50th UK–Cape round-voyage, having steamed 700,000-miles carrying 35,000 passengers with no breakdowns or delays.

The *Windsor Castle* leaving the fitting-out basin at Cammell Laird, Birkenhead, on 13 July 1960, prior to sailing to Southampton. Her shake-down cruise from Liverpool to the Western Isles was cancelled due to industrial unrest on Merseyside.

After just seventeen years in service the *Windsor Castle* was withdrawn following rocketing fuel prices and the impact of Boeing 747 jumbo jets. Her 124th and final voyage for Union–Castle ended at Southampton on 19 September 1977.

The ship was sold to the Greek construction tycoon John Latsis and renamed *Margarita L*, after one of his daughters. She was used as mobile offices and was based in the Arabian Gulf as Latsis oversaw various desalination projects. Following his death the liner was converted into an accommodation ship and berthed at Jeddah from January 1979 until June 1991, after which she was laid up at Eleusis Bay, Perama, near Piraeus.

In 2003 a Merseyside group was established with the aim of bringing the *Windsor Castle* back to Birkenhead as a hotel and conference centre. Under the direction of Mr Alex Naughton, the RMS Windsor Castle Trust hoped to berth the ship in Cammell Lairds fitting-out basin. A Dutch company was set to operate her as a hotel.

In the event it was discovered that the ship had deteriorated more during her lay up than had at first been thought and her DC electric system would have been very costly to change. The low price of steel had extended the *Windsor Castle*'s life, but the death-knell sounded with rising scrap values and the cheap, unregulated labour available in the shipbreaking industry at Alang.

Mr Naughton acknowledged that the attempt to bring the *Windsor Castle* home to Birkenhead had been 'an honourable failure'. At the end of April 2005 the old ship sailed from Piraeus, via Suez, for demolition at Alang. 'She sailed under her own steam to India, making her last voyage with dignity and elegance,' commented Mr Naughton.

There are a couple of stories about the *Windsor Castle* which are worthy of recording before they are lost for ever. One concerns a sixty-four-year-old passenger, Mrs Margaret Fuller, who fell overboard in November 1976 as the liner was some 250 miles off the Angolan coast, and some 1,400 miles from Cape Town. Mrs Fuller's husband alerted the crew at 9 a.m. that his wife was missing and after a brief search it was assumed that she might have fallen overboard. Captain Patrick Beadon turned the *Windsor Castle* round and retraced his course, making allowances for currents and wind direction. Three hours later Mrs Fuller was sighted, still treading water.

The *Windsor Castle* enters the Mersey following her launch by the Queen Mother. (Photo: *Shipbuilding and Shipping Record*)

The ship came to a stop just fifty yards from Mrs Fuller and a lifeboat was launched. Her rescue quickly became a race against time as onlookers claimed that they saw a shark circling her.

Another forgotten story concerns the race between the Birkenhead-built *Windsor Castle* and a Halewood (Liverpool) built Ford Corsair 2000E between Cape Town and Southampton in May 1967. It came about when Union–Castle claimed that after air travel, its mail boat service provided the fastest form of travel between South Africa and the UK. The Ford Motor Co. disputed this and the Ford Corsair, driven by rally drivers Ken Chambers and Eric Chapman left the dockside at Cape Town at the same time as the *Windsor Castle* departed for Southampton. The liner's 6,000-mile sea voyage was pitched against the 9,700-mile road route.

Chambers and Chapman contended with pot holes, petrol shortages and armed Congolese soldiers, and reckoned they had to deal with twenty-four tyre changes and thirty-seven puncture repairs. Their support team was locked up for several hours and held at gun point on one occasion. It was, of course, necessary to fly the Corsair across the Strait of Gibraltar and the Strait of Dover, and taking this into account, the race was declared a draw, although the Corsair actually arrived on the dockside at Southampton the evening before the *Windsor Castle* was due!

The *Windsor Castle* leaving Cape Town. (Photo: *Shipbuilding and Shipping Record*)

BIBLIOGRAPHY

Periodicals

Journal of Commerce
Liverpool Daily Post
Liverpool Echo
Sea Breezes
Shipbuilding and Shipping Record
Ships Monthly

Books

Great Passenger Ships of the World, Volumes 4 and 5 (Arnold Kludas), 1977
Last White Empresses (Clive Harvey): Carmania Press, 2004
Lloyd's Register of Ships – various editions
Saxonia Sisters (Clive Harvey): Carmania Press, 2001